ENGLISH COUNTRY LANES

For all my friends who have been known to travel slowly and for their various offspring, both extant and threatened, who will undoubtedly travel slower still.

ENGLISH COUNTRY LANES

A Celebration Of Travelling Slowly

written, photographed and designed
by

Gareth Lovett Jones

WILDWOOD HOUSE

First published in Great Britain by
Wildwood House Ltd, Gower House, Croft Road, Aldershot, Hants
GU11 3HR, England.

ISBN 0 7045 3070 8

Typeset in Great Britain by
Guildford Graphics Limited, Petworth, West Sussex.
Printed in Hong Kong by South China Printing Co.

Contents

Acknowledgements

The author and publishers wish to thank the following for quotations used in the book:

Blackie and Son Ltd. for the quotation from *England And The Octopus* by Clough Williams-Ellis

William Collins Sons and Company Ltd. and the author for the quotation from *The Peregrine* by J.A. Baker

Constable and Company Ltd. for the quotation from *The Old Road* by Hilaire Belloc

The Countryside Commission for the quotation from the 'National Household Survey'

Irwin Dash Music Company Ltd. for the quotation from 'There'll Always Be An England' by Ross Parker and Hughie Charles

J.M. Dent and Sons Ltd. and the author for the quotations from *Roads And Tracks Of Britain* by Christopher Taylor

Faber and Faber Ltd. for the quotation from *High Windows* by Philip Larkin

Anthony Shiel Associates Ltd. and the author for the quotations from *Daniel Martin* (published by Jonathan Cape Ltd.) by John Fowles

The literary executor of C.E.M. Joad for the quotations from *The Untutored Townsman's Invasion Of The Country* (published by Faber and Faber Ltd.)

The literary trustees of Walter de la Mare and the Society of Authors as their representative for the quotation from 'The Journey'

Methuen and Company Ltd. for the quotation from *The Wind In The Willows* by Kenneth Grahame

John Murray (Publishers) Ltd. for the quotation from *Collected Poems* by John Betjeman

The National Trust for the quotations from 'The Glory Of The Garden' by Rudyard Kipling

The National Farmers Union for the quotations from 'Caring For The Countryside'

Penguin Books Ltd. and the author for the quotations from *Green And Pleasant Land?* by Howard Newby

Rodale Press and the author for the quotation from *The One-Straw Revolution* by Masanobu Fukuoka

Maurice Temple Smith Ltd. and the authors for the quotations from *The Theft Of The Countryside* by Marion Shoard and *Agriculture: The Triumph And The Shame* by Richard Body

Gareth Lovett Jones offers grateful thanks for assistance with information to:

The Planning Departments of the County Councils of Berkshire, Cheshire, Devon, Dorset, Hampshire, Hereford and Worcester, Leicestershire, Norfolk, Shropshire, Somerset, Suffolk, East Sussex, Wiltshire, and Yorkshire

The Keeper of Rutland County Museum, the Curator of Cromer Museum, and the City Archivist, Chester City Record Office

The Bicycle Association Of Great Britain, the Cyclists' Touring Club, the Department Of Transport (Highway Planning And Construction Department), the Forestry Commission (Arboricultural Advisory And Information Service), the Nature Conservancy Council, the Ordnance Survey, the Ramblers' Association, the Royal Society For The Protection Of Birds, the Tree Council, the Woodland Trust, Wye Agricultural College, and the Youth Hostels Association

Special thanks also go to:

Christopher Taylor for a detailed and patient response to a long list of queries which were couched in what was at the time the profoundest ignorance of his subject,

Angela King for supplying full documentation of sources for material quoted from Friends Of The Earth's 'Paradise Lost?'

Bob Vickers for a series of highly illuminating working tutorials in book design,

and Marion Shoard for extended and sympathetic help in answering questions and supplying information used in the final part of the book.

Part One:

Introductory

"There'll always be an England
While there's a country lane,
Wherever there's a cottage small
Beside a field of grain."

Ross Parker and Hughie Charles,
'There'll Always Be An England', 1939

There is a myth of the English countryside, and even in this last quarter of the 20th century it still retains something of its potency. The imagery of this myth has accumulated in myriad shapes through seven centuries and more of English culture, but it has always been and still remains most prominent in the culture-and-water of popular cliché. We see it, in passing, barely conscious of its existence, in the guise of badly printed reproductions of 'The Hay Wain' adorning the lids of chocolate boxes and the covers of 'Get Well Soon' cards; or in media reports on rural events which open with phrases such as "the sleepy little village of X, nestling in the heart of the Y-shire hills, where narrow lanes lead confusingly in every direction and time seems to have stopped altogether". We see it, and do not see it, when we buy milk in cartons whose waxed panels are decorated with artwork showing cows in bliss on golfing grass, and a tidy farm track winding past some thatched bucolic cottage complete with smoking chimney. We tolerate it daily, if not hourly, as cheap return nostalgia-trip commercials for Euro-mountain butter, rape margarine, and various brands of bread and beer, all of which claim spurious links with a rustic past through the employment of red-cheeked actors now ensconced as typecast yokels. Yet, contrary to every expectation, there is a depth implied in trivialities such as these. They could not possibly survive unless we, the consumers, were not in some way prepared to accept them, and take them consciously or unconsciously to our hearts. Somehow, if we let them, they will touch us.

I think that the urban Englishman retains some mental image of a better world, 'out there' beyond the most recent extensions of the urban fringe, where the motorway does not (yet) penetrate and there is not a supermarket, let alone a hypermarket, for half an hour's drive in any direction. He holds on to this image self-amusedly, perhaps even self-critically. Yet despite all the disclaimers he may make, it persists for him as something *almost* real. In this abstractly ideal rural world he believes – despite himself, since his common sense, indeed his very experience of the country, for the most part tell him otherwise – that some form of better life may perhaps, somehow, be lived, if not necessarily by him. He clings to the idea that there – but let us not be too precise – there somewhere, in the 'heart' of the countryside, it might in an undefined way be different from the familiar (the drear, the

(Opposite)   Near Nuffield, Oxfordshire.

11

appalling) reality of everyday urban life; if only he might find the way to transport himself, to spirit himself, away to it.

Oddly enough, this idea is cherished not only in the hearts of urban people. Some country people are just as prone to it. A lady who sold me two ambrosial doughnuts in a cake shop in Sturminster Newton, Dorset – which is as 'quaint' a small English town as you will find, if not the prettiest, though in very pretty country – told me with delight and a contagious sense of magic how she was going to drive down to Devon with her children over the forthcoming Bank Holiday weekend. It was as if, somehow, rural Devon was more special than rural mid-Dorset: *Devon*, for her, was the great Beyond. There are even some farmers in this country – alas, for the vanity of human wishes! – who will go to any length to avoid missing an episode of 'The Archers.'

For those looking further than the milk cartons and the British Rail Weekend Break posters, there is ranged the work of writers, painters and musicians, each dealing with specific sources of inspiration in the landscape, yet all ending up, like it or not, in the same unplanned conspiracy by which the myth is re-entrenched. It is all the same whether it is Paul Nash, for example, placing overblown full moon and sinking sun in haunting equilibrium in a single image, Ted Hughes casting in iron language the revelation of a group of silent horses in a frozen moorland dawn, or Thomas Hardy setting down layer by layer a 'documentary', beguiling narrative of life in a woodland hamlet which never quite existed and in which – it is a part of its beauty – man must suffer unjustly. Perhaps most pervasive of all are the composers; Elgar, Vaughan Williams, Bax, Moeran, Britten, Tippett, all of whom created music which was either deliberately expressive of notions of landscape or later became identified with it through appropriation by films and television, to the extent that certain pieces can hardly be heard today without listeners automatically attaching their own iconography. So, directly and indirectly, we have fed off such works: they have supplied us with correlatives, solidifications, of our own nebulous feelings about the landscape, and in the process the myth has been further complicated.

This myth of rural England is one that deserves to be treated with a certain cautious respect. It is too simple to see the clichés as the substance, or to plot their origins solely in patterns of social conditioning. Howard Newby takes such a position in his book *Green and Pleasant Land?*, where he attacks the widespread failure of the urban majority to see what is actually involved in the running of the countryside in economic and social terms, laying partial blame for this on the rift which has taken place between the notion of an idealized 'picturesque' landscape and the awareness of the actualities of farming practice. He sees this rift as having originated in the late 18th century revolution in taste, during which landscapes came to be treated as aesthetic objects, created to order as improvements upon nature in many private parks, whilst the economic basis of wealth – the farm – was literally tidied away out of sight of the big house. In the same way, the pursuit of 'pleasing prospects' by cultured or would-be cultured individuals led to the imposition of artificial preconceptions on what was actually there. If a view could be found, whether in the natural arbitrariness of wild hill country or indeed in the farmed landscapes themselves, which could be seen to resemble the generalized ideals of contemporary landscape painting, it was treasured and enthused over. The use of the Claude glass, a device reflecting a miniaturized, subdued version of its subject, seen broadly in terms of light and shade with – as it were – a layer of varnish imposed upon it, is a prime symptom of this early and sophisticated form of alienation.

No doubt we do derive something of our current attitudes to the country from this source, just as we also derive a great deal from the arts. But I think that the myth of rural England has another, and pre-existent, source within ourselves. It is something about which no-one who is touched by it can do very much: simply, it is there, rooted in the psyche. It is not specific to this country: just as there is a rural England myth so there are comparable myths in other parts of Europe. Pastoral art, for example, in the broadest terms a surfacing of the idea of the 'better place to be found somewhere beyond', has existed in Europe for over two millenia, with even more ancient counterparts in fairy tales and legends the world over. Dealing with the English variant of what he calls "the desire to create imaginary worlds other than the world that is the case", John Fowles (speaking in the voice of his eponymous character Daniel Martin) takes the legend of Robin Hood, the 'greenwood myth', as an example of "the notion of retreat, in both the religious and the military sense". This, he says, enshrines "a dominant mental characteristic, an essential behaviour, an archetypal *movement* . . . of the English imagination".

Was there ever a time when some ideal was not perceived in, or projected upon, 'the country'? Even when all of us lived there; even during the long ages in which we were forced to fend off the ravening wolf-packs in order to survive at all, 'rural' ideals were created by us in the shape of local gods – gods of trees and streams. Something more than the reasoning mind perceived was felt and agreed to be there. Such ideals in nature, and such ideals of places in nature far beyond the known world, yet contained mysteriously within it, have remained with us, and we will continue to imagine them in the English countryside wherever conditions allow. We will do so, I think, even when we become as well informed about the nitty-gritty of everyday rural life as Howard Newby would like us to be, because it cannot be helped. Disperse the myth with well-tailored argument, qualify it with complex new understanding, it will return nonetheless.

Why Country Lanes?

"Men, indeed, whose pleasure it is to explore even their own country
on foot, and to whom its every phase of climate is delightful, receive,
somewhat tardily, the spirit of The Road. They feel a meaning in it;
it grows to suggest the towns upon it, it explains its own vagaries, and
it gives a unity to all that has arisen along its way."

Hilaire Belloc,
'The Old Road', 1904

The country lanes have always played the most important part in my own
individual variant on the myth of rural England. If there is a mystery in
the landscape then the lanes have been my means of penetration into it.
In both senses of the phrase, the lanes have led me on. And, of course,
I have never quite arrived where I expected to arrive: the lanes of reality,
despite all the force of one's imaginings, lead only to another part of the
same reality. Yet, endlessly and tantalizingly, their promise is renewed, and
since there is something close to an infinity – a universe – of lanes in England,
for me exploring them has become an end in itself, and subject in itself.

This book is something of a harvest; and, as the foregoing remarks have
no doubt already suggested, it is also and without apology a highly personal
piece of work. I have been exploring the lanes since I was first considered
old enough to go long distances on a bicycle, and I began to photograph
them at a not much later date. It quickly became my life's plan to cycle
along every country lane in England (and for some reason, despite my Celtic
forefathers, it has always been the English lanes which drew me most strongly),
to *go* everywhere and to *be* everywhere. But then I began to realize exactly
how many lanes there were. In Suffolk, for example, there are 2,845 km.
of unclassified roads; in Somerset 2,938 km.; in Shropshire 2,335 km. Even
so, I was not absolutely deterred: I modified my plan so that through regular
exercise and a pulse- and bran-laden diet I could contrive to live into my
90s, mobile till the last. Failing that, there was always the prospect of reincar-
nation.

Many of the pictures in this book were taken during the summer of
1980, but there is a sprinkling of images which date back over more than
a decade. For the most part, my explorations for the book were carried
out in territory already well known to me, where it was often the case that
I photographed again scenes and objects that I had photographed many
times before. It is my firm belief that the smallest area of landscape is inexhaustible from the points of view both of exploration and creation. On my 1980

journey I made countless new discoveries in each area, even in such country as that around the Stour valley in Suffolk, which I have visited more times than I can possibly remember. This, then, has been my experience. Whilst my other mobile friends were catching the next fast yak to Macchu Picchu or paddling their way up brown New Guinea backwaters, I have been in Essex, or Berkshire, for the 40th time, weaving my way in between the commuters and the factory farms. And it has sufficed.

For as long as I have been aware of them, there has seemed to me to be a magic in the lanes, even, at times, when they were not obviously beautiful. A while ago I came across two pictures, one of which used to hang in my room when I was a child, the other having entered my parents' house as a gift when I was six or seven years old. The first is an illustration of the nursery rhyme in which the cow jumps over the moon: it shows a bright night, and – behind the leaping cow, the cat with the fiddle, the dog, the plate and the spoon with smiling faces and tiny legs – there is a yellow lane, curving away to a close horizon; along it, past a small tiled cottage, there runs prosaically a line of telegraph wires. It is not a masterpiece of children's illustration, this picture, but art does not need to be great in order to affect the imaginations of children deeply. From a very early age I must have been made to feel by it that lanes are a natural part of the landscape of fairytale, and looked at it before I dreamed; and I do not think it is too fanciful to say that the second part of this book has come into being as a result of a (partly conscious) desire to make a kind of child's storybook out of the lanes' actualities.

The second picture is a small painting done by an old lady long since dead who lived three doors up from my childhood home. Both she and her husband were amateur watercolourists, and left behind an impressive collection of elegant, small-scale works, some of them painted in the Far East, many more painted in England. This picture shows another lane: it has very broad verges and mature trees, and could almost be a parkland drive but for the presence of two low, functional-looking barns, one of which has a red roof. I cannot look at this painting now without recollecting a trip I was once taken on by the old couple in their well-sprung Austin 7. Rightly or wrongly, I believe that on this trip we travelled along the lane which appears in the painting. By deduction I strongly suspect that the lane must be somewhere in Cheshire; but despite the fact that subsequent explorations have made me as familiar with the Cheshire lanes as any others, I have never been along it again. The painting hangs on my wall now as a perpetual challenge to find out where it was done.

But there is another and much more generalized kind of 'lost place' for which I have also found myself searching as I explored the English lanes. I was born just in time to catch a glimpse of the hindmost end of the old rural England, in which many villages were still occupied primarily by country people – many of them pensioners by the time I met them – and the cottages up the back lanes had only been taken over in certain areas, close to the towns and cities, by the influx of holiday-homers and urban refugees which by the beginning of the 1980s had almost totally transformed the social structure of the countryside. So I saw villages in many of the English counties *before* the developers with fine pointed teeth had begun their mass architectural and environmental rape in those areas of country previously little influenced by the town. I saw the gardens, meadows and donkey pastures between old farms and cottages which were subsequently and very quickly 'infilled' (to stoop to the jargon), first with horizontal-rectilinear 1960s bungalows, and thereafter with jam-packed estates of 'desirable"executive" residences'.

I soon understood that the country people whom I most liked and cared about, those whose world had been a village and its surrounding fields, were being supplanted even as I came to know them (and since I had few rural relatives, this was mainly through passing chats along the lanes or in pubs). The youngest of the new 'rustics' seemed, to a man, to be hell-bent on getting out as fast as they could (but to where?) on their quietude-shattering mo'bikes, or in their souped up, big-wheeled Minis and Cortinas. At the other end of the scale the old landworkers were being replaced by another class entirely: the politely unfriendly, territorially hypersensitive urban middle classes. There were – of course! – many notable exceptions in both camps. But the feelings of loss which I experienced as I travelled have been vivid enough at times nevertheless. The more I explored the country, the more desperate and frustrated grew my pursuit for the vestiges of the old way of life there, and this pursuit quickly established itself as the strongest single motivation for my photography – paradoxically perhaps, since I have rarely photographed country people. Thus, in photographing the lanes and their paraphernalia, I have not only been recording the artefacts of the pre-urbanized countryside; I have also been seeing them filtered through an awareness of the fact that these things and places were alive and significant for people fixed in the old communities as they are no longer, in a manner which it seems cannot ever be re-created. Another way of putting this would be to say that, to my eyes, the lanes are haunted.

Nowadays I am a little more wary of idealizing the past. I admit that this romantic sense of loss is based to a degree on feelings more pastoral than practical. I acknowledge the hard, atrocious facts of rural history, and I would be amongst the first to point out the absurdity of regretting the loss of a way of life which was not worth having in the first place. Indeed I would go further: it is not simply absurd, it is positively sinister to eulogize on such a subject from a position of remote ignorance, encompassing the utter degradation which was the daily experience of so many 19th- and early-

20th-century farm workers, for example, in what must therefore emerge as just another product of the fantasized history of an Olde England that never was.

But there is another side to this particular coin. Even Howard Newby, in his entirely justifiable crusade against the wrong-headedness of urban attitudes to the rural world, acknowledges, for instance, the loyalty of old-time villagers to their own small patch of country, the sense of identity which many of them had from this, and the certainty with which they regarded life from within the bastion of an unchanging set of *mores*. When on top of this you meet a man, landworker or farmer, who has been palpably contented by a lifetime bound up with the land and the forces of nature as collaborator rather than as tyrant (and intensive farming is nothing if it is not a tyranny over nature), no matter how his earnings have compared with the national average, then it is very difficult indeed not to believe that *some* things worth keeping have almost disappeared from the face of the English earth. Such thoughts become all the more hard to resist when one also confronts the many physical changes which have taken place, and which threaten to take place, in the fabric of the long-established rural landscape.

On Guide Books, And Why This Is Not One

Once upon a time, I met a Canadian couple in Colchester. They had just bought themselves first-rate touring bicycles in London and were started out on a cycling tour of Europe. The country between London and Colchester is hardly the most exciting in England – some would say it is amongst the dullest – but it does offer a wide variety of routes across its empty landscapes, along a complex network of lanes. This couple had come, however, not through the mid-Essex claylands with their many timber-frame and plaster villages such as Thaxted and Stebbing, and the plentiful sprinkling of Tudor and Jacobean buildings to be found on the roads in between; nor via the lanes which lead down to and back from the resoundingly bleak, level marshlands around the coastal estuaries (worth seeing precisely because of their bleakness). Instead they had cycled out of London along the Mile End Road, and followed the A12, the next worst thing to a motorway, through a nadir of urban strip-development, to the constant and threatening two-note accompaniment of large diesel engines. In despair on the first day, when there was also torrential rain and a headwind, they put up in a B & B in Billericay. *Billericay*! I was not entirely surprised to find that they did not so far think very much of England.

These people possessed the motivation to get out there on bicycles, which is without any doubt the best way to explore the English countryside. But what they patently lacked was information – such as the fact that good maps are available which would show them every detail of a cross-country route, or indeed the knowledge that the lanes existed at all, and were freely available to the public.

Most foreigners come here, often conditioned by garish brochure photographs, in search of the 'real England' – yet experience even less again. All they find in the hotels and amenities of the tourist traps and the motorways inbetween is a suave anglicized variant of North American culture, a trans-Continental Nowhereland in which certain monuments – the Tower, Windsor, Blenheim, the villages of Broadway and Bourton on the Water in the Cotswolds – are marketed as little more than three-dimensional projections of brochure images, to be consumed via photography (the evidence of having been there providing later confirmation for the tourists themselves since, I am convinced, they do not quite believe it at the time) and summarily departed from. Yet when foreign travellers begin to perceive the real density and complexity of the English landscape, then their simultaneous excitement and sense of frustration at not having more time can be a wonderful thing to behold. Since I often use Youth Hostels when I am travelling, I have met many cyclists from other countries (and it is particularly the people from the wide-open-space countries such as Australia, the States, and Zimbabwe who seem to respond in this way) who have complained to me that they have to move too fast in order to complete their planned itineraries. How good it would be, they say, just to stay here in North Devon, or mid-Northamptonshire, and *really get to know it*. These people are cyclists, and even so they feel frustrated. Unlike the Tower-snappers they have begun to realize just how much there is to see. Yet even when they have the time to do things in detail, all but the very few lack an effective method of exploration.

For the home resident there is a somewhat subtler problem. Most of us know that the lanes exist, and most of us have had some experience of them, even when this is nothing more immediate than the occasional Sunday afternoon drive with the relatives, or a trip to a country pub. But in our day-to-day lives we move outside the *dimension* of the lanes. Our dimension is that of urban streets, shopping arcades, trunk roads, double yellow lines, roundabouts, sodium lights, petrol stations, car parks; and that of the railways and their landscapes; and that of the motorways and theirs. We get from our own backyard to our place of work and our friends' backyards along these routes. They are our reality. For the most part, the lanes are not.

Any book on the lanes must therefore act by definition as a reminder of their beauty. But the question remains: if such a book is to encourage its readers out into the lanes, how exactly should it set about it? It seems to me that there are two methods of encouragement, and that they are diametrically opposed. The first is to make specific and detailed recommendations, devising routes which the reader will follow like the good reader that he is. The second is to provide a generalized appreciation of what *may* be found along the lanes, using details only as examples, and to try to persuade the would-be traveller to go out and find things for himself.

Paragons of the first approach, the Automobile Association has in the past few years produced a series of publications which could not easily be surpassed for their thoroughness as routing guides. These books, for example *The AA Book of Country Walks* (1979), a selection of walks all beginning and ending comfortably at a car park, or *Hand-Picked Tours in Britain* (1977), a selection of pleasure trips for motorists which makes partial use of the lanes, are the very acme of predigestion. The first book has its basis in the assumption that the reader is as a matter of course a more or less helpless metropolitan, car-bound creature who lives in subdued terror of any place where there is no cement and is likely to pass out at the sight of his first cow, and who *ex hypothesi* requires to be coaxed and seduced out of the overheated, carpeted interior of his car by a combination of paintings which show the tiny area (walks are between 5 and 10 km. long) as an aerial view, and by a text sometimes supported with drawings dealing with each and every stage in the walk – it seems right down to the last daisy – so that there is no chance whatsoever that he will ever get, or feel, lost. The picture which one takes from this of technophiliac, naturaphobiac man would be very sad indeed if it were not so wonderfully silly. Can we truly have come to this, in only two centuries of physical and social separation from the land, that we are considered to have need of such flagrant cosseting?

Surveys have been conducted which suggest that we have. The Countryside Commission's 'National Household Survey' (1977) identifies a 'conservatism' in people making trips to the country which inclines them to stick to familiar routes to the familiar venues, "and is reinforced by an uncertainty about where they can and cannot go in the countryside". The majority of countryside visitors (and how very sad for them if this is true) never get more than a few hundred yards from their cars, and most seem to be perfectly happy if they are supplied with a view, a place to park to look at it, a refreshments kiosk and a toilet to nip into before the journey home. Alas, no matter how much I may wish to reject it, this uninspiring picture has been borne out for me on a number of occasions by direct experience. Once, for example, I was cycling in the depths of the aforementioned Essex lanes one winter's dusk, near the strangely atmospheric village of Pleshey, when I was hailed by the driver of a car full of people from Harlow New Town who wanted to know the way back. Now Pleshey is not more than 16 km.

from Harlow, but there was a subdued anxiety in this driver's voice as he asked for directions (needless to say, he had no map), and I may be imagining it but I fancied that there was an expression of disturbed surprise on the faces of his passengers to see me, a bare-headed cyclist, out in this devilish lonely place as dark night fell. Another time, the relatives of a friend were staying at my house: they were a forthright, solid couple, down from the North for a short holiday, and new to the countryside of central southern England. On three separate occasions they stalwartly ignored every piece of advice we tried to give them on the hidden beauties of the surrounding area, refused the loan of maps, and drove along the most choked and ugly trunk roads to each mass-consumption destination (Blenheim, etc.). Could neither read an Ordnance Survey map? Or were they also, in truth, secretly afraid?

Other organizations than the AA have responded to this state of affairs in the best British avuncular tradition. On the ground one finds guidance for the nervous motorist in the shape of signposted 'Leisure Drives', developed by regional Tourist Boards and making use of both major roads and certain lanes. In addition to signposts placed at every junction, some Boards also produce leaflets with directions and details of what to look for. Users follow and do not deviate from the approved circuit, see what they are told to see, and get home to tea well before the afternoon has ended.

This gizzard-cramming phenomenon is not, alas, limited to guidance for the helpless motorist. Helpless cyclists (are there such beings?) can also now get assistance, in publications such as the *Cyclists' Touring Club Route Guide to Cycling in Britain and Ireland* (1980). I find it absolutely impossible not to be ambivalent about a book such as this. On the one hand it is almost exclusively a guide to routes along the lanes, which is of course right-headed, and many of the routes are well chosen: the book cannot fail to be of immediate help to those who have not cycled in the countryside before and who do, for whatever reasons, good or bad, feel the need of a pointing finger to help them on their way. It also enables one to plan lengthy journeys around the whole of the British Isles along country roads linking places of interest, for the most part avoiding drab Subtopia. But it is nonetheless a *guide*, giving specific directions which the less inventive reader is likely to follow to the exclusion of other possibilities.

It is time for me to lay open to scrutiny my own view about methods of exploring the lanes. This exists, as the reader may perhaps already have guessed, in emphatic opposition to the trend just described. To put it as simply as I can, I believe that it is useful but by no means essential to be informed about the places one visits, but that it is never good to know a lot at first, and that it is positively harmful to follow the detailed directions of another individual (or worse, committee) who has been there long before you. The lanes, as I have said, are endless. They go in every direction, parting and rejoining and doubling back upon themselves, and a very small area can be explored time and again, constantly yielding up new and unexpected pleasures. Like *The AA Book of Country Walks*, the *CTC Route Guide* does it all for you, telling you where to go and what to look at. It eliminates randomness, and in so doing makes impossible both the sense of intimate knowledge of a landscape and the high philosophic state which can be experienced at times, and entirely unpredictably, by just pootling around on a bicycle in some small and localized network of lanes. Again, like *The AA Book of Country Walks*, the *CTC Route Guide* subtly smothers inspiration: if you know, as you must, that others have been there before you, planning and approving the route (and making sketches of stile 'A' and gate 'B'), then what can be new? What can be fresh? How can it be possible to experience the exhilarating sensation of discovery through which it seems that somehow, miraculously, the landscape has materialized out of nothingness only moments before you arrived there, and that *you* are the sole and honoured discoverer of this new world? If Wordsworth's daffodils had been drawn by some graphic artist employed by the AA before he himself had arrived at them, I doubt that he would have written the poem.

As its title implies, the emphasis in the *Route Guide* is on getting from A to B, of a course to be run, of starting points and destinations. Naturally, this can answer a perfectly real need: there are always times during travelling when one wants to rise early and cover (relatively) huge distances, to feel the land passing copiously under one's wheels, with the big skies spreading in every direction as if in apotheosis of one's own heroic efforts. In other words, there can be a real need for a sense of *saga*, and on such days one must have a route of some sort in order to cover the ground. But surely – if one is to be a real hero – it is far better even then to plan one's own route? To venture into the unknown, even if at times it sorely disappoints, is better than to move always in the known.

I have two reactions to the tabulated conservatism of the majority of those who go into the countryside. The first is to jeer rudely, in the hope that some of those who do already know far better may be either shamed or goaded into getting – let us say – *four* hundred metres from their cars next time. The other is to reflect rather more calmly that if so many of those who get themselves to the country are identifiably apathetic or timid, then there must be something fundamentally lacking in education on this subject. Marion Shoard observes in her book *The Theft of the Countryside* that at present "most people need to be led by the hand into the countryside and shown what it can offer them". I would like to see very much more such leading done, as a matter of course when people are at a more impressionable age, from Junior School level and upwards.

The Actual Intentions Of This Book, And How They Are Realized

My reaction to the gizzed-cramming guides has been to try to produce an antidote to them here. *English Country Lanes* is an *anti-guide*, and its central philosophy is best summed up in the simple words GO AND FIND IT FOR YOURSELF! For what you discover independently in the English countryside will stimulate your imagination far more deeply, and remain far longer in your memory, than all those items which you expect to come across at regular intervals, on predetermined journeys, no matter how interesting these may be in themselves. Clearly there is some balance to be struck so far as information is concerned: it is always useful to have *some* idea of what is in an area before you get to it. At the same time it is a common experience that when one begins to know and love a stretch of country, one also comes to want to learn about it; and there is no better time to read and learn than when that bond has already been made through exploration. The kind of reading one does in the circumstances – on the history of the county, or on the history of the creation of its landscapes and buildings – will be of an entirely different order to the superficial 'TV' knowledge born of leafing through guide books or route guides.

But for those concerned with exploring the lanes for the lanes' sake, all that is needed to begin with is the vaguest idea of what may be rewarding areas to try (and very few areas are totally unrewarding when they are looked at in the right way), and some method of exploration. The ten small networks of lanes covered in the third section of this book are thus included only as examples of what *may* be discovered by slow and savouring exploration of compact areas of country, and not by any means as places to which the reader must perforce go if he is to see anything at all. Some of these areas are indeed very lovely, and possess lanes to match, but they are not offered here as the 'cream' of the lanes, as *The AA Book of Country Walks* somewhat absurdly offers its selection of routes. Each of us does of course have his favourite places, and I have included several of mine here – fearing, during less confident and no doubt less morally defensible moments, that I might be betraying them to invading hordes already darkening the horizons as they march en masse in search of solitude. But in the matter of lanes and paths there is no such thing as 'the cream', or if there is then it is, thank God, beyond classification. The networks of lanes immediately next to those described here may be quite as pleasant; they may be more so, they may be less so. But even where I have an opinion on this I shall not be letting on since, I insist, it is up to you, o gentle but unlethargic reader, to find out such things for yourself.

Other of the networks are not obviously beautiful, and I chose to include them for precisely this reason. One of the greatest pleasures in the lanes lies in the chance discovery of small and unexpected beauties along them, or in the country they traverse, which one would never guess to exist at all if one were flashing by in a car. Such beauties are present in varying degrees along all country lanes, and not merely in those areas generally noted for their landscapes (or indeed for the richness and variety of their lanes); they exist in parts of Cambridgeshire and amongst the Somerset Levels, as well as in Shropshire and Devon, and it was one of my intentions to emphasize the fact. Again, those stretches of country into which the uglinesses of the suburban and technological world do not noticeably penetrate, however immediately unimposing they may seem (especially to the motorist), are in my view beautiful by default. Homely and undramatic they may be, but they are nevertheless 'unspoiled', and satisfying for that reason alone; in England today, the sense that the beauty – or non-ugliness – of a stretch of country spreads unimpaired in all directions is a thing greatly to be valued in itself. Overall, my bias was rather more towards the lesser-known stretches, and away from those parts which lie within government-designated Areas of Outstanding Natural Beauty, or which contain noted beauty spots or other tourist honeypots to which motorists at present flood in their thousands. (Two networks do, however, partly coincide with A.O.N.Bs.)

The complexity of the lanes in the networks was a considered factor in their choosing: by no means every network offers quite so many byways-per-square-km. as do most of these. But once again my motive was merely to supply examples. The message remains: this is the *kind* of richness and complexity which lies in wait out there, not the 'best' of it. Seek, and ye may get lost in every county, metaphorically if not literally, along an entrancing variety of lanes and back lanes. The harder you look, the more likely you will be to find the quietest routes (see 'Advice' section ahead), along which your sense of remoteness from the madding and motorized crowd will be rarely broken into. Even in the 1980s there remain many areas in which it is possible to think of towns as places in the country, rather than of the country as a series of compromised and trampled spaces between the suburbs of a single great coast-to-coast town – the common experience when driving so many trunk roads. In the same breath it is worth saying that no one network, either those dealt with here or elsewhere, has uniformly beautiful lanes, and that it is very much in some networks rather than in others that the apparent continuity of unspoiled landscape can be most vividly experienced.

For the same reason that the networks are offered as examples only, the captions to pictures in Part Three have for the most part been deliberately kept a trifle vague. If you want to know exactly where each picture was taken – well, that's just too bad! Were there to be any reader who nevertheless insisted on pursuing the chimera of geographical accuracy where it is not relevant (rather than simply taking the point), then all I can suggest is that he go off for a ride or two in the country concerned and conduct his own investigations. But he will be winning no prizes from me – no, not so much as a *plastic* hare – even if he comes back with grid references for every picture in the book. Inevitably the text for these sections mentions specific lanes and specific points of interest; but they are by no means a comprehensive list, and I hope that there will remain many pleasant surprises for the traveller even in these ten networks, if he did happen, by sheerest chance, to find himself exploring them. On one subject only have I attempted to be exhaustive and specific, and this is in the detailing of what is ugly, disappointing, and indeed at times worth going out of one's way to avoid. This is not quite so perverse a scheme as it may at first sound, as I hope to demonstrate later.

One question which was often in my mind whilst I photographed the lanes was: would it be possible in some way to define their beauties, so that one arrived at what might be described as an 'aesthetic' for the lanes? Would it be possible, then, to produce some abstract of features – the kinds of trees growing or their siting, the presence, height and density of hedges, the narrowness or enclosure of the roads, the ways they bend, the frequency of all those laneside items such as gates, stiles, old signposts, triangular greens at junctions – to which one might refer when trying to establish what pleases people most along the lanes? Particularly now, when the landscape is changing so rapidly, considerations of this kind are potentially valuable, and I have therefore attempted to record as many of the lanes' individual beauties as possible, in the knowledge that they may not survive much longer.

But the lanes vary as greatly from region to region as does the country through which they pass. There is no such thing as a typical English country lane, no matter how hard the woolly travel writers of the 1930s may have tried to persuade people otherwise. So, for example, in my own wanderings I moved from the largely hedgeless, broad-contoured, timber-and-thatch-cottaged country of west Suffolk, with its lanes ribboning away across the present farming landscape very much like certain storybook illustrations, to the Parliamentary Enclosure landscapes of Rutland with their broad-verged, walled-in lanes and buildings of deep brown ironstone; from the semi-wooded, half-English half-Welsh countryside of western Herefordshire, whose lanes' complex windings may have first taken shape in Dark Ages forest, if not earlier, to the sweeping upland around Avebury which has a network of still unmetalled wire-fenced tracks and farm roads; from the die-straight, narrow farm roads running across the peat of the Somerset Levels to the beech-hedged lanes that climb and drop, and climb and drop, down the small, steep valley sides of that elevated region of mid-Devon around Chulmleigh from which one can see Dartmoor always to the south, and Exmoor always to the north. There are many other small areas, for example in the Cotswolds, northern Shropshire, Warwickshire, Northamptonshire, Sussex and Kent, which I shortlisted (and some of which I photographed) and then lamentingly excluded since this was not, after all, a thousand-page book, and all of these have their own further distinct identities.

The idealized 'journey' which makes up the second part of the book is, therefore, in one sense, a conscious extension of the grand tradition of the woolly travel writing of the 1930s. It has come into existence for no better nor worse reason than that I love the lanes far too much to have been able to resist compiling it. I hope its presence here will not serve to obscure the fact that each area – each 'lanescape' – has its own aesthetic. I have pointed a finger at some of the most obvious features of the networks explored in Part Three, but no more. However, if the surviving non-intensified farming landscapes of England are to be preserved – and restored – as I hope they will be, and if the most desolating of the new prairie zones are to be modified and given some worthwhile identity of their own, then a very great deal more such finger-pointing and noting of what is special in each area will have to be done in the near future.

Some Further Details Of The Author's Brief

A number of other factors influenced the content and shape of this book, some of which came into play only when work had begun on it. First, I think it is worth mentioning that a certain amount of consideration went into the overall choice of angles of view in the photographs. Except in hedgeless landscapes, what motorists see along the lanes for much of the time is the lanes themselves. This is also true to a certain extent of cyclists, but even in the highest-hedged and narrowest lanes cyclists are free to stop in gateways and to enjoy the views that motorists only dream of. There was a case, then, for producing photographs not only *of* the lanes, but also *from* them. Thus in this second category, with only a handful of exceptions, the photographs are of views which can be seen by someone standing in the lanes themselves; the exceptions are those in which I clambered over a gate into a field and walked a few yards in order to do better justice to the subject. With unprecedented honesty, I have noted these few moments of 'cheating' in the relevant captions.

There was also the problem in each area of where to draw the line between lanescapes and 'village views'. I was determined from the start that this should not be yet another book making capital out of 'the glories of the English village'. This, after all, was to be a book about the lanes. But lanes run inexorably into villages, and in certain areas – for example in the country of the Newmarket hinterland – the villages have evolved in such a way that they sometimes straggle down a miniature network of four or five lanes of their own, a farm here, a cottage there, and plenty of land inbetween. In most areas there are also what may be loosely described as 'hamlets'; clusters of perhaps only four or five houses, with no church, usually though not always outlying settlements of some larger village. I decided to compromise here: some hamlets are included, especially where they have blended into the lanes to the point where car passengers are likely not to notice them at all, and I have permitted myself the freedom of sometimes photographing the village 'back lanes' – the lanes leading away from the main thoroughfares where the calendar shots are always taken, which often only have a house or two dotted along them. These are especially rewarding where they run directly into fields as cul-de-sacs (except for the unfortunate motorist), and no subtopian commuter growth has taken place. In the case of the non-nucleated, straggling kind of village, every lane can be a back lane and I had to judge each place on its merits. Again, I hope that the captions to such photographs as were taken in these spots will help to keep the picture clear.

Finally, I should mention that this book does not dwell for very long on untarred routes: bridleways, 'roads used as public paths', farm roads, Roman roads, ancient trackways, lanes made originally as boundaries between estates – all those routes which are now increasingly and confusingly to be found lumped together under the umbrella term 'green lanes'. These do occur, of course, in all the networks, much more in some than in others, but only in certain cases did I spend any amount of time exploring them: the complex of upland tracks around Avebury could not possibly be ignored, and in both the Somerset Levels and the country around Hartland in Devon there are tracks, or metalled roads dwindling into tracks, which are very useful for the cyclist seeking to find routes where the motorist does not venture.

But from the start this was planned as a book which would celebrate the experience of cycling along the (relatively) smooth surface of tarred minor roads, and the sense of freedom which can be a part of such travel. The difficult rides or walks with one's bike which are to be expected along the rough gravel, hard earth, ruts or mire of unmetalled tracks are not quite of the same order, fun as they may nevertheless be if one is in the right mood. Let me say, though, that for those desiring to penetrate the countryside to its 'innermost heart' by bicycle, the roads with no tar on them are very difficult to equal.

Pootling

As bicycles are flooding back by their millions to the garden sheds, garages and glasshouses of the great British public, I predict with barely suppressed anticipation the imminent emergence of a new cult – it would be tautologous to call it a 'movement' – and I earnestly hope that in its own small way this book may contribute a thing or two to its growth. I am referring to the cult of the pootlists*: those enlightened few, soon to be many, who use their bicycles when they are enjoying them for their own sake – rather than simply enjoying them whilst getting to work, or whilst doing the shopping – for no grander purpose than to *pootle* around the country lanes.

It may be that the reader is unfamiliar with the term 'pootle', which has yet to find its rightful place in the O.E.D. Let me explain then that, as I understand it, 'pootle' has emerged as an inspired combination of 'pedal' and 'footle', but that the pejorative overtones – the notions of scurrilous time-wasting and aimlessness – implicit in the latter are entirely absent in the new compound. The pootlist is never shamefaced or apologetic – indeed, he is quiet the opposite – in discussing the fact that he has done nothing very much and, what is more, has done it randomly, and taken rather a lot of time over it. He is more likely to return after a day's cyclo-pootling (to use the term's more weighty committee version, the essential French translation of which, for the record, must be *le cyclo-poûtlisme*) ready to shout his small-scale exploits to the rooftops.

One thing I must make clear to those who as yet know nothing about the subject, and this is that pootling is utterly distinct either from racing cycling or from the use of bicycles in the countryside by those who live under the fond and commonplace delusion that cycle touring must, by definition, be some form of sport. These are they who open a conversation with their peers *not* with any attempt to discuss their experience in the country (since very probably they have experienced little of it), or what they have learned from people along the way (since they will not have stopped to meet any), but rather with the predictable, dull, achievement-oriented conversation-stopper, "How many miles did *you* do today?" So far from being a racer, or an achiever, the pootlist is involved in the diametric opposite of a race. He travels not to reach a distant goal in the shortest possible time, but so that he may experience both the places he traverses and the act of travelling in itself: he does, indeed, travel in the longest available

---

* I refer to pootlists/cyclists throughout as male. This is for the sake of simplicity and consistency only, and not in any way because I think of them as exclusively male. Truth to tell, some of my best friends are female pootlists.

time. Whilst as the days pass he may well find himself growing fitter than he has been for many a month, his first concern in using his bicycle in the country is not physical exercise – and even less is it any kind of competition, unless this be some private competition with himself – but to live life as fully as life will allow.

I have to admit that I do harbour a bemused admiration for the cycling heavies: in their own way many of them are idealists. Nevertheless, if the layman wishes to identify the mad cyclists of the cliché, I think he need look no further than amongst their ranks. Those who submit themselves to the incomprehensible rigours of 'L'Officiel Audax'; those who converge in packs in order to whisk themselves, heads permanently lowered, along traffic-infested trunk roads between cities on opposite sides of the island, and pre-ferably before lunch, and those who cycle the countryside in blind imitation of them, are depriving themselves of what, I must maintain, are by far and away the greatest joys that the bicycle has to offer – the joys of travelling slowly.

It is one of those unfortunate little ironies with which life is so bedevilled that the racers, whilst quite mad, can look far saner to the undiscriminating outsider who has been conditioned by watching sport on television than the pootlists themselves. The pootlist's customary ragbag kit – the sawn-off shorts, sometimes worn in ludicrous combination with lightweight hiking boots and socks with the wrong pattern, the oversize balaclava or, worse, sou'wester, the flapping tentlike waterproofs, the fingerless Scrooge gloves – might all have been especially adapted from original designs by Giles. The pootlist is very often to be encountered in the most unexpected places, and under the most unexpected conditions: munching nuts and raisins like some outsize rodent, for example, whilst sheltering under a bank of yews in the kind of downpour in which the quietest rivers break their banks and roads them-selves become rivers – and, what is more, appearing to *enjoy* himself. It should not be too surprising if the impression gained from behind the high-speed wipers of passing cars is one of unmitigated lunacy.

I am therefore confronted with a problem. How best might I describe the exhilarations – the rare exhilarations – of pootling, to such readers as have never yet experienced them, so that they will begin to see why (despite all such impressions) pootlists are in fact the very opposite of moonstruck? There may be just one fact which I have to advantage here, and this is that most of us do at least vaguely remember the pleasures of bicycling which we experienced in our youth. Perhaps even the most hardened advocate of the internal combustion engine has in this respect an Achilles heel (an Achilles cycle-clip?) that I may exploit to advantage. The bicycle is in any case still generally associated with childhood – which, of course, is why boys desiring to seem as men (and believing the myth that the moped is manly)

(Opposite)   Near Holt, Norfolk.

29

deride the passing cyclist. Many who rediscover the bike in later life do literally rediscover the machine of their childhood, and retrieve it from the spiders and dried-out potting compost. On top of this, it does seem that attitudes to the use of bicycles are now changing, so that the many not-quite-converted, the latent pootlists who have recently purchased new machines, may eventually convert themselves. The figures are certainly encouraging. Between 1970 and 1980 the annual rate of cycle sales doubled, whilst in 1979 they almost reached the all-time high of 1935, in which 1.6M machines were sold; and 1935, you may remember, was a year in which it was possible to take photographs of the bepedalled hordes in our inner city and industrial areas which made them look more like Dutch towns than the Dutch towns themselves.

The Joys Of Travelling Slowly

"I have always longed to be a part of the outward life, to be out there on the edge of things, to let the human taint wash away in emptiness and silence as the fox sloughs his smell into the cold unworldliness of water; to return to the town as a stranger."

J.A. Baker,
'The Peregrine', 1967

Perhaps I should open this heartfelt polemic by saying again that *English Country Lanes* was made by bicycle, and could not have been made in any other way. By this I mean not simply that I did all my exploring of the lanes by bike, and got from area to area by bike (with two exceptions where I hopped a lift on a train), but that what I photographed, what I saw, and above all what I felt in each place, was absolutely conditioned by my mode of transport. If I had been misguided enough to attempt a book on the lanes using a car, I would have missed 80 per cent of what mattered, if not more. I would not have seen the details in the hedgerows, I would have roared past even the more prominent subjects before I could properly register them, I would have worked in a state of sustained frustration and fear of holding up imaginary traffic if ever I slowed down, or worse, stopped. And never at any time whilst I was in a car would I have been able to enter into that entirely real and yet elusive phenomenon which is known as the *spirit of place*. For the bicycle can put its reflective user into a contact with the places he traverses such as enables him to sense their specialness, their individuality, perhaps even more immediately than if he were simply walking.

There is a bicycle currently available which is known as the 'Free Spirit'. It is not a very exciting machine in itself, but the name is striking: it describes far better than the zappy adolescent terms used by other manufacturers what is most significant about the bicycle: its rare power to free its user. The freedoms to be enjoyed in cycling the lanes are both physical and psychical, though there is no real dividing line between the two. I will begin with some of the physical aspects.

In the first place, there is the most obvious freedom of all: exposure to the air, the sun, and the weather. Most cyclists find that they can stay warm easily whilst they are moving, even on cool days. This is because of the alteration in the circulation of the blood which results from any form of physical exercise, the blood flow being redirected to the muscles and away from the intestines. It is thus frequently possible even in April to cycle in nothing more than shirt, shorts and plimsolls, whilst most of the rest of the British shuffle around in jackets and coats; and in May, a few days' cycling during sunny weather is enough to get a tan going – a month or more before most people will seriously consider removing their clothes. In high summer the stripped-down kit is an almost permanent feature for the pootlist, who will no doubt sometimes find himself feeling patronisingly sorry for all those poor, sad motorists, stuck by their sweaty nylon shirts to hot plastic seats as they burn along past him inside an endless array of mobile greenhouses.

And what of the rain, that much-dreaded, theoretical foe of all cyclists, which is used as justification for inactivity by so many who might otherwise ride? There are times, admittedly, when it can be too much, but in my experience such times really are quite rare. I was photographing for this book during what I later learned the media had christened "the worst summer for 25 years". It did rain a little, I must admit, and there were a couple of days during the three months I was out when it rained so hard, and gusted so hard, that I was glad to get indoors. But as to the rest, for most of the time that it was raining, or thundering, or blowing, or staying grey and heavy, I enjoyed it. The beauty of the English weather is precisely that it is so varied; and variety means rain, at least for a part of the time. On a bike, the sunny days stick in the memory particularly when they are framed by contrasting grey days: a brilliant Tuesday is all the more rewarding to the cyclist when he has had to pedal through a drenching Monday to get to it, even if he does not quite look at it like that at the time.

The rain can also be a positive pleasure when the wind is with you, moving mysteriously across the landscape in veils of greyness whilst the air currents guide you imperceptibly forward along the road surface, catching in the impromptu sail made by your cycle cape, and you travel in a 'silence' made out of the temporary concordance of your movement with the gigantic circling of the anti-cyclone. Again, in that marvellous kind of weather in which short, hard rainstorms alternate with periods of dazzling sunshine that make the wet roads steam, there is an exhilaration in beating each storm to the next stretch of cover – a distant tree belt or spinney, say – and this is all the more exciting when you are up on a windswept ridge and can see the weather coming at you, blackening the fields below as it draws closer. As the first drops of rain splash against your face you clamber into your waterproofs, and motorists will drive past you with all their lights on, quailing at the very sight of you because it comes as an uncomfortable reminder of what it might be like to stand out there, cut off from the fan-heated interiors of their cars.

And when the rain and wind are undeniably against you, it is still possible – sometimes, anyway – to treat them positively, as a test of patience rather than of strength. Continuing undeterred can lead after a time to a feeling of satisying completeness in having risen to the challenge. As in all physical activities that involve exposure to the elements, you can find yourself entering into an intimacy with your opponents; just so long as you do not push too hard at any one stage, or lose hope of reaching your destination, or begin to rail Tamburlaine-like at the heavens for chucking it down on you, as if you have been specifically chosen for the purpose. The cold water spraying on your face, the bluster of the headwind, even the obscurity of the road ahead, can become familiar in such a way that they no longer discourage. Except during the very worst days – which, I swear, one hand on my heart and the other on a copy of *Richard's Bicycle Book*, are genuinely infrequent – you can remain confident that the rain will stop eventually. Yet here you are in the meantime, out in it, whilst others run the stretch from pub door to car, or office to bus stop, cursing that they have forgotten their umbrellas. And when the sun returns, what a joyously renewed sense you will have of the beneficence of nature! After a day in the drizzle, to see the clouds draw away and the sun freshly exposed in a rain-washed sky, is the greatest satisfaction; as it is to feel its doubly energizing heat begin to dry out your clothes and to warm fingers chilled into inflexibility by hours of coolness; and to hear the bushes and trees dripping all around you, the birds singing once more, and the streams running full beneath the roads.

Another of the fears repeatedly expressed about cycling is that it is too much hard work. Any physical activity can be exerting at first, of course, but for those who are reasonably fit – or not unreasonably unfit – pootling may be indulged in with impunity. The whole point of pootling is that you should do no more than you are capable of doing; that you should match your journey to the current tone of your muscles, as well as to the 'tone' of your mental state. The wise pootlist always knows when to stop, and never bites off more than he can chew. The result of this is that there is a *gradual* and *gentle* move towards fitness, so gradual and so gentle that it may not even be noticed at first. There is a pernicious fantasy widespread in this country that it is necessary to flog oneself to death in order to be truly fit. This fantasy does, once more, have a lot to do with our prize-winning view of sport, in which achievement is all and no-one has much time for the runners-up. Those who use their bicycles on slow and easy journeys, travelling no faster than a cat can run, are, no doubt unknowingly, amongst the vanguard of a more mature approach to exercise. For them there is reserved the rare pleasure of *unexpectedly* discovering themselves to be fitter than they were, after the first few days of cycling are past. It is the greatest satisfaction to realize suddenly that you are capable of riding up a hill, or a slope, the very sight of which might have thrown you into a knock-knee'd panic on the first day.

Quite apart from its much-publicized physical benefits, it is now known that cycling can also act as an 'anti-depressant', partly for obvious psychological reasons – the sense of achievement at getting up off one's bum and actually doing something, especially when one has been feeling that exercise was the last thing one could contemplate – but also for as yet poorly understood chemical reasons: certain hormones are released during exercise which can act to reinvigorate the system. This is quite the opposite of the generally expressed notion that exercise makes you tired: it is only too much exercise too soon which tires. I find that in my case, a telltale sign of this 'anti-depressant' effect in action is what happens to my music-making. When I pootle, I whistle, and on a typical journey this whistling will begin with jaunty little numbers, bits of jazz and lesser Baroque mixed up together; but as the days pass and my sense of 'the bigness of the world' grows back, these will gradually transform into attempts at the epic and broad (tricky for the whistler at the best of times) in the manner of Brahms, Franck, Sibelius, and a lesser composer by the name of Jones.

As well as being exposed to the sun and the weather, the pootlist also moves amongst the scents and the stenches of the lanes, most of which the motorist does not even so much as guess to exist as he flashes past inside his box of glass and metal. But the cycle traveller drifts only gradually into each new sphere of olfactory influence, his surprise growing into delight as the scents themselves grow stronger. It may be something as simple as the smell of dried hay in a barn, which is as pleasing as that of a sweet China tea; or the zesty smell of cut grass in a meadow with its attendant sensations of renewal, and recognition that the summer season is arrived; or the heady, invigorating reek of fresh cow droppings, which can catch the nasal palate like the smell of some powerfully over-ripe cheese intermingled with the bouquet of a rough red wine. Even the synthetic smell of fertilizer has its good moments: it will overpower like a chlorinated swimming pool if one gets too close, but from much greater distances it can suggest the presence of the sea, even far inland. And perhaps even more delectable than the scents of the flowers, to my simple taste, are the hints one gets at eventide of other people's dinners, emanating most frequently, it seems, from unbeautified cottages standing close by the roadside: the smell of onions frying, the sharp autumnal tang of simmering blackberries, the smells of stews, which vary so greatly according to region that it seems the truly expert pootlist should be able to tell what part of the country he is in blindfolded, by distinguishing between them.

The cyclist will also quite often find himself making contact of one kind or another with the wildlife of the lanes, and the less wild life of the fields on either side. Some birds will play games with him – I am convinced it is a kind of game. Sparrows will dance along the hedges in a cloud, settling and taking off just before the cyclist reaches them; while finches and wagtails (the latter especially) will play 'chicken' with his front wheel, landing on the road surface just ahead of him, then fluttering nonchalantly on, bouncing through the air, to land again and wait for him to catch up. Swallows in quiet river valleys will divebomb him as they cull the insects he has attracted, flickering black shapes in every corner of his vision. Cycling into this calm and ceaseless gliding can be an entrancing experience, in which the traveller adds his own simple forward movement to all those other sophisticated acts of curving propulsion, and feels an indefinable connection between them.

Once in the Marches I had the strange experience of being escorted at dusk by a buzzard, which coasted on the air directly above my head for a kilometre or more; a silent, greyish outline of finger-tipped wings on a saturnine sky. It too was hunting, in this case for the mice or other small creatures which I might have disturbed in the hedgerow, but I could not restrain the idea that I was the one being considered as prey. And several times I have ridden past owls sitting on fence posts or gate posts like dun, feathered extensions of them, watching me pass with their rotating, jerking gaze and not budging an inch, as if they had been advised in advance that I was harmless.

At times like these one begins to wonder if the cyclist may somehow have gained exemption from the Fall of Man. Bullocks will galumph along with him beyond the hedges, and if he pauses, and is not too hasty, they will allow him to scratch their pink and shining noses. Hares will hop up the lane ahead until he has got sufficiently close to be struck by how big they are, and some will pause with surprising casualness knowing, presumably, that he can never catch them. A weasel may scurry busily along the tarmac, straight towards him (tarmac is no doubt a lot easier going than the natural terrain for such stump-legged beasts), and it will sometimes get extremely close before it identifies him as sentient and dives for the long grass.

34

The human animal is also generally friendly to the pootlist, and vice versa. People will smile and talk to cyclists, where with motorists they would never have the chance even if they felt so inclined, and cyclists will of course respond, becoming more mellow with each "good afternoon" or "lovely day" even if they have started out as gruff, blunt buggers. One hears stories of those who have cycled halfway around the world, partaking freely of the hospitality of many villages and settlements where they have been treated as brothers or sisters, and accorded an unqualified respect for their efforts of self-propulsion. This is not quite the case in England, though I have enjoyed many cups of tea, and glasses of homemade wine, in the homes of perfect strangers. People will sometimes ask the cyclist in and tell him their life story, or the history of the locality, and will talk of those they know in the area in a way that will make it familiar to him as it could never have been had he just passed through. One most excellent man I met recently in this way in the country near Appleby, in what was once Westmorland. I had been studying his barn – one of many strong stone barns in that vale – which was at the time missing a wall, its roof being jacked up on poles, and evidently in the process of conversion to a house. I soon learned that the farmer himself, a man of 67, was doing the conversion single handed, as well as just having taken up experimenting with cheese-making. He also made some of his own tools (his scythe was a masterpiece of bodging), and had plans already drawn up for a device which would make methane gas out of chicken droppings, once he found the time to build it: biomass conversion on the individual level, no less.

One of the greatest psychological freedoms of pootling along the lanes lies in being able to stop whenever and wherever one chooses. I admit that this is a skill which must be learned: the feeling that one 'has to carry on and get somewhere' – another of those totally absurd societary notions – is not easily abandoned. But once the cyclist sees that it is quite possible to stop anywhere, even halfway up a steep hill or in the narrowest crevice-like lane, he is in possession of one of the most valuable freedoms of all. What can be more pleasant than to throw oneself down in the warm sunshine of a May morning on some bank of short grass, with violets either side of one's head, in a place where perhaps no other person has stopped for months, or even years?

Being able to stop at will is a freedom in more ways than the obvious. When one pauses in a place, one focuses on it, seeing it for itself. Given a quarter of a chance, any spot in the countryside can take up this central position, its beauties becoming fully apparent only when they are dwelled upon, and seeming to spread out from them in every direction. Lanes which have beauty evident at every bend are rare – these indeed are the paradise lanes – but there are few, even in spoiled areas, which do not have something.

The beauty is also perceived more intensely through resting, through the good, full sensation experienced in relaxing muscles as the body, still capable of work, enjoys not working for a while. Birdsong is heard with additional clarity and increasing concentration, and the cyclist may open his eyes to see, for example, the tiniest of spiders working up its cable to his leg, or a black beetle scuttling across the road surface by his feet. The country grows in this way, the distance from the nearest urban sprawl seems greater, while towns dwindle beyond the horizon.

Near Wadesmill, Hertfordshire.

Once in a Youth Hostel I met a group of Americans – people absolutely atypical of most that I meet – who had to their own complete and complacent satisfaction 'done' Wales in an afternoon. They had driven north to south along trunk roads and they felt – despite anything I could say, which was quite a lot – that they really had seen everything they needed to see of Wales. After all, it was only a 'little bitty' country – with some 'real purty' hills, one of them reminded me – and you could fit it several times over into the foothills of the Rockies. It may be tentatively hazarded that these people were not likely ever to become aware of the joys of travelling slowly – nor, in particular, to know the actual extent of the land of Wales as measured by their own muscles.

The country can also grow for the pootlist when he is in motion. The more he explores an area the more he will become intimate with it, not simply in terms of its defining features but, more subtly, in understanding how its streams and rivers flow together; or in grasping the interrelationship of its lanes by doubling back upon himself to where he started; or in seeing hills, valleys and settlements from several angles, at each of which (it is almost inevitable) their 'personalities' will appear to be different. The best corners of any landscape or lanescape are by definition well-hidden, and they are usually to be found where they are least expected. It takes the slow, reflective exploration methods of the true pootlist to winkle out and fully appreciate such spots. There is in addition a somewhat knavish enjoyment to be had in finding one's way to locations so remote that even the locals rarely go there, nor sometimes so much as know about them when asked.

In such unhurried explorations the cyclist will grow increasingly responsive to the curves in the land surface, both the gentle and the steep, and once he has learned not to fear the hills (because he is equipped with an effective set of gears, and also because he has learned how to surmount the hills without dying at the top of them), he will begin to view them in a new way. To the motorist, the hills of England are often little more than a series of attractive picture postcards sellotaped to his windscreen, some of which require a change of gear. The pootlist, in extreme contrast, *navigates* by the hills. He comes to see England in terms of its uplands: the Cotswolds when approached from the north are a vivid reality to him, even when he is out of sight of them, and so too the Chilterns, or the Berkshire or Wiltshire Downs which rise above the fields like frozen tidal waves of green water – exciting, mysterious, places to be reached. He sees them for the challenge to his energies which they undoubtedly are, but realizes that this is a challenge which he can meet. Even when he is tired, the pootlist knows that he can moderate his efforts to suit such strength as he may possess. He also knows that the glory of being up there, and the downward release on the other side, entirely justify the work he has to do.

In an historical perspective, this knowledge of the land in terms of physical capability – rather than in abstract terms of 'driving times, barring traffic jams or other holdups' – places the cyclist as the direct inheritor of what was, until the advent of the internal combustion engine, the common awareness. In seeing England in terms of its hills, and in measuring the distances along the lanes against his own muscle power, the pootlist thinks as did all those millions in the past who had to make journeys by foot. But let there be no illusions: things are of course incomparably easier for the cyclist. Quite apart from the fact that for most of the time he travels because he wants to do so and enjoys the artificial assistance of his machine, the roads he uses are smoothly metalled. It is a heartening thought that a fit cyclist can if he or she chooses cover 80, 90, or even 100 km. along the back lanes in a day, where in rainy weather a horseman of the past would have been lucky to do 50. In 1740, for example, it could take no less than six days in winter to travel between London and Chester by stagecoach, and this involved setting off each day two hours before sunrise and arriving at the next stage two hours after sunset; whilst a writer in *The Gentleman's Magazine* of November 1752 flatly observed that the roads between London and Land's End remained as "what God left them after the flood".

Roads were either hedged or walled in by landowners on either side in order to contain them, with the result that their surfaces were churned into morasses of mud, or they ran across open commons or uncultivated land as an interweaving of tracks, each attempting to avoid the other in the constant search by traffic for the least-obstructed route. Road 'repair' was a parish responsibility until 1835, when supervised highway districts were established, and this usually meant little more than the occasional plugging of the largest potholes with whatever waste materials happened to be available.

One can get a vivid picture of the miseries of travelling in the 18th century by dipping into the works of Arthur Young, commentator on the rural society of his day, who in his *Six Months' Tour of Northern England*, for example, expostulates thus:

"To Wigan ... I know not in the whole range of language terms sufficiently expressive to describe this infernal road ... I actually passed three carts broken down" [due to "ruts which I actually measured four feet deep"] "in these eighteen miles of execrable memory."

Later in his perhaps understandably shorter *Six Weeks' Tour Through the Southern Counties of England and Wales* (c. 1770), he continues:

"Of all the cursed roads that ever disgraced this kingdom in the very ages of barbarism, none ever equalled that from Billericay to the King's Head at Tilbury. It is for near 12 miles so narrow that a mouse cannot pass by any carriage."

It is salutary to remember such things as these when the wind is against you, and to picture the endlessly repeating scenes of drivers lashing their horses and oxen so as to heave their vehicles through each new slough they encountered: salutary, and indeed refreshing, to remind oneself by contrast of how simple a matter it is to cover the distances now, 'even' by bicycle, and of how very reliable all metalled roads are in comparison with earlier times – excepting, of course, the occasional unexpected pothole or treacherous patch of loose gravel, the pootlist's bane.

For me, and I know few others who revel in this as I do, one of the most enticing freedoms in cycling the lanes is the freedom of the evening and night: the expansiveness of clear summer evenings when you know that the light will not be completely gone until ten or later, and during which you can trickle on, following your nose, not planning a route but simply letting the road unfold in front of you, taking turnings without consulting signposts, losing yourself without ever really getting lost. At such times you are able to travel so slowly that you can pick out every flower in the hedgebank, every leaf in the hedge, and feel the trees passing by above you, canopies of looming shadow under which the day's heat is still contained. You turn the pedals only each half minute or so – even less frequently when gravity is with you – and grow gently hypnotized by the continuous whirr of the freewheel as its sound merges into the susurrus of birdsong, and everywhere around you float the startling scents of evening flowers.

The lanes are empty. In the villages you may see a few children, having one last riot before bed, or the occasional gardener (more often male and old than any other, it seems) weeding out between the wallflowers on the lane side of his garden hedge, or some solitary youth, also cycling, heading for the stream to fish. But everyone else is inside, getting things done, or watching the box, or handing out the darts for the first match of the evening. As dusk falls so each new crossroads will grow in significance. I find that this is especially so on hilltops in the West Country, where the crosses are named – Bonny Cross, Borden Gate, Venn Cross, Kissing Gates Cross – the names lending a paradoxical intimacy to what is in fact unknown, and challenging one with the question: to whom were these names once familiar, and where are they now? If the moon shines in such places, it sometimes seems that it should be casting the dim shadow of some long-demolished gibbet across the road in front of you. Or will it be tonight that you will meet your double in the half-light, walking up some transverse lane towards you, his face fixed in a frozen stare? Highwaymen, hanged men and red-eyed goblins will lurk in the hazel and beech hedges, enriching the shadows. For others this may not be the case, but as far as I am concerned such mild fantasies are a positive part of the pleasure of cycling the lanes as night comes on.

When the afterglow is all but gone and one's eyes have been retrained to night-time sensitivity by the gradual, ungraspable dimming of the light, all old buildings along the lanes will have a new presence as they drift past you in the quiet, their stones reflecting the sound of your freewheel more clearly than the hedges do. The whitish-grey lane surface will withdraw in front of you to a vanishing point of sombre impenetrability, shifting its position so that you must at all times concentrate on aiming for it, especially on the downhill slopes. Along the lanes where there are no cars (and this also usually means where there are no pubs) the world will have stopped altogether. On warm evenings the darkness will further sharpen your responsiveness to the scents in the lanes, which linger most potently in the south of England in the three or four weeks where May blurs into June. The honeysuckle's sugars, the Continental suggestiveness of Scots pines, above all the intoxicating, sensual musk of the mayflowers, will be vivid in the darkness. Gradually the gap will widen between the daytime warmth held down beneath the trees and in the hollows, and the freshening chill of the sky-wide road. Every minute change in the lie of the land will become familiar to you in a new way since, as your sight is denied, your other senses all begin to come into exaggerated play: each downward plummet and upward swelling of the ground will become 'yours' through this intense experience of it, to be remembered years later in a way that little else in life is ever remembered.

As I have said earlier, there is more to the myth of rural England than may at first meet the eye. In those who care deeply for the countryside, the love of landscape and the quest (conscious or unconscious) for some kind of paradise on earth are, I believe, closely linked. That urban desire for a 'better world' outside the town can be greatly stimulated by travelling in the country, and it may well be that it is stimulated most vividly of all through the experience of travelling the lanes on a bicycle. There is no such thing in reality as a perfect landscape: the closest we can come to an actual physical perfection is perhaps in the landscaped parks and (as Edward Hyams called them, seeing them as a direct expression of native English taste) the 'paradise gardens' of the stately homes. But in such places, however lovely they may be, one must always feel a little deflated by an awareness of privilege, even if for the most part this is privilege past rather than present. The 'God's in His Heaven, All's Right With My Investments in the Colonies' which is implicit in the weed-free gravel paths and impeccably clipped hedges tends to choke off the deepest inspirations. The true Pastoral can only be made out of rustic environments; and it can only be imagined in them. And the vision of the better world will come to the cyclist in the lanes – always this is the case – in unexpected glimpses, instantaneous perceptions, after which there may be nothing more for days, or weeks.

Once, after a long day's cycling in persistent grey drizzle, I rode down out of a clinging hill mist along what starts as one of the highest lanes on Brown Clee Hill in Shropshire. The wide vale under the hill was not misty, and for a matter of a few seconds before it was hidden again by hedges I saw the landscape below me through the very bottom level of the mist. Relative to the closed-in murk through which I had been moving for some hours the land below was shining, illuminated in places merely with patches of less deep greyness where the cloud was thinner, the woods in faint grey-greens, the cornfields in the most recessive shades of remote, strange gold. It caught me off my guard, penetrating deep into my previously dulled aware-ness, so beautiful that even as my heart leapt to see it, I thought that I could not have stood to look at it for long. It was a revelation of an England I had never seen before (and once again, this is always the case – each time it seems entirely new): not England, but all that England might be. Then I heard a thrumming on the hill below me: an orange car; a brightly polished, new orange car; a man in it, making his gears scream, to save whatever time he needed, for whatever purpose it was. Normal experience was instantly resumed.

In a less dramatic way, the cyclist will come across many small beauties in travelling the lanes which briefly echo this elusive suggestiveness: glimpses over hedges of groups of trees by water, or a narrow enclosed valley, or the bending slope of a mown hayfield – things which, perhaps, in not being completely seen suggest more to him than if they were studied directly. Along the lanes themselves there are certain bends which, in certain lights, can seem as if they will take one to quite other than one's expected destination; and if, absurd and dangerous feeling that it may seem, such bends promise to lead the traveller into a past in which men were simpler and better creatures, more innocent than they now are, and in which life was the richer for its simplicity, then this too is the English Pastoral at work within one, and it should not be discounted, if only because that sense of innocence must in the last analysis have its source somewhere within oneself.

Certain Slight Disadvantages Of Cycling In The Lanes

Like all joys, the joys of travelling slowly are sometimes offset by little problems here and there along the way, and I think that it is only fair for me to mention some of these, if for no other reason than that my arguments in favour of cycling in the country would appear absurdly partisan were they to be left wholly unqualified.

The pootlist can be his own worst enemy in this respect. If – especially on beginning his travels – he misjudges his strength and at the same time puts himself too far away from his night-time destination at the end of the day, then he is creating his own difficulty, and a classic difficulty it is. But if, in addition, fate rewards him not with one puncture but with two (once, and only once, I had precisely five), and the rain which has been threatening to fall all day but which he has stupidly ignored begins towards the end of the afternoon, blotting out the last light of the sun in what is clearly going to be a 24 hour downpour, – and if, on top of this, the cyclist finds that he has even more stupidly misread his map and that there is in fact a long, slow, upward climb wher he expected nothing but downhill between him and a hot shower and bed, then he will be in an unusually good position to experience the less enrapturing side of pootling.

The unfortunate cyclist may find that his front light will not now work, or is angled upward so that instead of allowing him to see the road's edge it illuminates the branches of the trees that overhang it; the wind will of course be against him and will blow the rain, falling ever more heavily, directly into his face and down the neck of his cycling cape which (because he has not bothered to renew it) is of a primitive design, so that sooner or later the water begins to run in chill rivulets down his chest and between his shoulder blades. In desperation he may decide to cut the journey as short as possible by using a main road: but, naturally, when he reaches it he will find that it is the commuting hour and that the road is choked with traffic. Most of this is coming from the opposite direction and blinds him with one set of callously undipped headlights after another, whilst the vehicles on his side of the road soak him yet further by splashing the sheets of dirty rainwater that are running across the road up and underneath his cape. . . .

Such experiences are generally avoided by those who think ahead. But, human nature being what it is, most of us seem to need to have the experience first in order to learn to avoid it the next time. Misery can be a good teacher, so long as the novice pootlist is not totally put off by it, which is of course a very real danger in such situations. If he is not, however, then the next time – the next day, indeed – he will be a lot more careful. Yet even when care is taken there are sometimes unavoidable adversities. There is, for example, the *occasional* cowboy motorist who will not slow down in what until that moment has been the pleasantest, quietest kind of narrow lane, but who instead accelerates past down the rough gravel, flinging it in all directions, playing at Death Race 2000.

Then there are our four-legged friends. Now of course some dogs are genuinely friendly, even to cyclists and postmen, but I am sorry to say that in my own experience a very large number of others are not. However peacably, however generous-heartedly, you may travel, however deeply you may be caught up in your own quiet thoughts, if you move into the self-allotted territory of any such animal you will find the furry demon convulsing itself into an hysterical frenzy at your presence. Once, I liked dogs. The dumb ones I still like. But over time, repeated experience of totally uninvited canine aggression has nurtured in me a deep, passionate and *effective* loathing. I would recommend anyone planning to pootle to be prepared, at least: there may well be times when you find it necessary to boot away some such creature from under your very front wheel if you wish to remain in the saddle, and believe me, practice will eventually make perfect. One does of course need to discriminate. Some farm dogs will 'escort' you past their master's base much as if they were herding sheep; the Welsh mountain sheepdogs are particularly good at this, and their silent attention, like that of a good policeman, rarely gives reason for offence. But if you are attacked, remember that you have a right to fight back.

Entirely unbootable, alas, are the insects, which contend strongly with loose gravel for the grand title of the pootlist's bane. Especially vile are those tiny black insects which collect in the air when thunder is approaching, or gather in clouds in the cool and shaded hollows around streams and rivers at eventide, and seem to be drawn to one's facial orifices in much the same way that moths are drawn to candles. They will hit your face like raindrops, flittering into your eyelashes, creeping into your ears, hurling themselves in kamikaze fashion at your uvula (if you have been unwise enough to leave your mouth open), and they will seem to be crawling with exquisite slowness over your skin even when you have squashed them all into oblivion ten times over. There is no defence against them, except perhaps to ride with a stocking or muslin bag tied over one's head. At other times and in other places there will be the greenflies; and the mating flying ants; and the mosquitoes; and those long-legged flying things (I am no entomologist) which make straight for the eyes with the sole purpose of tormenting the very eyeballs with their seeming hundreds and thousands of bristling, spined and flailing legs, before they drown in your exasperated tears.

Some Practical Advice For The Poûtliste Ingénu

"The open road, the dusty highway, the heath, the common, the hedgerows, the rolling downs! Camps, villages, towns, cities! Here today, up and off to somewhere else tomorrow! Travel, change, interest, excitement! The whole world before you, and a horizon that's always changing! And mind, this is the very finest cart of its sort that was ever built, without any exception. Come inside and look at the arrangements. Planned 'em all myself, I did!"

> *Kenneth Grahame,*
> *'The Wind in the Willows', 1908*

THE THREE GREAT PRINCIPLES OF POOTLING

1 That the English lanes are in fact *worth exploring in themselves*, and are much more than simply routes to be got along as quickly as possible.
2 That the novice pootlist should vigorously attempt to make himself independent of predigestors and most guides, and strive to *find things for himself*.
3 That the best way to get to know the lanes in any broad stretch of English countryside so as to enjoy them to the full is to *explore small areas, slowly and in depth*.

Find Things For Yourself

There is a balance attainable in all things. I am not suggesting that the explorer of the lanes should go into them in complete ignorance of what he may find there, though he may: there is no law to stop him. What I am suggesting is that with only the vaguest idea of where to look first, the person who cycles the English lanes can – using the simple system described below – develop his own knowledge of any stretch of country and its major features, and that this knowledge is likely to be far more satisfying to him in the long run than if he uses a guide to isolate a handful of 'unmissable' features in the area, or follows a preappointed route.

How, then, to obtain such vague knowledge, if one decides to do so? I can recommend the Shell Guides*, which are county guides, although not all counties are yet covered; they are atmospherically illustrated, and they are not overloaded with detail. The trick with these as with other guides

---

* All books and periodicals are detailed in the Bibliography.

45

is to absorb something of what they tell you – knowing, for example, that certain parts of a county are likely to have more lovely landscapes or to be richer in interesting villages than others – and then to allow your accumulating experience, always using the information on the map, to guide you from there. The one risk you run in keeping it vague is that you may end up somewhere undeniably drear, like some parts of western Cambridgeshire, for example; but even this danger can be avoided to a great extent (see on); and, finally, there is no area of countryside *totally* devoid of interest, if you open yourself up to all the possibilities.

For general self-guidance in architectural terms, National Trust membership (which is cheap for what you can get out of it), and a copy (or the relevant pages, torn out to save weight) of the annual publication *Historic Houses, Castles and Gardens*, which covers numerous other privately owned stately homes, and the Department of the Environment's map of Historic Monuments (available at any such monument), will be sufficient to enable you to find your way – at such times as you choose to do so – to most of the major architectural gems in an area, barring ecclesiastical buildings, without any use of guides. It is perhaps worth noting, since no guide ever mentions the lanes except in a passing phrase, that in some areas there is a curious discordance between the quality of the buildings and that of the lanes. So for example in the Cotswolds, an area hardly paralleled for the richness of its vernacular buildings, the lanes are often (though not always) uninteresting, whilst in Cheshire the lanes can be very lovely, but the buildings along them are generally not so.

Having found things for yourself, of course, you may well discover that you have become sufficiently interested in an area to want to read about it. And this, I think, is the time to begin going into detail. Once one knows a stretch of country through exploration, its significance is utterly changed: it has become a set of realities, and the most obscure and academic essay on its history can therefore become instantly fascinating, because one knows what the writer is talking about. Under such circumstances one sees the guides for what most are: surface-scratching potboilers. For those who want general and reliable reading of this more detailed kind I can think of no better series than the *Making of the English Landscape* books, again planned on a county-by-county basis, and again by no means yet completed.

Maps

These are essential. The bicycle is the first, and the map the second, of the pootlist's two key tools of self-liberation. Once you know how to use a map, it will enable you to find your way anywhere and everywhere on the surface of the land where rights of way exist. If you are anything like me in this respect, reading maps will also stimulate your imagination: for me, a map of an unknown area is a far greater incentive to explore it than any guide can be, although I must say in the same breath that the anonymous computer-printout appearance given to the second series of 1:50,000 Ordnance Survey maps by the change of typeface (to be continued, alas, throughout the reprinting) makes them far less attractive and suggestive of historical associations than they have always been in the past. Whether or not the maps touch your imagination, however, you will still need them. I have found ideal a combination of small-scale (the OS 1:250,000 Routemaster series) for covering larger distances when one is not bent on exploring in depth, and large scale (1:50,000) for the areas one intends to stay in. One small warning here is that you should not expect to find *every* metalled back road on the 1:250,000 maps: this can make navigation in complex networks of lanes rather difficult, but generally for through routes these maps will suffice. The 'expense' of buying 1:50,000 maps which so many complain about is in my view more than justified by the countless perceptions they will give you of the ins and outs, the nooks and crannies of the landscape and lanescape, which you will never be able to search out with such consistency and confidence using a smaller scale. Also well worth buying is a tough plastic map case which will enable you to keep your map permanently open at the area you are in, thus saving a lot of fiddling and frustration. This is invaluable not only for protecting the map when it is raining but also for sitting on, since it can be used as an impermeable seat when the ground is wet, and wiped down afterwards.

Explore Small Areas In Depth

All writers on the English countryside agree on two points at least – that it is incomparably rich in its variety of beauties, and that one need travel only small distances in order to experience striking changes in landforms, architectural styles and farming methods. But I believe that most explorers of this variegated landscape fail to come anywhere near to appreciating just how rich it is, because they pass straight through it. What I propose is an alternative to passing through, which will no doubt seem odd at first to many people but may seem less odd when they get around to trying it. Having selected a small area of country, the traveller proceeds to explore it by cycling along each and every lane that he can find, until there are few lanes left which he has not at some point traversed. Then and only then will he have a real idea of how rich this stretch of country actually is. It is obviously useful for anyone adopting such an approach to find them-selves a base within their chosen area; and in my experience there is no better place to stay than on a farm, since in this way (quite apart from the warm hospitality you so often receive) you are as 'close' to the country you wish to know as you can be, barring sleeping out in it under the stars.

Systems of Exploration

The problem, of course, lies in finding a way of singling out your chosen area from the countryside which surrounds it. How do you give yourself limits within which you can begin to familiarize yourself with one small sector of the Great Unknown? Various approaches are possible, and all are firmly based on the availability to you of the relevant 1:50,000 maps.

1 The Network System

The areas of lanes dealt with in Part Three were all explored using this system which is, I think, the best and simplest way of delineating each chosen patch of country. It involves nothing more than the marking up of the four or five main roads ('A' or 'B') which encompass an area crossed otherwise only by lanes – preferably with one of those felt-tip pens containing ink that you can see through – and then keeping to the lanes within this arbitrary frame. The major roads become your 'boundaries' and within them every lane is a potential subject for exploration, with certain possible exceptions (see on). The map opposite shows the sixth network of lanes to be dealt with in Part Three (see page 188). Here the yet-to-be-patented network system can be seen operating in all its earth shattering simplicity. The boundary trunk roads are the A4113 running eastwards from Knighton to Walford, the B4530 and the A4110 soutwards from Walford to Mortimer's Cross, the B4362 westwards from Mortimer's Cross to Presteigne, and the lane over Stonewall Hill (chosen here for convenience) from Presteigne back to Knighton. Within these borders lies a territory of lanes completely and deliciously uninterrupted by other major routes and ripe for exploration, and the only problem remaining is how best to plan a route around it. This may take the shape of a figure (or several figures) of eight, with the explorer coming back several times to a central and increasingly familiar spot: again, this may sound crazy until you try it, at which point I think you will find that it is not. Or the route may take the shape of a further subdivision of the network into pockets of lanes, one for exploration here in the morning, another for the afternoon, and so on. There are many possible variations, and naturally I would expect anyone experimenting with the method to evolve their own.

It is not always quite so easy as in this example to find a main road for every boundary, as is illustrated by the actual choice of boundaries for most of the other networks: it can prove necessary to extemporize a little, according to the terrain. But then, why not? Such a system does not *have* to be conformed to like something out of Exodus Chapter XX – it is, finally, nothing other than a convenient means to a delightful end. Equally, the explorer does not *have* to regard it as his bounden duty to pootle along each and every lane when he does not feel like it, and he can even abandon his bike altogether if the fancy takes him, forget the lanes, and go off along the paths and tracks on foot (pootling the field paths is, of course, the subject of another and yet-to-be-written book). All that really matters is that at the end of his stay the pootlist feels that he has experienced something of the essential personality of the area – and through his own independent efforts.

<u>*A typical lane network:*</u>   *this is network number six in part three.*

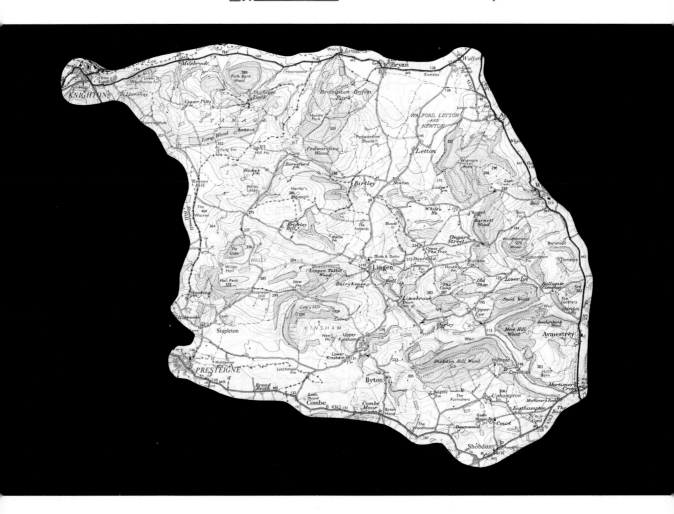

This generally takes a little time: most stretches of English countryside are slow to yield up their real magic, and it is often only on the third or fourth day that one begins to get a feeling for an area, however small. Yet the growth of familiarity with places is one of the greatest pleasures which pootling has to offer: there is a wealth of experience buried in tiny tracts of land – not simply in a geographical or an aesthetic sense, but in a philosophical sense as well. There is indeed an infinity hidden in 300 or 400 square km. of country – and no area can ever be truly exhausted. Time is also an important factor on a purely practical level. Even the smallest networks can still possess many kilometres of lanes. Some small networks in Devon, Shropshire, Essex and Kent, for example, have between 150 and 250 km. of lanes and/or unmetalled tracks in them, and since the pootlist rarely does more than 80 km. a day, and often does a great deal less, a single network can keep him occupied for several days at a time if he so chooses. And there are so many networks! At a rough estimate there are, for example, about 80 networks in the county of Norfolk. At a minimum of two days' pootling per network this means that it would take a traveller over five months to explore the lanes of that one county, were he dedicated (or mad?) enough to try.

The other three approaches are less fully refined methods of exploration than adjuncts to the first, and I mention them here in passing for what they may be worth.

2   The River Valley System

This is a variant on the network system which I have found very satisfying at times. In this case instead of marking off a sector of country, one follows a river valley from the source to the sea, or vice versa, staying always within the confines of the flood plain. This is particularly useful in the low-lying counties of the east, where river valleys often contain the most interesting country.

3   The Village- or Building-Based System

Those who insist on reading some kind of guide book before they travel may use the guide – though, ideally, as loosely as possible – to establish that a particular area of country is richer in interesting architecture than others nearby. They will draw up their networks in this area, knowing beforehand that they are sure to find *something* interesting to look at on their travels, even if everything else proves deadly dull, which of course it will not.

4   The Map System and the County System
These are simply methods of pre-selecting a larger stretch of country in which one's much smaller lane networks can then be located. Sometimes a particular OS sheet will seem to contain enough in itself to last you for as much time as you have available; but if you are more inclined towards history then marking off the limits of a given county on a series of sheets and then choosing your networks within those boundaries can also prove very rewarding, allowing the kind of exploration in which real knowledge is quickly accumulated.

Narrow Lanes, Gated Roads, By Roads and Unmetalled Tracks

The best metalled lanes for pootling are often (though not always) those yellow roads which the 1:50,000 maps conveniently mark as being slightly narrower than the rest, to signify that they are made up with not more than 4.3 metres' width of metalling. With only a little experience, these become quite easy to pick out. They often tend to have more kinks and bends in them than other lanes, or they will run not directly from village to village but go instead by erratic circuits linking up sattelite hamlets and farmsteads. These are not just the back lanes, they are the *back* back lanes. In other cases they may be found running roughly parallel to the major roads or main lanes (see on) which, because they are easier routes for motorists, tend to carry all the traffic. At their best these lesser lanes are so lightly trafficked that grass can be found growing through the tarmac down their centres, whilst along some older metalled single-track lanes one will find a strip of grass there because the centre was never metalled in the first place.

In some cases metalled lanes run 'through' the fields themselves, either joining villages (again usually as an alternative to a more efficient route) or running up to and through farmyards. These lanes are signposted either as *gated roads* or as *field roads*. There are subtle shadings of difference in what this means from county to county, but the broad picture appears to be that gated roads are always metalled with tarmac whilst field roads may or may not be tarmacked, and are often not so; however in both cases carriage-way rights still exist – in other words, people can drive their cars along them if they so choose. Generally they do not so choose, since such roads tend to have farm gates closed across them to keep the cattle or sheep in – although nowadays these are sometimes replaced with cattle grids – so that even the exploratory motorist is put off by having to stop and start at every gate. They can also be quite rough to drive along, even where tarmac is supplied, since they are a very low priority for any highway author-ity. But for the pootlist they are a joy. It is a particularly satisfying experience to cycle such *public* roads, knowing how few other members of the public ever get on to them. Gated roads are also, in a sense, the metalled roads that are closest to the countryside through which they pass. There is a very real distinction between travelling a gated road in the Leicestershire upland, which passes through a series of hedged fields but is not itself separated from them by hedges, and travelling the new 'field roads' created in prairie farming country by the recent removal of all or most hedges. In the first case there is an intimacy with the landscape, and a sense of being contained within it; in the latter, one may well be physically close to the crops or earth on either side, but there is no sense of containment – indeed, quite the opposite.

Lanes signposted as *by roads* are sometimes the narrow lanes of the first paragraph, through routes joining nowhere in particular with nowhere else in particular, but they are more frequently cul-de-sacs, at least for the motorist, petering out into an unmetalled bridleway, or simply running into a field. These are of course worth exploring precisely because of the fact that they do not go anywhere: there are quite possibly more corners of the old England, with just the cottage of the song standing in bushes next to some overgrown dew pond, down lanes such as these than along any others.

Untarred roads and tracks are to be considered for exploration according to your mood, and also according to the area in which they are located. Some counties have distinctive and complex networks of tracks along which entire journeys can be planned if so desired. These are particularly in evidence, for example, in the Downs of Dorset (835 km. for the county as a whole), Hampshire (800 km.), Wiltshire (727 km.) and Berkshire (322 km.). The second major factor in the use of unmetalled lanes is the weather: if it has been raining – and especially if it has been raining for more than a day – my advice is to stick to the metalling, unless you want to spend a lot of time poking accumulated mud out of your mudguards and off your chain and gears or, of course, unless you have a mountain bike.

The things to remember when using tracks – in just the same way as with very hilly areas – are to allow even more time than for normal pootling, and to anticipate the drawbacks before they arise. So for example on un-metalled roads you will find that you have to keep your eyes on the surface in front of you for more than half the time, and if you dismount to walk the bike you are almost guaranteed to end up in the nettles, or to catch your shin on a pedal. Even in dry weather, mud tends to lie in wait in hollows between high banks of brambles, every inch of which is frequently churned from bank to impenetrable bank by the hooves of horses. Desperate short cuts in such circumstances are not to be recommended: one invariably ends up dragging the bike along the narrow, overgrown edge of a barley field or, even worse, trying to wheel it over gluelike ploughed earth whilst the hares gallop away into the crops, laughing up their furry sleeves.

Learn To Avoid The Horrors Of The Countryside, Or At Least To Be Prepared For Them

To a greater or lesser extent, like every stretch of lowland England, each of the networks in Part Three bears its share of scars. What is ugly and what is not ugly in a landscape depends very much upon who is doing the looking, but to any eye which has become attuned through long exposure to the shapes, textures and colours of natural objects and of the older buildings, there is little that has been added to the countryside in this century, and almost nothing that has been added since the Second World War, which does not seem at times to be quite staggeringly ugly. For this reason I have tried to achieve a more realistic – though by no means 'balanced' – view of the actual appearance of the countryside than is generally in evidence in a book of this kind, by adding to each section a brief set of notes describing what *in my opinion* are the area's major uglifications.

In principle, of course, most English people travelling in their own country know only too well already about the characterless mini-suburbs recently attached to characterful old villages, the unscreened sewage plants, the pylons, the road-widening schemes which turn stretches of lanes into miniaturized motorways, the gravel pits, the rubbish dumped in woodlands, and so on, and so forth. But even if the traveller is not a foreigner who is unprepared for such things, I believe that it is still useful to have a reminder – a stating of the obvious, if you like – to which one can refer back. For after all, if we are going to go cycling in our own countryside, then why *should* we waste half a morning navigating around some aerodrome, or cycling along some lane long since put into service as a busy route for the commuting businessman? If these things can be recognized beforehand, they can be avoided, and the real beauty which may lie only a matter of a few hundred metres away from them (on a more devious and complex course through the lanes) enjoyed instead.

So, a few examples. Pylons, aerodromes, open-cast mining or quarrying are easy: they should all be clearly marked on an up-to-date map, and the private railways which sometimes serve both quarries and rural industry (marked with the symbol denoting 'mineral line') are an instant giveaway. Disused aerodromes are also indicated: at best these will be flat expanses of re-arablized emptiness, at worst acres of cracked concrete dumped upon by locals and in use by learner drivers busy jumping their clutches. Factories are sometimes marked on the map as 'works' (or 'wks'), but even if they are not, another way of anticipating them is to look for isolated single blocks of the bedroom pink somewhat oddly chosen by the Ordnance Survey to denote built-up areas, at sites such as the place where a railway line crosses a road, or at the junction of a lane and 'A' road. Water towers are marked as such ('Wr Twr'), as also are power stations and caravan sites (the caravan symbol is marked in the blue colouring also adopted by the Ordnance Survey to pinpoint places in the countryside where jolly fun is to be had, and to which – again – the motorist may drive).

Distinguishing what may be good old buildings from bad new ones is never easy, but one clear indication of subtopia in a village is where a cul-de-sac is marked (a white road completely surrounded by pink on all sides), or on a grander scale where a road runs away from the village high street and makes a complete self-contained circuit to double back on itself without going anywhere: such layouts are a hallmark of the spec builder and the suburban planner. But in general any large block of pink attached to a nucleus which is itself solidly based on the old lane circuit is nowadays likely to be a piece of suburbia, especially where a lane can be seen running directly to a nearby town, or to a main road which then leads – perhaps over a much greater distance – to a conurbation.

These lanes are in themselves generally worth avoiding, since they will of course be used by motorized commuters now living in the new housing. The trick here is to distinguish which of the many lanes running to such a village is going to be the busy one (usually only one is busy), and the way to do this is to look at the whole map and try to work out which nearby urban centre the traffic is likely to gravitate towards. Some such lanes, which I will call *main lanes* since a phrase is needed to distinguish them, are routes which act as links not only between the villages and towns along them but also between urban areas that may lie on either side of the country they traverse. These are definitely to be avoided since many are in effect *ersatz* main roads, used by the local motorists who know and prefer them. They appear on the maps as unnumbered yellow roads, but to cyclists they can have the dread feel of 'B' or even 'A' roads.

Such main lanes fall into the third tier of the Department of Transport's classification of the highway system: they are members of the 'Classified Non-Principal Road Network', which is defined as including all roads of importance to their immediate locality. This group also encompasses the 'B' roads – supporting my theory that main lanes are for the most part 'B' roads in disguise – and another category, 'C' roads, which were given letters and numbers in an earlier system of classification not centrally, but by some county highway authorities only.

It may be useful if I supply one example of a main lane as a point of reference. In the Rutland network (p. 160) there is a 'lane' which runs westwards of Oakham through Braunston to Tilton on the Hill. West of the B6047 an extension of the route connects with the A47 into Leicester. The 'lane' is marked on the map as a yellow road of the wider variety

(4.3 metres of metalling or over). This can in itself be an indication of a higher level of use. However, in an area such as this where Parliamentary Enclosure roads have made the creation of wide strips of tarmac easy, it is not necessarily the case. What makes this into a main lane is the fact that it provides a convenient link between Leicester and Oakham (much expanded by recent suburban growth) for all those motor commuters who work in the former town and live in the latter. It cuts off a large corner of the route along the trunk roads through Uppingham – which is itself a bit of a bottleneck – and is, relatively, far quieter to drive.

For pootling purposes, all trunk roads are by definition places to avoid. The serious pootlist will quite simply decide never to cycle along such roads, making exceptions only where circumstances force him to do so (going into towns or at river crossings, for example). 'B' roads are also to be shunned, but may perhaps be considered when the cyclist is in less high-principled mood, especially where they prove to be relatively quiet and unspoiled, and he wishes for whatever reason to cover the ground quickly. Again here, the area he happens to be in has direct bearing on what such roads are like: to date there are some 'B' roads in mid-Devon, for example, which have not been upgraded and remain far more like lanes than main roads.

Generally speaking there is no real reason why the traveller should not plan entire routes around the country along 'the Unclassified Road Network' – in other words, the back lanes. It is simply a question of time. The lanes take longer to ride because they bend, or have more steep gradients per km., and of course they offer far more temptations than the major routes to go slowly or stop. So if a cyclist wishes to use them to cover the distances from area to area, he must first work out roughly how long it is likely to take him, basing this on past experience and awareness of his present state of fitness, then add ten per cent, and plan his next night's stopping place accordingly. The lie of the land is particularly important for the pootlist involved in long-distance sagas. In my experience one of the most difficult cycling terrains is that of the West Country, where the sheer frequency of one in four hills plummeting down to little streams and immediately clambering back up again on the far side can be daunting, unless you are psychologically as well as physically well prepared. Here one should plan to do not much more than 70 km. per day if one is using the lanes to get across country. In landscapes with easier gradients, of course, a fit pootlist can (perhaps to his own surprise) nearly double that distance and still find himself capable of conversation at the end of the day.

The rewards of sticking to the lanes for long distances are those of pootling in another shape. The cyclist remains for the most part in the country: he avoids conurbations and all the tat of the main-road world – the garages and the Little Chefs, the industry, the shopping parades, the spaghetti junctions and the litter – seeing it only at some points where he crosses the trunk roads at right angles. Best of all, he stays away from the traffic itself; and after a while, whenever he approaches a busy main road he will be able to smell it before he sees it. To his newly sensitized nostrils the metallic taint upon the atmosphere of unburnt petrol, carbon monoxide and friction-eroded rubber will drift distinct across the last fields like the poison gas that it is.

Time And Timing

The true pootling convert cannot go too slowly. Along the lanes that really interest him, an average of 15 km. per hour is breakneck, and even 10 km. per hour is rather fast. He will be perpetually dismounting in order to peer over gates, examine flowers, enter churchyards, make notes, write poems, take photographs or kiss (or be kissed by) his lady poûtliste. Something just over walking pace is in fact a very good speed to ride on a bicycle, since one can look around, taking in all manner of details. The perpetual gentle forward movement can work in much the same way as a well-designed tracking shot in a film, concentrating attention and intensifying one's responses. There is great pleasure simply in freewheeling, allowing gravity to do all the work in moving you forward. This applies quite as much to the descent of steep hills as when you are on gentle gradients. After all, why waste the effort you have put into climbing the hill in a short, sharp, pseudo-motorized zap down the other side? The true pootlist will use his brakes, and relish the descent. For those who object that if one is to travel at walking pace on a bicycle one might as well forget the bicycle, I have what I believe is an unanswerable reply: walking, especially when you are carrying a pack, takes more effort than cycling, and this is notably so on the downhill parts since the walker, unlike the cyclist, cannot freewheel, unless he happens to have his roller skates with him. There is also the important consideration that the cyclist can accelerate when he wishes – I am far from suggesting that *all* cycling in the lanes be done at 10 km. per hour! – covering large distances at will, and enjoying doing so all the more by contrast with the slow, reflective pace he may earlier have been keeping. Not so walkers, unless they jog, which I have none too often seen them do.

In order to go slowly one must have time, and one must therefore allow time, even on a day trip. There is nothing more frustrating than travelling through a stretch of country which you know to be abundant in places to discover, and not having the time either to discover them or to relish them when they are discovered. There is no entering into the spirit of place if one is busy rushing through the place. (I might mention that it took me

56

something like 12 years of cycling to recognize this consciously: some people are indeed slow to learn.) This principle applies all the more emphatically in hill country. Alas, few will believe me who do not already know this, but hill-climbing on a bike has much more to do with the time available than with effort. If you allow enough time, and then more than enough, you will feel that you are not pressed: if you feel you are not pressed, you will be far more inclined to set a pace to suit your actual physical state. Furthermore, you will be able to walk – and to stop – whenever you want to. After all, why should one not do so? The terrible compulsion from which so many of us suffer – again, I did so myself until one day the Lord spake unto me out of a particularly strong gust of wind – to get to the top of each hill as quickly as one possibly can, is another of those products of social conditioning which the pootlist will gradually erase in himself. Why should one not pause to enjoy the view at many stages on the upward slope, as well as from the top? The view is different at every stage, and is often much more interesting half way up than at the summit.

One further point about timing. To my eye, the countryside in summer is at its most beautiful in the direct light of early morning and during the two to three hours before sunset. In winter such lighting can be enjoyed on clear days virtually from dawn until dusk because the sun never rises very high in the sky, and whole cloudless days can pass as extended, chill imitations of a summer's evening. But in summer, when the contrast between a hazy midday and the clarity of a sidelit morning or evening makes the latter all the more cherishable, one must try a little harder in order to seek them out. This means either rising at 5 a.m. at the latest or – a little easier for some people – staying out into the evening. In May and June there is light in the sky until 10 to 10.30 p.m., even in the south of England, and it is another of the many pleasures of pootling to remain out so late, witnessing the length of the longest days for oneself. It is a strange thing that most travellers seem to make a point of arriving at their destinations just as the beauty of the late afternoon or early evening is *beginning*. I suspect that this has to do with food. At six or seven we British eat, or at least set about preparing, a cooked meal. No matter if we miss the very beauty that we have come to see. No matter if we are not really hungry. At this time, we eat. The pootlist also eats, of course; the difference being that he carries all the food he needs with him, eating whenever he wants to, and on summer's evenings he can live for nights at a time on cheese and bread, fruit, nuts and chocolate which require neither a dining room nor a kitchen for their consumption. His table is a flowery laneside bank, his roof and walls a sheltering oak, and his television set (that other dinnertime essential) is the beauty of the place in which he finds himself, which he views afresh from his resting state.

Kit

It may seem a trifle superfluous at this stage to advise the reader to buy his own bicycle if he does not yet have one, but there is a point to be made here. Possessing your own bike alters your attitude to cycling: it makes you far more enthusiastic about the whole business than if you simply borrow a friend's machine for a weekend, and it is incomparably better than trying to ride in the country by using a cycle hire scheme. Cycle hire schemes are, in general, to be avoided: they shackle you to a base you may not want to return to, they take money that might have been spent on the first instalment for your own new bike, and – worst of all – you are usually supplied with one of those ludicrous sideplate-wheeled, sausage-tyred parodies of the velocipede which will give you backache, thigh-ache and bum-ache in a matter of ten km., no matter how fit you are.

If you wish to know which bicycle to choose, or if you wish to refine your knowledge of cycle technology, then the well-known *Richard's Bicycle Book* (1975) is invaluable. Richard Ballantine's book is a splendidly well-organized how-to-do-it manual which most idiots really can understand: it makes all the points about cycle maintenance and knowledge that any pootlist could possibly need, and its existence makes it entirely superfluous for me to repeat any such information here. There is just one area of argument in this book with which I cannot quite see eye to eye, and it is this. Ballantine encourages us to do our own maintenance, and, further, to maintain preventively by overhauling our bicycles at regular intervals. This is right and fair enough, of course. But I do not believe that novice pootlists should allow themselves to worry *too* much about maintenance. Bicycles are extraordinary machines. They can be treated atrociously, shamefully neglected, even allowed to go rusty, and they will still somehow work when they are needed – for most of the time, anyway.

Once, on a summer's evening in the Hebrides, I met a local gentleman next to a ruined forge above a murky lochan. He was playing a harmonica in the dusk, all by himself. He smelled strongly of stale talcum powder, and from the breast pocket of his tattered jacket there dangled half a dozen wilted narcissi. We talked; I learned much local gossip; and then the musician pulled what, for want of any better word, might be called a bicycle from behind a pile of broken granite blocks. We rode companionably on together until we reached a stretch of road which sloped down steeply and directly towards a sea cliff high above the Atlantic. "Excuse me," he said, "if I go on ahead, but I have no brakes you see." I watched him gradually gain speed as he plummeted towards the cliff edge, putting out his large feet in order to scrape along the road and slow himself down only at the point where the road began to curve back and away from nothingness. I myself used my well-maintained brakes, with their newly inserted Weinmann blocks, and took the hill more gingerly.

I am not, be it noted, upholding this man as an example to be followed. I am simply trying to emphasize the point that bicycles will keep on working in some manner or other even when they are falling apart. The pootlist does not have to be an expert cycle technician. He may in time become one. He may choose to be one for the love of bicycles as things in themselves. But in order to *pootle* – in order to get out there into the greenery and be free from all care – I would say that he needs to know very little more than the following:

(a) How to mend a puncture, and therefore
(b) How to remove and firmly replace both front and back wheels
(c) How to replace broken spokes, especially on the back wheel, and therefore
(d) How to remove and restore the freewheel
(e) How to tighten up the brakes
(f) How to adjust the gears
(g) How to fix the lights when they will not work
(h) How to oil the bicycle, and where to do so
(i) How to replace brake and gear cables, when and if they break

The chances of the bearings wearing out, the chain breaking, or even the brake blocks wearing down to the shoes are in my experience really quite slight, even on a longish trip. Obviously if you set up your bike before such a trip you are going to be a lot more confident, but even if you do not, please remember: you are still allowed to go. So long as you have the few basic tools (see *Richard's Bicycle Book*) and some spares (cables, bulbs, spokes, and at least one inner tube), you can rest easy as you pedal. If the worst comes to the worst and something does go wrong which you simply cannot fix, you can usually get yourself to a bicycle shop without too much trouble and there talk to the person who does the job so that next time you are a little better prepared. Of course, one has to think rather harder if one is cycling in such places as the Hebrides, where bicycle shops – indeed any shops – are rather thin on the ground, but in the English lanes cycle breakdown disasters are rarely real disasters. The danger of taking the bike too seriously is that it begins to dominate one's whole approach to travelling, just as awareness of the camera can dominate the photographer to the point where he turns into one of those excruciating bores who spend all their time talking about lenses and 'f' stops instead of taking pictures.

A Note On The History Of The Lanes

At no stage could this book have had pretensions to being a history. Apart from the fact that its emphasis is celebratory rather than analytical, the history of the lanes is so intimately bound up with that of the locality in which each network is situated that most generalizations tend to become meaningless. I have, therefore, adopted a pragmatic approach: it seemed to me that the best method would be to investigate, for example, the West Country hedgebanks as they are to be found around Chulmleigh in Devon, or the wide-verged Parliamentary Enclosure lanes and the craft of hedge-laying as they occur in the east Leicestershire upland, and so on, according to the networks chosen. Once again such material is offered only to give some idea of the enormous range of variations which can be found in the lanes, and is not intended as any kind of 'typical' selection.

Those wishing for an expert, accessible and down-to-earth introduction to the history of British roads might be well advised to turn to Christopher Taylor's *Roads and Tracks of Britain*. Taylor, a well-respected field archaeologist, is at pains to debunk the myths: the hunter of 'ley lines' is established with very little room for doubt as a self-deluding fantasist, imposing what he wants to find on the known or the likely reality with little respect for either, and the prevalent image of the prehistoric trackways as lines of communication built for arcane, mysterious purposes is supplanted with another picture, less mystical but far more likely to conform with actual events, in which the roads are shown to be long-distance trade routes which were, however, "only one part of a highly complicated pattern of routes which stretched into every corner of Britain in the centuries before the Roman conquest". A repeated observation in the book, well worth bearing in mind as one cycles the lanes, is that it is at best difficult, at worst completely impossible, to date the origin of roads (other than Roman roads, or those built in later centuries for which documents exist) with any certainty, and that this situation is very unlikely to change. In his introduction, Taylor writes that:

"We may see a delightful green lane wandering across the downlands of Wessex, apparently linking groups of prehistoric forests with burial mounds, or we may follow a minor road across miles of countryside from one medieval town to another, but there is no actual proof that one is a prehistoric track and the other a medieval highway."

It is not only the novitiates of Alfred Watkins who have been guilty of wishful thinking. Even before Watkins wrote *The Old Straight Track* prece-dents had been set amongst the ranks of conventional archaeologists themselves through their over-valuation of the significance of the long-distance tracks found on the open uplands of southern Britain. So Taylor furnishes an example of a route which in 1940 was almost wilfully regarded as a 'major prehistoric trackway' (the Jurassic Way as it passes through Northamptonshire), and another still regarded as such with a lot more evidence to support the view (the Icknield Way as it passes through Cambridgeshire), the precise importance of which has nevertheless been called into doubt by later research. In both cases the existence along the routes of prehistoric sites such as burial mounds and hill forts was taken as evidence of their importance. But in recent years aerial photography has shown that in the country at some distance from both routes there is a plethora of prehistoric settlements not previously recognized on the ground, which bear nothing like the logical relationship to the 'ways' which had appeared to be the case with sites identified until this time.

This of course excludes all the many other sites in the surrounding countryside which do not even show up as crop marks in aerial photographs but which we may, on the evidence, reasonably assume to have existed. So what does this suggest? First, it invalidates the old view that prehistoric people lived almost exclusively along the lines of the known and supposed trackways, on the strategically 'safe' chalk uplands, never penetrating into the hostile, unconquered forests of the lowlands. Settlements there were in precisely such lowlands, and – the second inference – these must have been linked by roads of some kind. The 'remains' of these roads, Taylor suggests, are in evidence all around us as the roads of today, still in use in a somewhat different shape and by a somewhat different kind of traffic.

Another extremely interesting observation made in Taylor's book is that whether or not certain parts originated in prehistoric, Roman or Dark Age times, the overall network of roads, including the lanes and by roads, was substantially complete by the 11th century. Thus, apart from roads built on later private estates, during the Parliamentary Enclosure period, in urban and industrial areas, and of course during the present motoring boom, most of the British roads as we know them today run along approximately the same routes as they did 900 years ago. Furthermore, in many parts of the country, for example in Cornwall, Devon and the Marches, it seems reasonable to assume that the system of roads, 'complete' by the time of the Norman Conquest, had in fact evolved during prehistoric times. Such networks were thus very ancient even in the Middle Ages. But we may go yet one step further, to propose that virtually the entire system of British roads (with the foregoing exceptions) *may* be prehistoric in origin. Taylor acknowledges that this could indeed be the case, but he also observes that even if it were, it could not be proved.

The great appeal to us of the ridge trackways, and the long unmetalled stretches of Roman roads and drovers' roads, is, I think, that they run across the country for hour upon hour without connection with modern settlements. Travelling such routes one moves in an environment in which it is almost impossible not to project one's own sense of antiquity on to them, whether it is relevant or not. Because of the way that they look and because of the proximity to some of them of visible and identifiably ancient sites, many of which (like the Uffington White Horse or the nearby 'Wayland's Smithy') have irresistible atmosphere, these tracks have become symbols in our minds of all that lies buried in the unknowable past of this island. This habit of projection is not new: consider the number of 'Grimm's Ditches', 'Grim's Dykes' and 'Devil's Dykes' to be found around the countryside, superstitiously named by the Saxons who had no idea of the features' original strategic function.

What Taylor gives us that is both new and extremely thought-provoking is an overall view of the antiquity of our roads. Certainly it is far easier to imagine prehistoric farmers whilst one is standing up on the Ridgeway in an autumn dusk looking out over the great green sweep of the Vale of the White Horse than it is on some thundering trunk road, but ultimately the view of all roads as ancient is far more intriguing. And for the cyclist in the lanes it is an unqualified stimulus to the workings of the imagination: the metalled lanes may seem less old than the trackways, but if you keep with you the awareness that except in Parliamentary Enclosure landscapes whatever route you are following is likely to have come into existence in the Dark Ages at the latest, I think you may find the lanes quite as exciting in the long run.

Many of the beauties to be discovered by the traveller in the English lanes are immediately obvious. Yet all lanes depend quite as much for their individuality upon their less striking features – the patched-up gates, the disused pumps, the stiles, the roadside 'weeds', even at times the telegraph posts – as upon the old buildings or the hedgerow trees which stand along them, or the landscapes through which they pass.

What follows here is a photographic record of a journey through the lanes of England which no-one has ever quite made. Its pictures are drawn from those I have accumulated in 15 years of cycling the lanes: a distillation of a mere handful of images out of thousands. In the circumstances there could never have been such a thing as a judicious selection, nor are the photographs meant to show what is in any way generally typical, even if they happen to do so in some cases. Finally, this is what it must be – a personal celebration, which depends for its content quite as much on pure chance as on any other factor.

In exploring the lanes for yourself you will, I am sure, develop your own ideas about what features contribute most to their person-alities. In the meantime – for the sake of argument – let us travel alongside a hypothetical, oddly lucky and attentive cyclist as he enjoys the beauties of the English country lanes for the first time . . .

Part Two:

A Celebration Of The Lanes

This wanderer may first be attracted by the old buildings that stand along the lanes, many of which fit into the scene as though they had been designed for that sole purpose.

(Right)   Approaching Bingham's Melcombe, Dorset.
(Below)   Approaching Stoke, Devon.
(Opposite)   Approaching Thriplow, Cambridgeshire.

Wherever they are encountered such buildings impose some sense of their period on the lanes that run by them.

(Above)   In a back lane at Great Bardfield, Essex.
(Left)   In a back lane near Streetly End, Cambridgeshire.
(Opposite)   Near Ashdon, Essex.

These places can be either live . . .

(*Opposite, top*)   *Near Shalford, Essex.*   (*Top*)   *Near Nedging, Suffolk.*
(*Opposite, bottom*)   *Near Poslingford, Suffolk.*   (*Bottom*)   *Near Great Bardfield, Essex.*

. . . or dead.

(Opposite, top)   Near Stansfield, Suffolk.
(Left)   At Stapleford, Leicestershire.
(Above)   Near Monk's Eleigh, Suffolk.

Other such remnants of England's rustic past may be live, in a manner of speaking . . .

(Left)   Near White Colne, Essex.
(Below)   Near Stone, Kent.
(Right)   Along a farm track at Wissington, Suffolk.
(Opposite, below)   Near Wembworthy, Devon.

. . . or again, dead.

(Left)   On a farm track at Miller's Green, Essex.
(Above)   Near Cratfield, Suffolk.

The cyclist will travel past, or under, ancient arches, and over bridges both ancient . . .

(Above) Near Dunwich, Suffolk.
(Left) Near Winchelsea, Essex.
(Right) At Hockenhull Platts, Cheshire.

. . . and less so. Occasionally, where there is no bridge, he may have to share the lane with a stream.

(Above)   Footbridge to a bridleway
near Little Walsingham, Norfolk.
(Right)   A back lane at Clee St
Margaret, Shropshire.
(Left)   Near Lownard, Devon.

Gradually this traveller's attention will move from the more striking features to all those other, lesser artefacts that give the lanes their individuality.

(*Opposite, top*)   *Near
Grimpo, Shropshire.*
(*Opposite, bottom*)   *In the environs of
Guiting Power, Gloucestershire.*
(*Left*)   *Stone gatepost near
Wykey, Shropshire.*
(*Below*)   *Near Welham, Leicestershire.*

(Above)   Newly laid hedge near Belton, Leicestershire.
(Below)   Hand-clipped field hedge near Radnage,
Buckinghamshire.

(Opposite, top)   Near Deerfold, Herefordshire.
(Opposite, bottom)   A stone's throw from Ansty, Dorset.

(*Opposite, top*) *In a cottage garden in a back lane
at Burwash Weald, Sussex.*
(*Opposite, bottom*) *In the vicinity of Bures, Suffolk.*
(*Above*) *Near Brinkworth, Wiltshire.*

(Above)　Near Great Bardfield, Essex.　　　(Below, right)　Near Burwash, Sussex.
(Below, left)　Near Byton, Herefordshire.　　(Opposite)　On the way out of Stogumber, Somerset.

He will come across signs of different kinds, both informative . . .

(Above)   Norfolk.
(Right)   Herefordshire.
(Opposite)   Devon.

. . . and otherwise.

He will discover reminders of a time when water was not on mains supply . . .

(Right)   By Eaton Mascott
Hall, Shropshire.
(Below)   Stream-fed water trough
near Stoke Wake, Dorset.

. . . as well as laneside memorials of the beliefs of others who have passed that way.

(Opposite) Near Releath, Cornwall.
(Left) Near Great Walsingham, Norfolk.
(Below) Near Sampford Courtenay, Devon.

The communication links of the urban universe are a constant and – for those who need it – a reassuring feature of the lanes, and attached to them the cyclist may occasionally notice curious reflections of the world he moves in.

(Above)   Near Waldron, Sussex.
(Right)   Near Ipsden, Oxfordshire.
(Opposite)   Near Oakford, Devon.

He will find objects abandoned along the roadsides, decaying relics of a remote way of life . . .

(Opposite, top)   Near Witheridge, Devon.
(Opposite, bottom)   Near Pilsdon, Dorset.
(Above)   Near Maldon, Essex.

. . . as well as other objects – some relics, some not – which in any case remain very much in use.

(Below)   Hop poles on a farm track near Kilndown, Kent.
(Opposite, top)   Fence posts near Ongar Street, Herefordshire.
(Opposite, bottom)   Near Field Dalling, Norfolk.

From the beasts of the fields, the cyclist will enjoy varying receptions . . .

. . . but wherever he goes, he will find himself travelling in the invigorating company of those other, less mobile creatures of the lanes.

(Opposite, top)   Near Sidestrand, Norfolk.
(Opposite, bottom)   Near Swaffham, Norfolk.

(Above)   Near St Keverne, Cornwall.
(Below)   Near Acton, Suffolk.

In many places, the blossoming of the lanesides will transform the plainest vistas into idylls . . .

(Above)   Not far from Lyddington, Rutland.
(Opposite, top)   Rather further from Burgh
next Aylsham, Norfolk.
(Opposite, bottom)   Yet further again from
Upend, Cambridgeshire.

. . . whilst from day to day and hour to hour, the weather will make countless further transformations.

(Opposite, top)   Hole in the storm clouds near Oakford, Devon.
(Opposite, bottom)   Retreating storm near Blaxhall, Suffolk.
(Above)   Approaching storm near Tumbler's Green, Essex.

(Above)　Near Blakeney, Norfolk.
(Right)　Near Blaxhall, Suffolk.

After the storms clear, if he is in luck, the wind will blow this traveller on . . .

*(Left)   Near
Thurston, Suffolk.
(Above)   Near West
Beckham, Norfolk.
(Right)   Near
Lavenham, Suffolk.*

. . . and the lanes themselves will lead him on: into the shadows or into the light – as if toward some paradise on earth which, it seems, lies just around the next bend, or the next.

(Above)   Near Diddlebury, Shropshire.

(Top right)   Near Oakford, Devon.
(Bottom right)   Near Sampford Peverell, Devon.

At times he will be presented with tantalizing choices; whilst at others it may even seem as though . . .

(Above)   Near Shudy Camps, Cambridgeshire.
(Opposite, top)   Near Wood Ditton, Cambridgeshire.
(Opposite, bottom)   Near North Molton, Devon.

Following pages:
(Left)   Near West Putford, Devon.
(Right, top)   Near Plaish, Shropshire.
(Right, bottom)   Near Bridge Street, Suffolk.

. . . if they were given the slightest chance, the lanes would carry him up into the sky itself.

And as the days and weeks pass, he will come to follow them in the hope that they may.

Part Three:

Lanes To Get Lost In

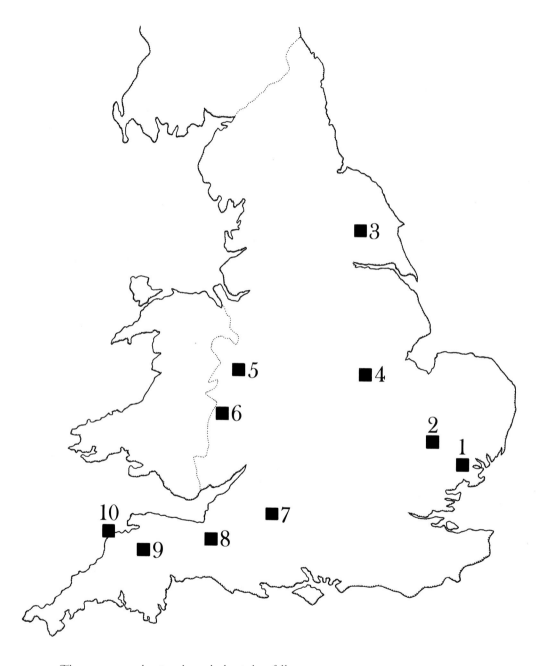

The essays on each network can be located as follows:

"When the high road
Forks into a by-road,
And this leads down
To a lane,
And the lane fades into
A bridle-path,
Green with the long night's rain,
Through a forest winding up and on –
Moss, fern and sun-bleached bone . . .
And this thins out
Into open wild,
High under heaven,
With sunset filled . . .
And a path is sought in vain . . .

. . . And every thorn, and bird, and flower,
And every time-worn stone
A challenge cries on the trespasser,
Beware! Thou are alone!"

Walter de la Mare,
'The Journey', 1942

The following ten networks are offered as *examples* of the many and various lanescapes to be enjoyed throughout England. It is not in any way being suggested that they are the only lanes in the country worth visiting. All were explored according to the methods set out in Part One. Such places you may yourself find, in applying these methods in other areas. All place names mentioned in the text may be found on the relevant Ordnance Survey 1:50,000 maps. Those elements which in my opinion make the networks less than they might be, in the best of all possible worlds, are noted at the end of each section.

Lanes Of The Box, The Brett And The Stour Confluence

Suffolk and Essex
OS Maps 155 and 168

Bounded by: A1071 west from Hadleigh to junction with A134; A134 south to Great Horkesley; lanes east through Boxted and Langham to Gun Hill, by Dedham; A12 north to junction with B1070; B1070 northwest to Hadleigh.

This stretch of country may seem to those who already know it either too popular or indeed too populous to be an appropriate subject for pootling explorations. Dangerously sandwiched between Colchester and Ipswich, studded with lovely 'honeypot' villages such as Nayland, Stoke by Nayland, Polstead and Boxted, its southern half world-famous as a part of 'Constable's Country', and most of it now designated as an Area of Outstanding Natural Beauty, it may at first sight seem far too likely a tourist trap to be worth getting to know by bicycle. It is true enough that you will not often enjoy that easeful sense of remoteness here which is to be had in parts of the Marches or Devon, or indeed in the less well known parts of East Anglia itself, but even so there is a rich complex of lanes in this small area, most of which are used by few but local residents. The tourists, and even the weekend trippers from the nearby towns, tend to stick to well-beaten major routes and leave the rest alone.

I think also that it is fitting to begin with an area in which the effects of prairie farming, and of hedgerow removal in particular, are now all too apparent. Certainly the area's fascination for me, intensified by inevitable recollections of how Constable saw it, is that it is now several landscapes in one. The 'old' landscapes can still be found in fragments along the lanes – juxtapositions of Tudor timbering, cornfield, hedgerow, oak and cattle pasture – and one can pursue them, tantalized, from place to place, trying to fit the old world back together again. Yet in other stretches nearby you move in a hedgeless expanse of 100 to 200 hectare 'fields' which seems to have more connection with the Cambridgeshire Fens and the 21st century than with the remains of pastoral Suffolk and Essex. And there is now a third type of landscape here, which has been created simultaneously with the prairies through the planting of poplars and some willows, particularly cricket-bat willows, since the Second World War. The poplars are to be found in neatly laid out stands in the valley bottoms – for example, in the Box Valley near Stoke by Nayland, and Polstead – where the younger trees can give a paradoxical, vegetable newness to the place in contrast with the immemorial timber and thatch which is seen against them, and certain poplar-backed meadows now bear a distinct resemblance to landscapes not by Constable but by Monet. In another and rather more rigorous fashion, the new blocks of poplars to be found along the lane from Boxted to Nayland, for example, now entirely modify the original appearance of that part of the valley as a series of water meadows and cornfields.

The villages are of course reason enough in themselves to explore this area, and there is great satisfaction to be had as you travel the lanes here, in knowing that each new settlement you approach (with one or two marked exceptions) will be a place worth seeing. But, as so often in East Anglia, it is the individual buildings which stand along the lanes quite as much as the villages themselves that contribute to the area's personality. There is hardly a lane which does not have a thatched cottage at some point along it, and in places you will confront superb examples of the larger timber-framed yeoman's house, such as the one – not to be too specific – which stands at a cross somewhere to the east of Higham. Were you to be looking for an ideal vista of the 'olde England' which never was, the calendar England, then you would find it here in the juxtaposition of this house's shrub-shrouded timbers and, at the right time of year, the golds of the unhedged wheatfield that spreads in front of it.

In other places small clusters of thatched cottages are to be found, grouped with the usual randomness, rather as if they have sprung from the ground like living organisms – this impression is needless to say much damped where modernization has occurred – for example at Stoke Tye near Stoke by Nayland, which is down a back land marked deflectively to the motorist as 'By Road'. Scotland Street, on the hill to the west of Stoke by Nayland, is a winding extension of the village so abundantly dotted with timber-framed cottages that on one's first descent one wonders if the revelation of thatched roof beyond thatched roof will ever end. In many cases the plastered cottages are painted in brilliant colour washes: oranges, mustards, and a somewhat violent pink, a reddish-purple like the colour of blackcurrants and cream mixed, occasional blues. When the cottages are seen over the crops, their lower storeys obscured by growing wheat, it sometimes seems as if these colours are intended as statements of the buildings' separateness from the fields around them – as indeed they may be. This is even more noticeably the case in winter, when the cottages are isolated against the sombre heaviness of the ploughed earth, and the statement becomes a shout. As a general rule in the prairie lands of East Anglia, the villages and farms today are like oases of habitation in a desert of rationalized productivity, tree'd or hedged-in areas isolated amongst the open expanses of crops. One does notice that even the farmers tend to like trees in their own gardens.

What is for me the greatest characteristic pleasure of cycling the East Anglian lanes of the 1980s can best be experienced in the north of this network, on the gently shelving 'upland' where – another paradox – the old landscape has been the most spoiled. Here, on clear sunlit days in the early morning and again especially in the late afternoon and evening, the cyclist can sometimes feel as though he is travelling not in an area of lowlands slightly indented by streams and rivers, but instead across the great flat expanse of some high and apparently limitless mountaintop. This, I believe, is an experience specific to cycling; in any case, I have never known it when travelling in East Anglia by train, car, or even on foot. When the wind is behind him, and the sun is sinking lower and illuminating the landscape with a light ever more intensely yellow, the cyclist can feel he is so high above the rest of world that, if he raised an arm, he might be able to touch the scudding clouds. There can be no doubt that the removal of trees and hedges, which I have attacked in the final part of this book, has served to intensify this illusion of altitude: there is now so little left to separate the earth from the sky.

The confluence area to the south of the network provides an entirely different experience for the pootlist. In doing so, it is notably atypical of what is to be found elsewhere in East Anglia. Here the three rivers have cut their valleys relatively deep into the clay, and in doubling back upon yourself around the area you will descend and climb many 'big' hills – again, in East Anglian terms only! The contrast between the apparent unending flatness of the upland and the suddenly revealed, sometimes enclosed and intimate landscapes of the valleys is constantly fascinating. On the lane from Boxted to Nayland, the cyclist can have the experience of dropping 'over the edge' into the Stour Valley down one of the longest hills, and if he has by chance approached through the flat, drear, suburbanized zone which lies to the south, it can indeed seem here that he is descending into a different and older world.

The contradictions of this landscape are also evident in the relationhip of the lanes to the surrounding farmland. Where the lanes are incised below the level of the land and the hedges have been removed, one can have a curious sense of intimacy with the fields, huge as they are, and in winter with the earth itself, by being brought so close to it. So also one often notices strange juxtapositions of some narrow winding lane, evolved to connect small enclosed fields in the earlier landscape, with this same new spaciousness. For isolated stretches the cyclist can travel along lanes enclosed by old high hedgerows. He can pass through small areas of sometimes idyllic pastoral landscape (cattle are still kept in the water meadows, where these have not been ploughed up) – such as that along the stream behind Thorington Street with its daisied pastures enclosed by low, rounded hillocks – and then out once more into the wide spaces. Even in the latter, vestiges of the old landscapes can still be evident in the lines of mature hedgerow trees which have been left in places along the lanes, – the lane from Polstead to Polstead Street, for example. In one way the trees' isolation makes them more striking than in hedged landscapes, since each stands single and individual, apotheosized against the sky. Perhaps the most baffling aspect of travelling the East Anglian lanes today is that when one is in the patches of old enclosed country, the new expanses seem inconceivable, even when they lie only a few hundred metres away; whilst in the new landscapes the 'oases' of hedged fields themselves dwindle into insignificance.

Along with the hedges have disappeared many of the laneside flowers, and anyone coming here in early summer from the Marches, say, or Sussex, will be quick to notice the contrast, and the lack of variety where flowers do occur in the roadside banks. There are one or two good tracks to be sought out, however, where trees, hedges and flowers remain as abundant as elsewhere in the country: for example, the pretty bluebelled bridle road which runs past a Hall to the east of Boxted, or a very 'green' lane running east of Withermarsh Green (itself a delight) near a farm whose owner evidently cares about preserving landscape features. Several of the metalled *upland* lanes around Withermarsh Green retain their hedges, neatly kept, so that here one can get some idea of what hedged Suffolk used to be like, where the hedges had not been allowed to grow to tree size. There is a little-used back lane between Nayland and Stoke by Nayland which also has its fair share of good old hedgerow oaks and bluebell banks. Along it, if he stops in the right gateway, the pootlist can find a particularly perfect Suffolk view in which the tower of Stoke by Nayland church, a dream in late-Medieval brick, rises on the slope above the Tudor Sheldrake's Farm: the curving lines of this hummocky landscape are like an exaggeration, or inspired parody, of the gentler slopes in evidence in most other Suffolk terrain. Here, in fact, is a perfect test case for the figure-of-eight principle: there are lanes (as opposed to the 'B' road which also runs here) radiating in three directions from Stoke by Nayland, and all are worth exploring. How could this possibly be achieved by travelling direct from one place to another?

For those who seek it, it must be said that the texture of Constable's landscape paintings can still be found in the reality, but not along the lanes. It is necessary to walk the meadow paths, or along the banks of the Stour, and the best stretches in both cases are just outside my chosen area: the meadows between Dedham and Flatford Mill, for example, which still have many fantastically twisted old willows lying askance them, and are without a doubt the best approach to Flatford Mill, if you *must* go there! The lane which figures in 'The Cornfield' can also be located, still unmetalled, though to preserve its mystery I will once more leave the detective work up to you: suffice it to say that it is a little to the east of the network in the environs of Stratford St. Mary, and that even if you imagine the church tower over the meadows – which it is not in reality, since the painter invented it to improve his composition – the lane bears little resemblance now to the one which has entered the nation's corporate imagination. One Constable vista which *is* within the network lies along the track to the north of Langham, where the juxtaposition of farmhouse and church in 'The Glebe Farm' of 1830 can still be seen, though unsurprisingly the trees and foliage of the painting have no connection with what grows there today.

An attempt is now being made to maintain and indeed to restore something of the look of the landscapes as recorded by Constable to this area. The Dedham Vale Landscape Conservation Project, initiated by the Suffolk County Council planning department, is dedicated to encouraging the conservation and new planting of all those landscape features – the lines of willows, the hedges, the small woodlands (and perhaps, eventually, the elms, too?) – which still serve to make Dedham Vale what it is. The project's sphere of influence extends across the network of lanes explored, and anyone pootling along them in the future can hope to see quite a lot more tree planting, and perhaps even some new hedgerow planting. The native species of poplars and willows in particular are being planted at the moment, including the black poplar, which has long been very rare.

The Dedham Vale project may prove significant not only as a pilot for similar schemes in less famous areas of East Anglia, but, also as an indicator of the extent to which planning authorities can succeed in persuading land-owners whose interests may well lie quite elsewhere that landscape conserva-tion is a good thing. For – apart from the power to plant and conserve on publicly owned land – the planners have very little real power (at present: see Part Four) to control the appearance of the countryside. It is also highly relevant that this project came into being in the first place for a negative reason, viz. that the Anglian Water Authority had proposed a land-drainage scheme which would enable farmers to convert the remaining rough pastures of Dedham Vale, with their ponds, weed-filled ditches, drainage channels and footpaths running diagonally across relatively small, hedged-in fields, into the same vast, profit-making wastes of tilled earth that one finds further west along the valley. No amount of tree planting could possibly substitute for the character of such meadows once they had been ploughed up; and the planners have only limited powers to prevent such – in non-agribusiness terms – monstrously destructive activity from going ahead.

(Opposite)   Superabundant foliage in surviving hedgerow: near Willy Lott's cottage.

Avoid or be prepared for:
The country to the south of Boxted, as described (hence the inconvenient lane 'boundary' to the south of the network); subtopian housing estates at Stratford St. Mary, with traffic to match; odd, not entirely ugly, waterworks on dead-end lane to Stour north of Langham; distinctly ugly and depressing water-tower/hill landmark by Raydon; line of pylons scarring entire north of area, especially the desolate lane from Layham to Hadleigh, further desolated by slabs of modern housing dropped into the curves of the river landscape at Layham; subtopian 'infilling' with miserable little bungalows at Whitestreet Green and Polstead Heath; similar, even more ghastly, intrusions of brash individual houses into otherwise beautiful back lane at Bell's Corner east of Polstead; unscreened sewage plant sited by the Box with clodhopping insensitivity on 'white' lane – in fact metalled – between Calais Street and Stone Street, south of Boxford; brand-new (1978) superlane by Pott's Farm, west of Hadleigh, built to transport minerals from a pit earlier opened up amongst the fields there.

Main lanes: *Stoke by Nayland to Polstead and Bower House Tye; Boxted Cross to Gun Hill; (yellow roads through Nayland and Stratford St. Mary are old main roads, their traffic now re-routed, and are therefore quite quiet).*

Buildings to give the lanes their sense of period:

(Left, top)   East of Higham.
(Left, bottom)   In a back lane, Shelley.
(Above)   Near Shelley Priory Farm.

Intimations of enclosure:

(Opposite, top)   'Over the edge' from the upland down a steep, short descent into the Brett valley. Near Giffords Hall.

(Opposite, bottom)   Nayland church, seen from a track behind the village.

(Above)   Backward view of the bridge carrying the lane over the river Brett, near Shelley.

(Left)   A half-open lane, idyllic from this angle, near Stoke by Nayland.

After the hedges:

*(Above)   One time when the hedgeless landscapes can
have a certain beauty: a clear Summer's dusk. North of
Polstead.*
*(Opposite, top)   A lane in the French style near Boxted,
given its present appearance through postwar poplar
planting following hedge removal.*
*(Opposite, bottom)   Big fields and isolated, trimmed-
down hedges to the east of Higham.*

Lanes Of The Newmarket Hinterland

Cambridgeshire and Suffolk
OS Maps 154 and 155

Bounded by: B1061 south from Newmarket to junction with A143; A143 east to
Wickham Street; main lanes north through Wickhambrook and Barrow to A45 by
Higham; main lane southwest through Gazeley to Ashley; B1063 to Newmarket.

You will not meet any tourists along *these* lanes. This is the kind of country
which most people would not so much as dream of traversing for its own
sake, always assuming they knew it to exist in the first place, and I chose
to explore it for precisely this reason. Apart from its proximity to Newmarket
and the thoroughbred world whose impeccably laid-out studs take up most
of its northwest corner, and the fact that the wearisome poet John Lidgate
was born in 1375 in the village which shares his name, this is a stretch
of country without major historical associations, particularly striking architectural features, or obviously beautiful landscapes. Yet – and this of course
is the point – it is full of pleasures nonetheless.

Several landscapes run into one another inside this network, and the
lanes also change accordingly. In the northwest the B1061 runs up the 'high'
ground that is the easternmost extension of the chalk ridge of which the
Chiltern Hills are the best-known part. Just outside the boundary I chose,
the straight lanes which run from this ridge down the barely perceptible
slopes of Chilly Hill and Hungry Hill towards the Fen and the Icknield
Way (here coincident with the A11) are amongst the most fearfully lonely
in England, and definitely to be avoided by those who suffer from agoraphobia.
The basic layout of this upland landscape is that of Parliamentary Enclosure,
but there is little left to show now of the work of the early-19th century
commissioners, except the straightness of the roads. Most of the hedges are
gone, and such blocks of woodland as remain have little impact on the prevailing emptiness. But cross the B1061 at Dullingham and enter the chosen
network to the south of Newmarket, and you will find the same Enclosure
layouts modified in quite the opposite direction. Here, instead of removing
hedges, stud owners have further subdivided the originally fairly large fields;
they have planted many tree belts, some entirely surrounding the paddocks;
and fields used for exercising the horses possess not only substantial hedges
but also fences which run along inside them, the latter rounded off at the
field corners, presumably to stop the horses from stalling during exercise.

What one sees here is, by and large, a 20th-century landscape founded on the skeleton of a 19th-century one: most of the planting and fencing was done during the early years of this century when racehorse breeding and training was rapidly expanding into a much bigger business than it had been. It is a totally different world to the country either west or south of it, self-contained, ordered, 'finished', its extreme affluence evident in the appearance of every stud building; it has no precise equal elsewhere in England, even in other horse-breeding areas. It is also perhaps a trifle sterile, a trifle unmysterious.

The effective southern boundary for the studland (though there are one or two isolated studs to the south of it) is the broad but surprisingly quiet 'lane' which dips and climbs from Dullingham to Cheveley. This has the unmistakable wide verges of an Enclosure road, boxed in by hedges that are neatly tailored to the standards of the area, as well as many tree belts, some of which have been planted only very recently. The use of yellow gravel here and nearby augments the feeling of luxuriousness, which dissipates very quickly, however, as one moves further south. This road is bisected near Stetchworth by the Devil's Dyke (marked on the OS maps as Devil's Ditch, but take your choice), a bank and ditch construction which runs 12 kilometres between Reach in the fens and Wood Ditton. Like the Wansdyke mentioned in the Vale of Pewsey network, this massive earthwork was built as an attempt at defence against invaders approaching from the southwest, and perhaps especially along the Icknield Way. Its date is uncertain; all that can be said is that it was made after the third century A.D. Eight kilometres to the southwest, outside the network, lies another smaller construction of the same kind, the Fleam Dyke.

The older buildings in the villages and along the lanes in the northwestern part of this network are principally of flint, sometimes cornered with yellow Cambridge brick which weathers to a grim greyish colour, giving a comfortless appearance where the houses are built entirely out of brick. Amongst these villages only Dullingham (the older part lying to the west of the B1061) is worth visiting: here a string of typical Cambridgeshire thatched houses, some of them plastered, are dotted attractively along a well-tree'd road flanked by the hall parkland.

But as one travels southeast towards the beginnings of the central Suffolk claylands, the depressing Cambridge brick becomes less evident, and flint gives way to plastered timber-frame and thatch. The villages in this back-of-beyond country have had their share of hideous council and speculative housing developments, and subsequent 'infilling': they are especially prone to the latter where they are, like Kirtling Green, just a series of old houses dotted along a once elm-lined lane, with small fields inbetween. But many keep their character, at least in part. At the northern end of Cowlinge, for example, there is a delectable row of tiny thatched cottages; Wickhambrook has pleasant surprises along its many back lanes, which here link a number of 'Greens' or sattelite settlements (and all such back lanes should of course be fair game for exploration, even if at times they disappoint); Ousden has a characterful straggle of old cottages running up what in other parts of the country might be called a small combe (but n.b., infilling here also); and in the north, Higham is worth seeing not because it is obviously beautiful but because there is, at present, hardly a modern house in the place, and the old houses would appear (since they are unchintzified) still to be occupied by genuine country folk. Best surprise of all in these lanes is a hamlet of memorably varied thatched houses spread along a bend in a lane – let us say, somewhere in the vicinity of Lidgate, itself a pretty village in its own way. Completely unpolluted by the activities of the speculative building shark, this place is as near perfect an example of a Suffolk hamlet as you will find, and it is not in the guide books.

As the villages change to the south of the Dulligham–Cheveley road, so do the lanes. The broad, straight, tree-lined roads of the studland quickly give way to much narrower and more winding routes, some of which even keep their hedges. For what is generally regarded as prairie country *par excellence* (if that is the right phrase), there are a surprising number of hedges here, when one starts to look for them, although as often as not they 'enclose' vast fields whose earlier inter-field hedges have long since gone. Along the narrow lanes in the country south of Cowlinge there are high blackthorn hedges, so that one can at times feel entirely cut off from the world here; and there is a similar small area near Wickhambrook. Where the hedges are cut low or grubbed out altogether, one can have curiously long views – not down, as if off hills, but out *across* the gentle rolling of the land, with its broad sweeps of green or dazzling yellow, gold or brown. Above the Kennett Valley at Dalham is the one place where the traveller does have any sense of elevation on something like a proper hill, but from many lanes elsewhere it is possible to see for the kinds of distances which only hills allow in other regions of England.

Sadly very rare now, but still visible in places, are patches of undrained marshy ground at the lanesides where the lane runs parallel with a brook; distinctive and once common landscape features in this area, these too have fallen victim to the modern East Anglian farmer's manic assiduousness. One place where you will find such 'bad farming', however, is along a lane in the neighbourhood of Ousden. Here there stands a small farmhouse, still without an electricity supply, which is owned by a rare individualist whom I had the pleasure of meeting whilst photographing his property. He came up to me along the lane with the help of a pair of crutches he had made for himself out of hazel branches, and he was dressed in clothes which he might well have been wearing when he first bought the land, just after the Second World War, for £3 an acre. This was a time, he recollected, when there was a lot of land around those parts that nobody wanted very much. He had made the choice at some point (and there are a few others in East Anglia – even in East Anglia – who have done the same) that he would not join the elevated ranks of the barley barons. The result in landscape terms is that his farm, with its large, leaning barn buried deep in a thicket, remains – for so long as this man remains – as a scene from old Suffolk which might well have been painted by some 19th-century romantic–realist such as Leader. When I explained what I was doing in the area, he gave a sharp nod of his head and commented somewhat drily, "You're after what's been left, then, aren't you?" "Exactly right," I replied.

Most of the defining characteristics of the network can be found together in the northward-draining Kennett Valley. This boasts a length of relatively quiet 'B' road, between Lidgate and Dalham, which is positively enjoyable to cycle. With crops in them, the vast fields here can be quite beautiful as they sweep down over the contours, and on a May evening the oil-seed rape will startle with its brilliance. From the south the approach to Dalham (a Suffolk village noted in most guides for its prettiness) is good: a few thatched houses, no infilling, some sense of the place as it was. But the approach from the east is better. After the bare, dull upland there comes an entrancing descent under an avenue of mature oaks and sycamores, no doubt once planted as part of the parkland of Dalham Hall. This gives the most powerful feeling of 'coming in to somewhere', so much so that the village, pretty as it is, does not seem quite enough when one arrives in it. Beyond Dalham, from the lane to Ashley, you can look down from Cambridgeshire into Suffolk, and the village with white-coned mill on hill and church amongst trees looks for all the world like a realization of a design by some topographical artist of the 18th century. Relative to the surrounding country, the landscape here has an almost epic sweep to it; but this is, I must stress, only a relative impression.

Exploring the lanes in this network, then, as in so much of East Anglia and other areas where farms have been rationalized, the traveller who cares about the countryside will be split and doubly split in his reactions. Split because the old village and laneside buildings, still in places enclosed with their hedges, trees and a few small meadows, remind from some angles of how it all looked, and was, until not so very long ago, but are now contradicted by almost all the modern building, since no attempt whatever has been made here to continue vernacular building styles, and the new houses speak through their hotchpotch of non-styles only of suburbia and compromise. Split because the relatively few areas of country that are still hedged remind one of how *this* all looked and was – a landscape that was known to those who lived and worked in it as a series of specific places – whilst the new defoliated plains speak frequently, and almost incessantly in winter or in bad weather, of desolation, loneliness, and a seeming cold-blooded, soulless efficiency in those who crop them. Split once more since these wastes can, at times, as noted, be physically beautiful in themselves; and even whilst they may be deprived of the specific sense of place to be enjoyed in enclosed landscapes, they can sometimes posses instead a bigger mysteriousness, a sense of the 'world-riddle' not dissimilar to that which is to be experienced in moorland or desert. Finally, this concerned traveller's opinions will be split because tree planting along the denuded lanes is producing in places a new kind of landscape, which could in time possess definite identity and appeal of its own – if, and only if, the work of planting is increased so that it spread from a few corners here and there where strictly convenient across the whole bared face of the land.

A track to Lidgate in 1970 and again (from somewhat further back) a decade later, after the brambles, the elders, the wayfaring trees and the guelder roses had been reduced to ashes. Of course, far fewer 'pests' can live here now . . .

Avoid or be prepared for:
Suburban spread out of Newmarket into eastern part of Dullingham, Stetchworth, Ditton Green, Saxon Street, Cheveley, Ashley, Gazeley (a particularly vile brand-new estate here, nearly as big as the original village, with some twee 'Georgian'-style houses), and even some bungalows down the very back lane to Dullingham Ley (one of which is called Wit's End, which at least stimulates some reflection about its owners); some infilling to be expected in most other places except Dalham; astounding water tower at Ditton Green (illustrated in Part Four); radio mast at Ousden which one cannot fail to see for several kilometres in any direction; easy-to-screen but unscreened sewage plant on lane west of Lidgate, not far from track to church, illustrated; indescribable council and commercial estates at southern end of Cowlinge.

(Opposite, top) Elms give this lane its personality, both in the foreground and in the distance but, alas, they will not last for long.
(Opposite, bottom) A marshy corner near Cowlinge. Note the new poplars.
(Above) A Suffolk lanescape much as it all once was, complete with reeds. Near Ousden.

(Above)   Lane to Lidgate from unspecified hamlet.
(Right, top)   At Meeting Green, near Wickhambrook.
(Right, bottom)   Little-altered lanescape at Baxter's Green.

Lanes Of The Yorkshire Wolds, And The Fringe Of The Vale Of York

Yorkshire
OS Maps 100, 101 and 106

Bounded by: Main lane south from Norton to junction with the A166 west of Skirpenbeck; A166 east to Fridaythorpe; B1251 northeast to junction with B1248; B1248 northwest to Norton.

"Oh yes, very nice," commented an old local at Birdsall when I told him I was staying at Thixendale, in the centre of the Wolds. "It's a bit of an outlandish country up there, though, isn't it?" Birdsall, which is more of a country house parkland with estate houses than a village proper, lies in a bowl of relatively high land beneath the steep ridge of Birdsall Brow. Climb that ridge, up a lane which begins broad and ends narrow, and you move from a civilized lowland landscape to a remote and haunted upland – which is no less under the firm control of man. "Their aspect is strangely vast, cold and lonesome," wrote Rider Haggard of the Wolds in his *Rural England* (1902). "The traveller across their expanse meets nobody, although now and again he sees a solitary farmhouse set in the depths of a territory of its own." This is quite as true today as when it was written, and it is very much a part of the appeal of the Yorkshire Wolds, to me at least, that they have lost little of their sense of isolation.

The Wolds are probably best known outside Yorkshire for their great quantity of deserted villages, of which Wharram Percy, lying in a combe between Thixendale and Wharram le Street, is both the most excavated and the most famous. Travelling the uplands here one needs to know little of the area's history to begin to sense the *absences* of settlements. Many signposts point along the lanes to Burdale, for example, as though there might in fact be something there, but when one arrives at the empty crossroads one finds a solitary farm, hidden away behind the embankment of an abandoned railway, and next to this rear the shining white chalk cliffs of an equally abandoned quarry. Beneath the embankment there is a postbox, its next collection time inserted dutifully into the slot; and one cannot help wondering just how many letters are ever taken out of it. Those occupants of the original Burdale who survived the Black Death, as also those of Wharram Percy, Raisthorpe (up the dale towards Thixendale) and Towthorpe (almost directly east, on the far side of the B1248) had all shut up shop and moved on by 1550, finally driven out by the enclosure of the surrounding lands under a new and more intensive system of sheep farming. Perhaps a third of the population of the old East Riding was killed by the Black Death in 1349, and it has been estimated that 129 villages were deserted in the region during the following century, many of these being up on the Wolds.

The first impression, then, in cycling the gently sloping uplands and the steep-sided Wolds valleys, is one of past activity and subsequent abandonment. Those who dug the prominent barrows (one of the biggest round barrows in the country, Duggleby Howe, lies northeast of Wharram le Street, just outside this network, but there are many smaller earthworks to be seen within it), those who settled the hills in the centuries prior to the Middle Ages, those who built the railways (the Malton to Driffield line, through Burdale, is one of four disused lines across the Wolds), those who excavated the quarries (there is one other large quarry in the network, just beneath Wharram le Street, which is now a nature reserve), have all moved on, and the relics of their former presence serve only to emphasize the reigning solitude.

In the upland contained within this network, and excluding the main road villages of Fridaythorpe, Fimber and Wharram le Street, Thixendale is the only settlement surviving and, as one resident told me, the only reason that Thixendale ever gets into the papers is because it has once more been cut off by snowdrifts. Even in midsummer it is a remote-seeming place: a handful of houses and farms spaced out along a lane, a small church, a pub, an erstwhile school which is now a youth hostel (and useful pootling base for the network). At night one can wait for literally hours for any vehicle to pass through Thixendale, listening to the cries of the sheep as they echo along the combe. Even in the daytime there is very little traffic along any of the upland lanes except farm vehicles and the occasional outside visitor in car or on motorbike, driving through to get to somewhere on the other side, and trying (probably unsuccessfully) to get hold of the country's elusive atmosphere as they do so. This part of the Wolds certainly does not encourage the casual visitor to stop; and it is blissfully free from picnic sites and official car parks, or even from shops selling ice cream other than surreptitiously. The Wolds are, in fact, a part of the Yorkshireman's rather than the tourist's Yorkshire, and it is notable that many of those Yorkshire persons who go there to explore the area do so on foot, and with the assistance of a stout pair of boots.

There are arguably four types of landscape within this network, whose personalities will grow more clearly distinct the longer the pootlist spends exploring them. The obvious division is between the lower-lying country to the west and the uplands of the Wolds proper, but each of these areas can be further subdivided. The Wolds themselves are made up of a sweeping chalk upland, deeply indented by a series of winding dry valleys which in more southerly regions would be called combes, but are here, naturally, known as dales. When one is on the top of this upland the most frequent impression is of an intensively farmed arable landscape which shelves gently but impressively over many kilometres towards the east coast, and from whose high western scarp one can command enormous picture-postcard views over the Vales of York and Pickering. The uplands have been heavily cultivated since the first half of the 19th century, so that it would be inappropriate in this case to assume that the broad expanses of wheat and barley are an entirely recent phenomenon. Many fields are however much larger than they used to be, and in some places (for example on the ridge lying eastwards of Wharram Percy) no hedges have survived at all, whilst in others they have been cut into such parsimonious, pathetic excuses for a hedge that you virtually have to get down on all fours and peer amongst the laneside grasses to find them. However, as in other chalk landscapes, the openness of arable cultivation can accentuate the swelling beauty of the land's contours, and certainly contributes to a 'top of the world' impression which is justified here by the hills' actual height.

As an experience, the dales are totally separate from this upland. One comes into them either abruptly (as on the lane running southwards into Burdale, which drops steeply down the valley side) or more insinuatingly, as in the unparalleled Water Dale, which snakes down over nearly 4 km. from Leavening Brow towards Thixendale, getting very gradually deeper as the lane bends this way and that around the spurs. I still remember the first time I cycled down this marvellous combe, which is like a landscape equivalent of a Rossini crecendo, getting gradually more impressive the longer you stay with it, and sustaining itself for far longer than you expect. The lane sits so very neatly in the flat valley bottom, bending just where the spurs bend, and after the first slope the gentle downhill gradient is barely perceptible. It seems Thixendale will always be there just around the next spur, but it never is, and the traveller new to this country is guaranteed to arrive at it only when he has finally given up looking for it.

Water Dale's apparently contradictory name is no doubt derived from the fact that springs rise to the surface here, as in other dales, after heavy rain, although for the rest of the time it is a dry valley with one or two patches of slightly damp ground where voluminous king-cups shine in season. Like all its neighbouring combes, Water Dale has steep sides maintained as rough pasture; these are nevertheless being recolonized in many places by hawthorn and gorse, which can give them a maquis-like appearance. Travelling down the dale one quickly sinks deep enough into the hills to feel entirely cut off from the expansive sweep of the upland, and the closeness of these steep (though never *very* high) slopes creates a feeling of intimacy which is odd in such lonely country. The dale's flat bottom is maintained as a series of pastures, supporting cattle and horses as well as sheep (though I am sorry to report that in other places, for example between Thixendale and Burdale, smooth and unvarying arable cultivation now holds sway). Cowslips can be seen in them, and even more so on the steepest slopes, peppering the grey-green grass with a star system of tiny yellow blossoms which becomes clearer, and ever broader, the more intently you search for it.

Is it perhaps because we know that so many antiquities have been discovered in country of this kind that the rough, steep pastures themselves seem ancient? Writing of the parish of Sancton, south of Market Weighton, local historian J.G. Hall observed in 1892 that "almost every field in and around the parish is rich in relics of the Britons, Romans and Saxons," and this is equally true of countless other old pastures in the region – at least, so long as they are kept as patures. There are times in exploring the Wolds – after one has passed by a dozen or more tumuli during the day's meanderings – when the evenly shaped, steep-sided slopes of the dales themselves will begin to seem like earthworks: sinuous, massive, interlocking barrows that might well conceal the remains of Stone Age chieftains by the score, buried with or without their chariots. Such an impression is all the more vivid when one penetrates the combes that have no roads. The Wolds do in fact provide an excellent test-case for a little tentative combining of cyclo- and foot-pootling. I have dwelled at some length on Water Dale because it is the only dale in the network whose full length can be cycled: but it is possible to enjoy this same experience on foot in several other dry valleys that wind their way down to Thixendale. Unfortunately in all cases the routes are for walkers only. None of these grassy bottoms have so much as a bridleway along them, but they do all have something of the essential, enclosing and ancients mystery just described, which is why I think they are worth mentioning even in a book that nails its colours to the crossbar. Indeed, the famed Wharram Percy itself – whilst it must have had several 'lanes' running to it in the Middle Ages – is accessible now only by way of a farm track, or along the line of the nearby disused railway, neither of which could have been described as public roads in the recent past.

To get to the Vale from the Wolds valleys, one must climb back up to the high land above the steep west- and northwest-facing scarp, and then drop over the edge. The most dramatic (and therefore perhaps the least worthwhile) drop in the network is the one-in-five hill down to Acklam: rather more gentle, and allowing more time to take in the enormity of the view and enjoy an easy, protracted plummet, is the hill down to Leavening. In both cases one arrives at villages set quite high on the slope, as is also the case on the lanes down to Uncleby, Painsthorpe and Kirby Underdale. This halfway country, which is neither the high upland nor the low-lying and relatively flat land of the Vale of York, provides the third discernible landscape of the network, and it is one that is well worth exploring in depth, even if this does mean a certain amount of clambering back up to altitudes you have not long since lost. To my eyes, the loveliest part of this under-Wold county is the area around Kirby Underdale, where two long and water-bearing combes run to join one another in a complex, rolling landscape of thickly hedged small pastures and prominent hanging woodlands. There are mature hedgerow and mid-field trees in all directions, and the steep scarp of the Wolds rises imposingly in the background. This is the kind of landscape in which it is very easy to shut oneself out from the greater world beyond: the lanes and tracks bend delightfully, the little meadows by the streamsides are full of buttercups (in one I saw two scarlet-combed roosters strutting neck-high amongst the brilliant yellow flowers, apparently as free as the wild birds above them in the treetops), and if one climbs either along the lane past Painsthorpe (and hops over a fence at the appropriate moment) or, more strikingly, up the track running south from Kirby Underdale, there are big, deep, exciting views of the high ends of the combes themselves where once more the cowslips proliferate, running in lines along the cattle path terraces.

In general, these foothills of the Wolds – whether at Kirby Underdale or further west towards Bugthorpe, at Acklam or further north at Birdsall – feel far more of a 'civilized' country than the Wolds themselves. Much of the land here is managed in what appears to be the old mixed farming system, with a small field of barley here, a meadow of cattle there, a few horses near the farm, and plenty of parkland-sized trees in every solid, well-kept hedgerow. The undulations made by the numerous small valleys in which the becks run down towards the Derwent continually surprise with their variety; as so often in England, the area of land is small and yet it has a seemingly inexhaustible complexity which grows more appealing the longer one spends exploring it. An additional pleasure here is that the villages and their sattelite farms are mainly built in an attractive, weathered light red brick with orange-red tiled roofs (most of these buildings are products of the Enclosure period, and the thoroughness of the transformation during Enclosure explains the absence of older domestic buildings in the area). The farmsteads in particular are satisfying as one passes them along the lanesides, set squarely into their hedged landscapes with no suggestion that the fine old barns will ever lose any of their present usefulness. I would go so far as to say that this high, lush, mainly pastoral zone is one of those rare stretches where the English countryside can be seen at its very best: each of the narrow, broad-verged lanes gives enticing views of the scarp beyond when one is travelling eastwards, and of the opening out of the Vale when one is travelling in the opposite direction. It seems for all the world like a stretch of lowland Herefordshire that has been somehow tilted onto a slope under the high 'down'.

The fourth landscape in the network is, of course, that of the low-lying country of the Vale itself, which just begins to be apparent to the east of the main lane which forms the network's western boundary. One drops down to this region from the foothills on the lane to Bugthorpe, for example, and beyond this village one finds oneself back on a much broader lane which run through an Enclosure landscape of the less interesting kind: very large fields, now scantily hedged, with few trees and not a great deal of personality. Arable cultivation predominates here, although this is not always the case. Elsewhere to the north can be found a rather more pleasing mixture of arable and pastoral, though always in large and only very gently sloping fields. The roads are unexceptionally broad here, with broad verges as in the East Midlands, and there is more traffic about. Even so, some of these wide lanes can be appealing: the road which climbs and winds very gently up to Birdsall is one such, not least because it has been planted as an avenue on the last stretch before the estate parkland. In this northern sector of the network there has been a certain amount of uncompromising hedge-removal, for example near Kennythorpe, but this does throw open some strikingly broad, uncomplicated views of the rolling green rim of the high Wold, and with such a completely controlled and ordered foreground that all the promise of the ancient, empty hills beyond is once again renewed.

Avoid or be prepared for:
For all its remoteness, this region of the Wolds is particularly badly infested with jets – these vile, eardrum-shedding memento mori will shudder over at exasperatingly frequent intervals, seemingly low enough to part one's hair; also sometimes to be encountered on the high Wold are other members of the military, disguised as rotting tree stumps or areas of duck pond, performing their indecipherable rituals grim-lipped and with a religiose solemnity; disused quarries are as mentioned at Burdale and Wharram – whether one finds them ugly or not depends very much on personal taste and the state of the weather; small industrial site with the obligatory and as always totally functionless 'screen' of conifers next to the main lane north of Leavening; hangar-like sheds of agricultural industry at Fridaythorpe; recent installation of poultry batteries and gleaming silver service units in the most prominent possible siting along the lane up to Fridaythorpe from Burdale; all the villages have something to recommend them – in the case of Kirby Underdale, Langton and Bugthorpe, quite a lot – with the exception of Leavening, which is not pleasant, having almost as many modern houses as old ones and no real centre, and Leppington and Kennythorpe, which have very little personality; Thixendale – whose personality was at best elusive – now suffers from one or two appallingly brash and irrelevant pieces of domestic modernism.

Preceding pages:
(Top left)   Dusk light at Gill's Farm.
(Bottom left)   Water Dale.
(Right)   A tempting farm track at Burdale.

(Opposite)   No longer on any lane: the shell of
Wharram Percy church.
(Below)   Dusk light above Thixendale.

Lanes Of The Upper Welland Valley And The Environs Of Robin-A-Tiptoe Hill

Rutland and Leicestershire
OS Maps 130 and 141

Bounded by: A606 northwest from Oakham to Melton Mowbray; B6047 south to Church Langton; lanes east through Weston by Welland and Ashley to Middleton; B670 northeast to Rockingham; A6003 north to Oakham.

The oft-noted quip about Northamptonshire that it is, or was, a county of *spires, squires* and *mires* could be applied with equal confidence to the sweeping hunt country of the Leicestershire upland. Since remnants of the appropriate types of holy house are to be discovered in this network, I shall dare to add to this musical catalogue not only *priors* but *friars*, and regret in passing that – from this point of view, at least – it is rather a shame that the people of the area have not been noted in the history books as incorrigible tellers of untruths.

But to the point. Throughout this section, as elsewhere, I deliberately refer to Rutland as a separate entity – England's smallest county that was – partly because its conversion to a subsidiary of Leicestershire (there is now a Rutland District Council) makes a mockery of the local history which a book such as this must and does willingly respect, and partly because Rutland remains nevertheless as a separate entity, in the minds of at least some of its occupants, as well as in the County Structure Plan which seeks to preserve the area's individuality. One small but telltale detail here is that in 1980 Oakham Town Council put back the Rutland name signs on major roads. Many had been removed, apparently by collectors, in the misguided belief that the world had no further use for them after the little county's loss of rank.

Once again I have manipulated my system of exploration, in this case so as to extend the original network further south into the Welland Valley, with the result that we are dealing here with two very subtly different types of country. The myth about the east Midlands landscape that it is not really hilly, and worse, that it is boring, will be seen for what it is by anyone who cycles the lanes near Belton, for example, or Tilton on the Hill, or Launde Abbey – the last being a religious retreat approachable in every direction only along lanes with steep gradients. However, not all gradients are so steep as in these vicinities, and the hill country (of which Robin-a-Tiptoe Hill is one of the more noticeable summits) is generally satisfying for the pootlist since expansive views, as it were miniatures of the breathtaking, and a real sense of height can be enjoyed after relatively very little climbing. It is also possible to get a long way up the gentler hills on the impetus from the last descent: the rate of loss of speed experienced by the loaded-up touring cyclist is interestingly similar to that of a fully laden lorry, so I will stress that this is the case only on the gentler hills. Due to the prevailing drainage pattern in the area, the easy, rolling gradients are on the east–west lanes, whilst those running north–south tend to be more switchback, dropping into and climbing out of the stream valleys: this is exactly the kind of basic geography of which pootlists become aware much earlier than most other travellers!

Until I began exploring the east Midlands I had always thought that the landscapes of the 'hunt' painters such as John Ferneley Snr. were the inventions of second-rate talent which could not quite deal with the full complexity of actual landscape. It was all the more surprising, then – since most of the hunt painters are indeed second-rate talent – to find that even in the 1970s much of this country looked as it does in paintings of the early 1800s, in other words 'oversimplified'. In many long views – over the Welland from by Slawston, for example, or the view of Tilton on the Hill from south of Marefield – the gentle sweep and dip of the hills, still divided into large, straight-edged rectangles of green by the Enclosure hedges, the church spires giving focus to valley or hilltop, the neat clumps of still-deciduous woodland and the attractive, bending and seemingly jumpable streams, look at first sight as though they might have been created deliberately and perversely in imitation of the paintings. Long views of vales will open up, with sometimes hardly a farmstead in them. Climbing out of Oakham towards Brooke, you leave behind the new housing estates, pass under the line of pylons, and top the hill to be confronted with an idyllic, rolling, hedged landscape complete with cattle pastures, Braunston locked into its trees on the right, and beyond it a dense horizontal pattern of hedgerows on the hill slopes south of Knossington. A little further to the south, from the ridge lane which runs west of Ridlington, the traveller can look down on Belton on its knoll in the Eye Brook Valley, for all the world like a flattened-out version of one of the hill-based Devon villages such as North Molton, seen from the Exmoor heights. As well as the long views, the upland also has a certain number of steep-sided valley ends, more akin in atmosphere to the Marches than to East Anglia, where the lanes are shut in on either side by small scrubby pastures that are sometimes shared by cattle and horses together. Many of these – even where they do not contain ridge and furrow patterns – possess mid-field trees and steep, crumbling banks, and have clearly not been ploughed for quite some time.

In the south of the network as one approaches the Welland such corners are not in evidence: the landscape becomes more spacious, though with delectable low, grassed and wooded upswellings of hills which rise out of the rolling flatness of the valley bottom. Whilst there is a lot of arable cultivation here (with large fields, for example, by Church Langton, and hedge removal south of Goadby) there nevertheless remain many pasturing meadows near the waterside. The valley is perhaps at its most satisfying (I say only 'perhaps') on the narrow lane from Welham to Slawston.

The east Midlands possesses the largest areas of landscape to have been virtually re-created during the Parliamentary Enclosure period (roughly 1750–1850), when land which had previously been farmed under the old open field system, or had been used as common, heath or marsh, was divided up by parliamentary act into newly hedged fields and then realloted to land-owners in proportion with their previous holdings or rights of common grazing. Whilst the larger landowners almost without exception benefited from enclosure, the same is not true of the peasantry – the cottagers and, especially, the squatters – many of whom had previously had access to common land only by custom and not by right. When the commons were cut up into fields and hedged such people only rarely got something in return for the loss of what had not been theirs in law, but upon which they had nevertheless founded their precarious livings. Even where commoners did have a legal right to compensation in land, what they were awarded was frequently too small to be of practical use to them. A family could not keep a cow, which it might have kept on common grazing, if the land given back to it was much less than three acres, and in most cases it *was* less. Under such circumstances the new peasant 'landowner' might find that his only practical choice was to sell out to the owner of adjoining land, and would thus be a landowner no longer. There is a certain irony, then, in the fact that the hedgerows in Enclosure landscapes which are now cherished by many of us as things in themselves, were at the time of their setting the most immediate symbols of a system which, whilst it created more work for the agricultural labour force than had existed previously, nevertheless deprived many of the poorest people of their livelihood.

It is also interesting to find that to some (though not all) representatives of the taste of that period, the hedgerows themselves seemed despicably ugly. In trying to understand this reaction one should bear in mind that the newly created landscape of regularly shaped field shut in with neat lines of low, hand-trimmed hedges, was a very far cry from the wild-grown and variegated thing it has so often turned into by the present day. The peasant poet John Clare, who is regularly quoted in such matters because he was one of the very few of his class whose opinions have survived in print, wrote despairingly of the denudation of the common heathland which lay near his home village of Helpston (east of Stamford, not far from this network). His agoraphobic reaction to the 'naked leas' which resulted from the cutting down of trees and scrub is intriguingly similar to that of so many of us to the barley prairies of today.

And what of the cultivated landscapes which were obliterated through enclosure? The process may have opened up longer vistas on rough common land, but in farmed land it shut them in. The ridge and furrow patterning which is so common here as throughout the east Midlands acts as a reiterated challenge to the traveller's imagination: what *exactly* was it like, the old open field system of which these lines of low, grassed-over mounds are the remains? It can be reconstructed by artists working at the instruction of landscape historians, who may speculate in the abstract about how the open fields were laid out and how they functioned. But what were they really like, to work in, and to walk around in? Stand amongst the ridges and furrows and you can get some faint sense of how it might have been, but only within the confines of the later and much more immediate landscape. Could the open fields possibly have felt so bare and uniform as the agrarian prairies do today? Surely not: for even in a landscape with far fewer hedges there were still many intensively managed woodlands, and the division of cropping into strips (whose mounded shapes were produced through the repeated use of ploughs that turned the earth towards the centre) must have given a highly varied terrain, even if it was unenclosed. One can if one wishes go to Laxton in Nottinghamshire, where to date a small area has survived that is a direct descendant of the old open fields. But it is only a descendant, and not the thing itself. Until such time as some yet-to-be-founded museum of landscape has re-created it for us, the actual experience of the open fields will remain a mystery to tantalize all those who find themselves walking amongst the ridges and the furrows.

The effect of enclosure of the lanes was that wherever it took place the existing pattern of routes was replaced with a new and generally much simpler one. The new roads were built straight where possible, and to allow for by-passing of the sloughs which developed along them in winter they were made immensely wide: inter-village roads were 12 metres in width, roads between market towns were 18 metres, and the main road to London through Rutland was no less than 30 metres across. Much of this breadth became grass verge, especially after Macadam's innovation had arrived to dispose of the sloughs; and the verges came to be used for grazing cattle, although today you will see little save the occasional pet goat making use of them. They are however of continuous benefit to the pootlist concerned with finding places to splay himself out in the sunshine. In many cases where the lanes have little traffic, the metalled width has actually shrunk in this century to that of an average single-track road; and where the verges along such stretches are overgrown with bramble and cow parsley, the impression given is anything but that of the stereotyped highway-wide Enclosure road which is meant to dominate the east Midlands landscape. Such roads do still exist, of course, but every possible variation on them is also to be found, in this network as elsewhere. One particularly beautiful and intriguing lane runs from Braunston to Knossington: up to the point where it leaves the parish of Braunston, and the old county of Rutland, it does indeed have the appearance of a straight, wide, if switchback Enclosure road, but beyond this as far as Knossington it is a bending and narrow lane in the earlier style.

Leicestershire and Rutland were amongst the few counties in England in which the craft of hedge-laying survived intact after the First World War. This was due partly to the continued prominence of dairy farming in the region, with the resulting need for stockproof hedges, and partly to the demands of the local huntsmen for hedges which would act as stimulating barriers but could also be jumped without undue danger. The Midlands type of laid hedge is also known as the Standard hedge, and it can still be found in a broad belt of England between County Durham and Gloucestershire, although in the west the style tends to merge with those of the Welsh hedges of which, in striking contrast, there are several regional types with further stylistic subdivision amongst them. In the 1920s, Leciestershire hedge-layers went as teachers to other parts of the country, taking the Standard hedge with them. Ironically many of their pupils were unemployed industrial workers – a drift *to* the land which was short-lived at best. The most expert hedge-laying continues to be practised today, or so it is said, in Leicestershire, Nottinghamshire, and Warwickshire. Local variations on the hedges produced in the Midlands have been given their own names: the 'oxer', the 'double oxer', the 'bullfinch' (i.e. 'bull fence'?), a hedge so wide that no fox hunter could clear it.

Hedge-laying must be a satisfying job – once you have mastered it, which no doubt takes a good deal of time and patience. Its aim in all its variations is always the same: to make an impenetrable living barrier either out of young hedgeplants which have never been laid previously, or out of old ones which have grown up from what was a laid hedge in the past. The plants are laid by having their stems partially but not completely severed, so that they continue living when they are bent over, and are then woven around a newly driven line of stakes. They are held neatly in place by a top binding known as 'heathering' (otherwise 'edders', or 'winders'), which can be made out of hazel wands, sweet chestnut, elm, willow, or even clematis and briars, although hazel is generally preferred as the longest lasting. The laid stems are known as 'pleachers' or, depending on who you are talking to, and where, 'pleshers', 'plashers', 'pletchers' or 'plushers'. The interweaving of plants and stakes is sometimes referred to as the 'wattle', a term which was no doubt originally borrowed from vernacular building. In the hunt country, wherever the farmers are compliant, the stakes are sawn off level to minimize the risk of injury to the horses. However, it remains a mark of the hedge-layer's craft to finish off the stakes with an upward and diagonal cut in order to "make the white shine all one way", as they put it, and this too can be seen in some laid hedges in the east Midlands.

Hawthorn is by far the commonest hedge plant in the region, and it is still frequently referred to here as 'quickset'. In the old days this word appears to have had a punning double meaning: it could mean either the business of planting a hedge so that it would grow speedily, or it could mean the hedge as a thing in itself, a barrier that was 'quick', in other words living. Hawthorn was intensively cultivated in nurseries from the 1790s onwards to supply the necessary plants for the Enclosure hedges; previous to this, seedlings had been gathered wild from woodland. The hawthorn species *not* generally found in today's Midlands hedgerows but still found in the wild, *Crataegus oxyacanthoides*, is known as Midland hawthorn, without any doubt as a result of some 19th-century conspiracy utterly to confound the modern layman; the hawthorn which is used in the hedges, meantime, is called simply 'hawthorn'.

Were you to pay a visit to the Rutland County Museum in Oakham, you would find there a fascinating collection of local hedge-layers' tools from times past: a mallet (known as a 'beetle') for driving in the stakes, long and short-handled 'slashers', billhooks and trimming hooks – satisfyingly hand-crafted objects for work which is itself a handicraft. Similar tools are still in use today, but the regional variations in design which meant that you could tell which county (or even which part of a county) a man came from by the design of his billhook are now much reduced. The large firms which make the tools do still produce a Leicestershire (or Warwickshire) billhook which is absolutely *not* used by the Welsh hedge-layers, and a variety of Welsh billhooks (the Llandidlo, the Knighton, the Newtown, for example) which Midlands hedge-layers similarly eschew. The Leicestershire billhook is reckoned to be the best of the lot, and not just by the Leicestershire men.

Despite the frequency of laying, the use of machines for trimming the hedges has resulted, here as everywhere else, in quite a variety of shapes: hedges cut down into 'A's so low that a man let alone a horse could jump them, hedges box-shaped in cross-section, hedges trapezoidal. And, of course, machines and hedge-layers notwithstanding, there are still many hedges which have been allowed to grow as they please until they have transformed them-selves into dense, high strips of woodland: one such stretch runs directly south of Brooke – at least, until such time as the farmer gets there to 'tidy it up'.

The commonest hedgerow tree in the region today is the ash, which was much planted in the original Enclosure hedgerows and has now been given pride of place by the devastation of the elms. Those trees were, alas, not long since known as the Northamptonshire weed, and were probably as common in these parts also. But the ash, which grew in the company of elms, has trouble withstanding high winds on its own and is often to be seen, especially on the exposed uplands, mis-shapen and grotesque through the breaking away of its upper branches.

If blood sports have kept the hedges tall in northwest Norfolk, where there is much pheasant hunting, they have kept them low and solid in Leicestershire and Rutland. The hill country of this network is a part of the territory of the Cottesmore hunt, which is the oldest in England, whilst further to the east lies the territory of the Quorn hunt, an upland that has been used for hunting as a sport since medieval times at least. Compensation to farmers for damage to property is used in part for hedge-laying, and the Cottesmore even has its own hedging expert, who arranges competitions to help keep the craft alive and supplies stakes and binding materials as gifts for the farmers. It is impossible not to be impressed at the influence of the huntsmen on the landscape in these parts. There is no question that they have helped to run counter to the trend for hedgerow removal, which may nonetheless be seen in effect, for example, west of Cold Overton and north of Ridlington, although nothing in this hilly area matches the enlargement of fields in the Vale of Catmose, to the north of Oakham. I am pleased to report that I did meet a fox along the ridge lane to the west of Ridlington, and that it was not at the time being pursued by man or beast. It was basking in the sun in the green corn, and was disturbed by my passing, bounding away across the half-grown crops with the motion of a light sea craft hitting a series of big waves. It paused at the field's edge and turned its pretty feline face towards me – gauging me, no doubt, in relation to its other enemies – before dipping out of sight for good.

One further delight in this network is the abundance of gated roads, whose qualities were discussed earlier. These can sometimes be deeply potholed as the result of years of erosion by cattle droppings, since many of the fields they traverse are pasture. This will slow the pootlist down even further than may be his wont, but such erosion is satisfying since it is a sure sign that one is in 'deep' country, or to put it another way it shows that the highway authorities know how little the roads are used except by the farmers, and spend accordingly. The number of potholes on country lanes usually runs in inverse proportion to their popularity with motorists.

I have said nothing so far about the buildings in the area, yet this is another network of lanes along which there also happens to be an extra-ordinary richness of villages – both close-packed miniature townships such as Hallaton, Belton and Somerby, and remoter-seeming, random groupings of houses near a stalwart hall or church lost in trees, such as Cold Overton and Owston. The physical beauty of the buildings begins with the stone, which is of two kinds: the ironstone which was much quarried in this upland, and the oolitic limestone which was sometimes brought in from the famous quarries at Ketton and Clipsham, and was worked from the 13th century onwards. Though the grey-yellow limestone is a better building stone and has been widely used across the country (for colleges in both Oxford and Cambridge, for example, as well as for the rebuilding of the bombed-out House of Commons), I prefer the appearance of the ironstone, which comes in various shades from a deep golden-yellow to a gorgeous orange-brown, unforgettable in direct evening light when buildings made out of it can seem to glow amongst the trees. It is called ironstone, incidentally, because it is a source of iron ore; but there is never very much ore in it, and anyway it is low-grade material, which is one reason why the stone was used only for building and not for the establishment of yet another industrial wasteland. Veins of iron ore can sometimes be seen running across pieces of stone in the cottage walls, so that this is one of the few areas of Britain where it can be claimed that the stone walls rust.

Avoid or be prepared for:
Ugly and sinister hilltop water reservoir tank built into the top of Whatborough Hill; lines of pylons running north–south in both the west and the east of the network; radio mast between Oakham and Knossington; fantastically badly sited 'civic amenity site' (i.e. dump) at northern end of lovely gated road to the south of Somerby, complete with see-through wire fence and concrete posts; oblique views of open cast strip mining in Welland Valley to east of network beyond Rockingham, and the cranes of Corby on the hill to the south; in general, but with exceptions, despoliation of the outskirts of villages by speculative building of the bungaloid variety (the far from beautiful Victorian brick which can be seen in many stone villages, e.g. Belton, does not spoil because the traditional patterns were adhered to), with dire modern building ruining only certain centres where there was space to fill, e.g. bungalows and yellow-brick houses with 'Georgian' windows opposite fine church at Somerby, well-heeled 'executive' houses planted where there is (or rather, was) a view at Ridlington, bringing the smarter suburbs of Leicester into a village street of old gold stone.

Main lanes: *from Oakham through Braunston to Tilton on the Hill; Horninghold through Hallaton to Tur Langton, though not overwhelmingly busy; from A606 through Pickwell, Somerby and Burrough on the Hill to Twyford; Oakham to Knossington, recently widened; in general, the presence of commuters' cars at peak travelling times, though not on the field lanes and the like; lane north of Great Easton along Eyebrook reservoir becomes a car park for picnickers at weekends.*

(*Above*) *Field road near Owston, running through long-established pasture.*
(*Opposite, top*) *Slight incline as one leaves the Welland valley on a lane to Slawston.*
(*Opposite, bottom*) *A meadow near Dalby Hall. No poisons have been used* here.

Following pages:
(*Top left*) *Hilltop ash, always the last to open, on a lane near Burrough on the Hill.*
(*Bottom left*) *A lane near Loddington: low-hedged, but not very broad.*
(*Top right*) *Near Great Dalby. The hedge was broken by a Capt. J.D.A. Keith who 'took a bad fall', as they say, in 1962. The event is commemorated by a small plaque bearing the captain's name and the date, which is fixed to the fence that now plugs the gap. During the eighteenth and nineteenth centuries, the location of the death of a favourite horse was sometimes marked with a small gravestone. One of these was rediscovered in 1981 in a hedgerow not far to the east of this spot.*
(*Bottom right*) *Gated road to Somerby with ash trees, high hawthorn hedges, and grass up the centre of the asphalt.*

(Opposite) Wind-broken ash near John O' Gaunt fox covert.
(Above) Parliamentary Enclosure road with ash trees. West of Middleton.
(Left) Invaluable landscape feature: a mid-field hedge, long since useless as a barrier, now grown into a line of hawthorn trees. Near Belton.

Lanes Of The Wenlock Edge, Ape Dale, Caer Caradoc Hill And The Lawley

Shropshire
OS Map 137

Bounded by: B4368 northeast from Craven Arms to Shipton; B4378 to Bourton; lanes generally westwards through Presthope, Hughley, Church Preen and Lawley to crossroads by Longnorgreen; Roman road south to junction with A49; A49 south to Craven Arms.

It is quite possibly easier to find traces, or at least intimations, of an earthly paradise along the lanes and tracks of the Wenlock Edge and its neighbouring dales than it is in most of the rest of rural England, especially in spring and early summer, and again when the autumn is well advanced. This, as far as I am concerned, is one of the most beautiful of all lanescapes, and I cannot restrain myself from blurting out the fact. It is beautiful for being largely untainted by the grey fringes of the Megalopolis; beautiful for the winding narrowness and enclosure of its many lanes, along which even the gravel used in recent metalling is a warm and comforting pink; beautiful for the seemingly limitless variety of vistas of hills beyond hills, both 'within' the Edge and beneath it in Ape Dale, or above it on the slopes of the hills to the northwest; beautiful for the strips and clumps of oak woodland which still round off many hilltops and steep slopes along the Edge, against which there remains to be seen a wonderful variety of individual hedgerow, parkland and laneside-garden trees; beautiful for the floral luxuriance of its damper spots in the ditches and pastures; and beautiful, finally, for the contrast between this generally 'soft' landscape and the upper slopes of the Edge hills (and the entire upland around Caer Caradoc Hill) which remain wildernesses of bracken, some of them nevertheless passing through a brief phase of lyrical beauty under a smoke of bluebells before the bracken has sprouted back into prominence.

The loneliness of this country is one which can be almost too clear from certain observation points: the big vistas to be had of the long, apparently low and wooded scarp of the Edge from the high land above Enchmarsh, for example; or the exquisite Claudian landscape which is to be enjoyed from outside the porch of Wilderhope Manor, with Brown Clee Hill perfectly framed by the graceful sweep of the wooded foreground hillocks of the Edge itself. Although it is well visited by walkers, the Edge and its surroundings are still probably best known by certain striking views (one is just out of the chosen area, to the north on the B4371) obtainable from near to roadside parking places, and from postcards made out of photographs taken at the same points. But the specific appeal of the Wenlock Edge lies in the multitudinousness of its hidden dips and curves, the frequency with which one can find new and unexpected 'corners' within it, even after years of familiarity: new juxtapositions of slopes one knows (or thinks one knows) with others which have as it were emerged out of the landscape by dint of travelling a kilometre or less along some previously unexplored lane or track. The knowledge that this beauty extends almost entirely unimpaired in every direction does of course add to the sense of enchantment – a word I would not use since it has been so degraded, if it did not absolutely fit.

In place of the church towers standing against the sky which are sometimes to be seen at the ends of East Anglian lanes (where they bend out of sight), here beyond the lane foreground one constantly sees the wooded hilltops, tilted pastures, mature hedgerow and mid-field trees, all shutting in the view. Admittedly conifers now predominate in the woodland areas, and it is outrageous that they should, but there are sufficient oakwoods remaining (for example along the valley lane from Diddlebury to Middlehope or on the scarp near Strefford) for them still to affect the area's personality strongly. Even some of the coniferous woodlands here are worth a glance, since they have been left to grow to full maturity – something you do not see very often. Each of the many hillocks which go into the making of the southeastern section of the Edge is either capped with woods or has woodlands on its highest slopes, while meadows rise up to meet them with increasing steepness the higher they ascend.

A glance at the map will show that almost all the metalled lanes on the Wenlock Edge run diagonally across its 'spine', and that each of these follows a small stream valley, on either side of which there stand the steep-sided hillocks already described. No traveller approaching the Edge from the north could possibly expect a landscape of such complexity beyond the seemingly endless tree-clad bank which is the northwestern scarp face of the ridge. Though there is an overall likeness in these small valleys (they all run as a narrow passage from the south-east, gradually opening out as they get higher), each has a personality of its own. They are best explored by approaching from the south, even if this does mean travelling a little along the B4368 (which is generally not very busy). One of the most lingeringly memorable of these miniature valleys lies... how can I put it? Let me say that it is situated somewhere towards the southwestern end of the Wenlock Edge and has been named, and that a part of this name means 'stream valley'. At one point along it the lane crosses the watercourse, whose steep banks can be seen whitened by the flowers of wild garlic, and at intervals as one climbs one comes across simple and unspoiled cottages built of the Wenlock Edge limestone. Several of these are situated beneath the level of the lane, whilst others are built end-on to it, as if with the intention of giving anyone looking from an upstairs window the best possible view of approaching strangers. There are a number of old, tiny orchards here, and in April their blossom stands out bold and startling against the steep, sombre wooded banks beyond. At one point an old gate lies half open on a near-vertical field awash with bluebells; nearby a horse grazes on a cottage lawn. No cars pass. The idea of 'seclusion' in the English countryside finds real expression in places such as this, in the 1980s no less than in the 1880s.

Each of the transverse lanes will lead the cyclist literally into the centre of the Edge, its secret midst, a high intermediary zone enclosed by the scarp to the northwest and the line of hillocks to the southeast. Here there are a number of small and still distinctly quaint settlements – Dinchope, Westhope, Middlehope, Easthope (the suffix 'hope' itself means a small enclosed valley, separate from the main dale) – where for the most part the pootlist is likely to hear only birdsong, sheepsong, the barking of defensive farm dogs (never song), and the sound of the wind. Here one can feel entirely and satisfyingly cut off from the modern world which no doubt continues to flow down the two 'B' roads on either side of the ridge. It is readily possible to keep within the 'hopes' along the southern section of the Edge, where there is a metalled lane (the curious tower on Callow Hill lends this section a further likeness to a Claude landscape, without the use of tinted glasses), and one can get from Middlehope to Upper Millichope along what starts as a metalled lane and then becomes a track. One can also follow a new and ugly cement farm road to Wilderhope, which then turns into the most splendidly beaten-up stretch of unrenewed metalling you are likely to encounter, this eventually leading out on to the B4371, which follows the ridge the rest of the way to Much Wenlock. Only between Millichope and Wilderhope is there a real problem: you can keep up on the hill, but this involves using a footpath through the woods on the scarp – very pretty, but also very muddy after any amount of rain.

The lanes of the Edge – and something like this can also be said of many, perhaps most, of the lanes in the Welsh Marches, at least in Shropshire and Herefordshire – are quiet (very few commuters on the Edge itself, very few places for them to live), well-hedged (much sheep and cattle pasture, and hedges are laid, though not generally bound with heathering), narrow, bending, and with a luxuriance of wild flowers especially along the banks where the lanes have become indented into the land surface. This luxuriance is quite possibly matched today only in other parts of the Marches, and in Devon and Cornwall. Orchids can sometimes be found along the hedgerows, and in general there is a sense of natural abundance in the lanes. Ferns will grow alongside the hedgerow shrubs, reminders of an earlier covering to what is now a field landscape, and the more waterlogged laneside ditches will sometimes be found overflowing with king-cups. This being a pastoral area, there are also long stretches of thoroughly eroded tarmac, especially near farms, and here the verges will usually be trodden and squashed by the passage of many patient hooves into a brown slough. But elsewhere there are flowers, flowers and more flowers. Along one exquisite lane which drops and bends and climbs its way in the vicinity of the Lawley there is a laneside woodland which is entirely carpeted with a pink variety of scarlet pimpernel: if you happen to be passing in the early evening at the right time of year you will find the air there sweetened with its perfume, a gentle and delectable shock amongst the shadows.

The Wenlock Edge is only one of three distinct types of country in this network (whose somewhat vague northern boundary was chosen as a way of cutting down on an otherwise unwieldy area). Of the others the first is the landscape of Ape Dale, where the lanes run under the Edge. The roads which will seem to the pootlist to lie most distinctly 'beneath' the ridge are those which run roughly parallel with it, by way of a series of zigs and zags, frequently diving between tall hedged banks, through Alcaston, Wolverton, Harton and Easton, and then moving away north to Wall under Heywood (this latter stretch is another of those still mysteriously marked as white on the OS maps, although it is in fact tarred for its full length). Cycling these lanes, one has the seemingly endless, seemingly near-vertical barrier of trees on the scarp slope of the Edge always on the one hand, viewing it either from a slightly raised position or from as deep into the Dale as one can go. At the other hand, topping the fields, are the purple and orange summits of the Long Mynd and the third landscape in the network. It was on one of my journeys along these lanes that I encountered a local farmer driving a tractor to which a bulldozer claw was attached. In the claw there was a wheelchair, and in the wheelchair was an old lady. The farmer grinned and nodded through the racket of his machine; the old lady, who had perhaps not seen me, went past regally without a glance.

The third landscape here is that of the upland which is capped by the summits of Hope Bowdler and Caer Caradoc Hills and the Lawley: this is in effect a scaled-down version of a Welsh mountain landscape (Wales lies some 40 km. to the west). Amongst the many striking panoramic views back over Ape Dale towards the Edge is, for example, the vista to be enjoyed from the high fenced lanes round Hazler Hill (again for white read yellow), or from Yell Bank above Enchmarsh where one sees not only the dale but also the small amphitheatre of steep-sided hills of which Yell Bank is a northern extension, with Cardington placed exactly as one imagines a village in hills should be placed, directly in the centre of the depression and encircled by the upland. From a little further on along this lane one can also see the apparently flat patchwork plain of northern Shropshire, extending from the bases of the intervening hills to a distant horizon. One of the distinct pleasures here, as upon the Edge itself, is being able to discover the various small summits in ever new combinations. As you ride around the lanes you are perpetually glimpsing Caradoc, say, through a gateway – but then, what is the hill on the right? And if that is Willstone Hill, then what is the hill just beyond it?

To get into the centre of these hills there is only one road you can follow, and this is the very definitely unmetalled track (popular with weekend walkers) which runs from Cardington to Church Stretton under Caradoc and over a heather- and bracken-clad col known appropriately as The Wilderness. Here you climb out of the cultivated vale into the upland wastes, and at the ruined farm which stands like a frontier post directly under Caradoc – as also at the ruined Cwms Farm to the south – you can see the once enclosed and tiny fields now half-way returned to reed and fern, their hedges transformed into lines of gnarled and twisted hawthorn trees, some still bent over in mimicry of their laid shape, under which the sheep roam quite freely. Curiously, a part of one of the fields right by the farm was being cultivated when I was there, though nothing was coming up: it looked, in proximity to such a sad and remote ruin, like the work of some half-hearted wraith. The track as it passes this farm is crudely paved with the local stone – a country lane as many used to be before the rebirth of scientific roadmaking. However, down towards Cardington the 'metalling' is the bared rock of the hill, which lies in totally uncyclable ridges across the line of the track. Once again here one's sense of scale may be affected, and Caradoc can at times look like a great mountain, since it has a mountain's gaunt outline and texture, rather than what it is – a hill that can be climbed in 20 minutes. It is one of the many hills in the Marches (of which two others are also named Caer Caradoc) which claim unto themselves the final battle between the legendary Belgic prince Caractacus and the Romans, led by Ostorius Scapula. Whether or not the fight actually took place here, it is all too easy to imagine that it *might* have done, most dramatically perhaps on the broad shoulder of The Wilderness, with Caradoc's sombre rocky outcrops coldly echoing the clash of swords.

There are many spots along the lanes in this network where one has vivid impressions of the age of the manmade landscape, in a way that one can only rarely do in the east, or in landscapes altered by Parliamentary Enclosure. These impressions, I hasten to add, may be absolutely false, based on a romantic response to a particular clump of gnarled and windswept trees (nothing more, perhaps, than the product of 50 years to a century), or to the rough surface of some pasture which was last ploughed over for cultivation during the Second World War. Ironically, however, the chances are quite high in Shropshire, when one is looking at a landscape which one feels in the fullness of ignorance *may* be very old, that one is doing so in fact. The complex pattern of indented, densely hedged-in lanes and the many small fields which lie between them is something which grew up piecemeal over a very long period. In the first place, many fields were created as a result of enclosure (with hedges) direct from forest, moorland or other uncultivated land during the Dark Ages and later. In western Shropshire enclosed land and open fields appear to have developed side by side, each village having a number of open fields to its name, though these were never so extensive as those in the east Midlands. The picture is further complicated by the fact that hedging of these open fields began to take place here during the 16th century, so that by the 1750s there was relatively little for the Enclosure commissioners to do. The only fields which may seem to the layman to be older than is in fact the case are those abutting directly on to unfenced moorland, many of which were created as a result of the enclosure of common grazing in the 18th and 19th centuries. In most places in this network, as might be expected, the lanes retain the countless dips and bends typical of roads that have evolved unplanned as 'inroads' into a very much untamed landscape, over a period of centuries which are themselves now lost in unrecorded history.

The geology of Shropshire is complex, throwing up a wide range of good and mainly weatherproof building stones which, in the central upland area, could be worked close to building sites: hence the frequency along the lanes of small quarries now overgrown with shrubs and trees. Shropshire's limestone country is confined to the Wenlock Edge and the two dales on either side of it, and most of the building stone was taken from the Edge: to the south it is a darker, harder stone which weathers to a recessive greenish-grey, whilst in the north it is lighter and softer. However, nowadays no-one wants to quarry any of the still abundant Wenlock Edge limestone for building, as one frustrated potential customer told me, "because it's too hard". Strange that it should prove too hard for 20th-century man when the evidence exists on all sides that it was not too hard for his technologically far less advanced predecessors. The only people who do not find it hard, evidently, are the proprietors of the industrial quarries which lie immediately south of Much Wenlock, who have removed and pulverized a substantial portion of the Edge since they first set up in business.

The old building stone quarries on the Edge can be intriguing. Along a back lane at Diddlebury a stone house is to be found sited in one such quarry, whilst at Munslow a cottage (now robbed of much of its old personality by having been cloddishly 'done up') sits perched on the top of a miniature cliff face made by quarry men: a house founded **on rock** if ever there was one. There is also at least one lane across the Edge which appears to have been cut down into the rock of the escarpment: this is the lane running south from Longville. Similar gullies can be found in most hilly areas in England, notably in the West Country where they can be very deep indeed (look, to take just one example, in the wonderful complex of hills which lie to the north of Bridport in Dorset). *If* they are man-made, and it is possible that some at least resulted from centuries of water erosion, then the first and most obvious reason for their creation would be to ease an otherwise difficult or impossible gradient; and this might well have been the case on the Longville lane. But it is equally possible that such 'road improvement schemes' also doubled conveniently as quarries.

This network has its share of the Marches' perhaps over-famous timber-framed buildings, for example at Rushbury and Easthope. But it is the limestone which lends the most distinct character to the area, paradoxically by being subdued and not obviously beautiful – yet beautiful nonetheless. Old stone barns and farmsteads stand at the lanesides so undemonstratively that even the cyclist can go past them before he has noticed they are there. On dull days especially, they will merge in with the trees and hedges, almost as if they were themselves living organisms. It takes a certain amount of time in this area before one comes to appreciate fully the villages and hamlets, which as usual are at their best where they are most remote and unadulterated. Take, for example, the superb group of austere old farm buildings at Chelmick on its back lane near Hope Bowdler, which looks very much as if it has been hacked direct from the ground it stands on. Here there is a barn with woodwork that was long ago painted brown (brown or very dark green paint being almost as sure a sign of continued occupation by older rural people as new 'Georgian' windows are of the urban invader); this paint has by now faded and weathered to a colour which marries so harmoniously with the grey-green of the stone around it that one is tempted to wonder whether it was planned that way from the start.

Avoid or be prepared for:
Ludicrous white lollipop – a radar dome – planted on Brown Clee Hill by the Civil Aviation Authority makes nonsense of the hill's graceful outline from certain angles; Bungalow Disease affects certain villages, for example Aston Munslow and Rushbury, and individual buildings such as the brash object which has taken over a small field at Longville; similar creations at Dryhill and Hope Bowdler – greedily planted to take in the view through their gaping picture windows – reduce their immediate surroundings, places of solitude and infinity, to quasi-urban mediocrity; worse still, if possible, is the trendy architect's doodle which has appeared recently at Westhope, acting as vociferous denial of this otherwise wonderful little place's remoteness; opened-up pub car park at Cardington crudely urbanizes the approach from the east, but the rest of this fine village is thankfully unspoiled; picnic area at Wolverton Wood to

the north of Westhope draws some cars up the lane through Ticklerton, duly widened in places, and there is weekenders' car parking also on the ridge lane above Enchmarsh, and right along the track (which should be totally banned to them) from Willstone to Caer Caradoc; Manor Farm at Alcaston is now a timber-frame building surrounded by the farming equivalent of an industrial estate, and there is a Chukie Chicken manufactory at Upper Affcot; pylons graze the network in the west.

Outside Diddlebury: farmyard with hand-clipped hedges.

*(Top left)   A paradise of flowers: scarlet pimpernels,
to be sought here, and to be sought there, on lanesides
near the Lawley.*
(Left)   Coniferous and deciduous blend, above Diddlebury.
(Above)   Across the 'hope', from Longville to Broadstone.

(Top left)   Near Westhope.
(Left)   A track above Diddlebury, with Whitcliffe Hill
in the distance.
(Above)   Along the 'hope', from Westhope to Dinchope.

Following pages:
(Top left)   Remains of a deserted farmstead on the track
across The Wilderness, below Caer Caradoc.
(Bottom Left)   Wilderhope Manor.
(Right)   Caer Caradoc from a deeply indented lane
below Enchmarsh.

Lanes In The Vicinity Of Lingen, The Lyes, The Lugg And The Wigmore Rolls

Herefordshire
OS Map 137

Bounded by: A4113 west from Walford to Knighton; lanes south via Stonewall Hill to Presteigne; B4362 east to Mortimer's Cross; A4110 and B4530 north to Walford.

This is castle country. Within or immediately next to this network there lie the remains of no less than ten fortifications, mostly medieval, which range from the ruins of once-massive stronghold castles to obscure greened-over knolls marking the sites of defensive positions that were never anything grander than hurriedly built wooden towers encircled by palisades. In the west, Offa's Dyke runs parallel to the lane over Stonewall Hill which subsequently took its place as a part of the boundary between England and Wales, and Mortimer's Cross in the southeast is the location of the text-book battle of 1461 which put Edward Mortimer on the throne as Edward IV. When one first explores the area it can be strange to realize that one is moving amongst so much evidence of the battles and bloodshed of past centuries, since this country is now so noticeably, reassuringly remote from both the pressures of modern society and all but a handful of its population.

In the hills around Lingen, England shades off into Wales, both historically and – equally to the point for the reflective pootlist – physically, in terms of the landscape. For those who wish to come to grips with the meaning of the phrase 'the Welsh Marches' there could hardly be a better stretch of country, since the Marches were for many centuries the areas where as a territory England yielded ground to Wales (or, from the Celt's point of view, vice versa). The word March in its original Teutonic form of *mark* was used to describe the waste land lying between one village and the next – a somewhat indeterminate boundary zone at best. to the Saxons, the word *mearc* meant simply 'boundary', but their application of it to the Welsh borderland did not help to make this boundary zone any less indeterminate, at least until the Mercian king Offa ordered the construction of the 130 km. or so of his noted dyke during the eighth century. The dyke was a symbol, not a fortification, and the Welsh were requested not step eastwards of it on pain of severe penalties, which no doubt included death. The Welsh did however frequently step eastwards, in very large numbers, recapturing substantial parts of what are now Cheshire, Shropshire and Herefordshire. After the Norman Conquest, William of Orange found a solution to the dilemma of what to do to contain the wild Welsh in their mountains whilst at the same time finding distractive employment for a number of his no doubt equally wild following, by giving the latter *carte blanche* to hack their own petty princedoms – over which they were absolute monarchs – out of the lands which lay Waleswards of the old Anglo-Saxon kingdom. These territories came to be known as the Marcher Lordships, of which there were 140 in all, and the Marches were thus finally established as the districts lying immediately on either side of the border as laid down by Offa. The first Lordships Marchers (to use their other title) included such centres as Chester, Shrewsbury and Hereford, whilst to the west much of what were until recently the counties of Montgomeryshire, Radnorshire and Brecknock were also 'tamed' by the Norman warrior lords.

But it is in the country to the west of the English plain, where the hills gain stature and turn gradually into mountains, and castle ruins such as those at Wigmore and Stapleton stand high above the river valleys, that the embattled nature of this boundary zone can be best – if also, once again, most romantically – appreciated. From the lane which climbs out of Wigmore the pootlist can (almost – see caption) enjoy a view of the castle, most important stronghold of the Mortimers, sited on the flank of one of the hills known as the Wigmore Rolls and commanding wide views across the Teme Valley. At Stapleton the 'castle' ruins face up the valley of the River Lugg as though still in expectation of attack from the west; the impression given is, however, slightly misleading since the original structure was much altered in the 17th and 18th centuries, being demilitarized into a private residence.

Both this ruin and the lanes beneath it are reputed to be haunted by the ghost of a Lady Bluefoot, a mistress of the castle who was murdered, along with her husband, by a servant who loved her but did not have his love returned. In another version of the story – and there were no doubt many more – the lady's husband is the murderer. To him the Lady Bluefoot protested her innocence, telling him that if he killed her then white violets, symbols of her purity, would be seen growing around the castle every Christmas time.

The Lady herself has had her character altered in a verse which one can readily imagine the old women of the locality reciting by firelight to wide-eyed grandchildren:

> "Lady Bluefoot, all in black,
> Silver buttons down her back.
> Harrigoshee! Harrigoshee!
> Lock the cupboard and take the key."

In this case, as well as being a murder victim it seems that the good lady is also something of a kleptomaniac. Cyclists searching the castle ruins for white violets at Christmastide may be advised to padlock their machines.

There are two distinct kinds of hilly landscape in this network, and the quiet and cyclable main lane which runs from Walford through Lingen to Combe provides a convenient dividing line between them. It is my own impression that to the east of this line the hills and valleys are 'English' in appearance, but that to the west they become 'Welsh'. The lanes in both areas focus on Lingen; this may be nothing more than a silent village street with pub and combined post office and village store, yet when one is in the lanes it takes on the significance of a miniature capital to the locality since the signposts at almost every hilltop junction, east or west, point down towards it. And these lanes are quiet as anywhere in England: you will meet no-one in them except the farmers and perhaps the occasional friendly local. I sat for an hour by one laneside near Wigmore without a car going past – not a car, not a bicycle, not a weasel, not a mouse – and when a vehicle did finally pass me, it was a farmer's Land Rover, camouflaged with cow muck.

The lanes amongst the 'English' hills are single-track, and in the valleys the dominant impression one retains of them is of flower-bedecked deep channels slicing their way through the earth between wooded and steep-sided hills that utterly close out all the world beyond. On the upper slopes and tops here, both the landscape and the lanes are more open; there are tidy, squared-off hedges and broad verges in places (for example near Ongar Street) which suggest possible activity during the Enclosure period. There is a great density of many small hills, clustering together around the Lugg and its tributary streams, and amongst them there is not a single village, only hamlets and isolated farmsteads which are still well described by the word 'settlement'. The hill slopes provide a number of long, quite hard climbs which will be a good test of the pootlist's gearing, patience and muscles, not necessarily in that order, and conversely the descents can be dramatically steep and sudden. One distinctive focal point for the hilltop lanes is the Cross of the Tree to the east of Lingen where the original tree, no doubt an oak, has long since been replaced by a new one which is used for billposting local social events. The 'rolling' of the entirely wooded Wigmore Rolls and the other hills to the south can be very well seen near here on the lane to Lower Lye: the landscape forms into a series of green waves running (when facing east) from one's left hand to one's right.

Southwards above the Lugg Valley near Upper Lye the whalebacked Shobdon Hill with its cloak of conifers looks like a small scale version of some Austrian or Bavarian mountain, and from many positions it occupies a dark backdrop to the undulations of the lesser hills, and to the valley itself. By no means all the oak woods have yet been replaced here, and those which remain lend an ancient beauty to many lanesides (I say 'ancient' since to the English oaks are consciously or unconsciously associated with prehistory as surely as are conifers in Scandinavia). A particularly perfect oaken hill is to be seen rising above the flat green meadow behind Lingen. To the north of this, along the main lane, the absence of woodlands allows one to see the shapes of the eastern ridge of the 'English' hills more clearly, and these are oddly memorable. One landform is flat-topped like a tiny green mesa: an obvious site for a hill fort, yet none appears to have been built there. Another hillock next to it is shaped like a large, grassed-over pimple, entirely bare of trees or shrubs. Not far from these, in a field by Lingen, is the mound of a motte and bailey whose shape echoes them intriguingly.

The valley lanes in the eastern part of the network almost all give the impression of an idyllic lushness, with many low meadows backed by streams and woods in which cattle, sheep, or an isolated horse graze quietly as if they had been doing nothing else for centuries. In the Lugg Valley the lane from Aymestrey runs parallel with the stream and at much the same level as it, then climbs the hill; and there is a lane running from near Lingen which does the same in the opposite direction. In both cases one has the sense (as in climbing to the 'hopes' on the Wenlock Edge) of being admitted into the centre of the hills along the wooded valley as though one were entering a pass through mountains; and the absence of traffic, and indeed of buildings, only serves to intensify this impression. Where buildings occur they are generally unpretentious cottages, some of stone, some brick, others timbered, many set back from the lanes and hidden by the hedges and old orchards which surround them. One lane which runs eastwards past (to keep it as vague as I can in the circumstances) the scant ruins of an ecclesiastical house, is particularly magical. It begins as a trench between flowered banks which drops, climbs and again drops, taking a sharp right turn through a seemingly impossible narrow space between cottage and boarded barn, after which the presence of the ecclesiastical building is indicated by an ivy tree whose infrastructure is in fact a wall, behind which there is another wall to which a dead elm is knotted by a mass of tangling roots. The lane then continues along streamside meadows both yellowed and empurpled by buttercups and clover, with a steep wooded slope reaching up from it on the left, and leads towards what seems from this angle to be an entirely forested narrowing of the valley. The centre of the tarmac here has a greenish dusting of moss along it, which provides some indication of the frequency of traffic. This, in fact, is a Paradise lane, for all of a few hundred metres.

To the west of the main lane the hills are higher, and the highest has been named as a mountain – Harley's Mountain. These are hills on the edge of mountains, as opposed to those on the east which are hills on the edge of a fertile lowland, and though there is beauty here, there is nothing with quite the idyllic suggestiveness of the valley lanes to the east. Climb the lane running up from Birtley and you will find yourself in a subtly different landscape: the valley becomes a steep-sided 'V' in which the pastures are rougher with clumps of nettle and thistle in them, the hedgerows have more bracken, the farmsteads are even fewer in number (though Hick's Farm is a stone and timber-frame building in the Herefordshire manner), the trees are smaller and thinner on the ground, and even the woodland through which the lane passes at one point has a wilder look to it. Another telltale indication of the proximity of Wales, with its strange religious ways, is the small brick Primitive Methodist chapel which stands at the cross at Willey, serving a virtually invisible community of scattered farms and cottages. The apparently absolute isolation of this building – when I was there, a rook with a broken neck lay on the road by it, quite undisturbed – is belied by its lovingly mown lawn and tidy clipped hedges.

When one reaches the open upland it is all long views, either northwards across the Teme Valley from the white road (yet again, it should be yellow) that runs to the south of Stanage Park, or simultaneously east across the 'English' hills and west towards the mountains of Radnorshire-that-was, from the lane over Stonewall Hill. To climb this lane is a lot of hard work, since the gradient is too steep for all but the lowest of gears and the ascent lasts for over 2 kilometres, but the huge panoramas do reward one's efforts. The stone wall – at least, *a* stone wall – begins on the English side of the lane near the top contour, a ramshackle and rippling drystone affair that has spilled its flat stones over the bracken and grass of the roadside. Elsewhere the bare pastures of the hilltop are divided by wire fences, with occasional square, dull blocks of conifers and decorative rows of Scots pines; nothing could be more distinct from the hedged-in enclosures of the nearby upland around the Cross of the Tree. There is a real sense of height here; it seems that you would be able to see *over* the horizon were it not inconveniently obscured by mountains and hills on every side. And if you are in a silly mood – which as commited pootlist you should unquestionably be, even after a twenty minute slog – you can zig-zag from one side of the metalling to the other as you travel, so passing from England into Wales, and back again, without any of the usual hassle with border officials.

Pleasantly little to get upset about here. Main lane through Lingen from Walford has been widened in places, and has one or two bad cottage modernizations along it; lane south from Brampton Bryan also of 'B'-road proportions; isolated crass modernizations – a cottage near Lower Lye, for example, with a swimming-pool-blue plastic car port – and one or two vulgar bungalows (this is excluding development in villages and towns along the main roads); in general, the saddening, enraging replacement of oak plantation with conifers is to be expected, until such time as we find a way to stop it.

Near Ongar Street. Naturally, the broken sign is pointing in the wrong direction.

*(Above)   Wigmore castle. (This was taken about 150
metres from the lane in order to give a clear impression
of the ruin's siting).*

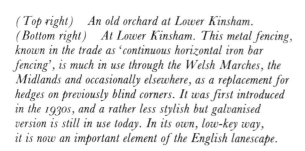

(Top right)   An old orchard at Lower Kinsham.
(Bottom right)   At Lower Kinsham. This metal fencing,
known in the trade as 'continuous horizontal iron bar
fencing', is much in use through the Welsh Marches, the
Midlands and occasionally elsewhere, as a replacement for
hedges on previously blind corners. It was first introduced
in the 1930s, and a rather less stylish but galvanised
version is still in use today. In its own, low-key way,
it is now an important element of the English lanescape.

(Top left)   Hedgerow tree in an inter-field hedge near Birtley.
(Bottom left)   Sturdy old mid-pasture oak, with a chimney
of the Hall at Lingen.
(Above)   Valley lane near Lower Lye, with a wooded backdrop.

*(Above)   The Wigmore Rolls with retreating storm, from
a spot somewhere in the vicinity of the Cross of the Tree.
(Right)   A steep descent through the wooded country of
the Wigmore Rolls.*

Lanes Of The Vale Of Pewsey, And Trackways Of Tan Hill And Fyfield Down

Wiltshire
OS Map 173

<u>Bounded by</u>: A345 north from Upavon through Pewsey and Marlborough to Ogbourne Maizey; lane west to A361 by Broad Hinton; A361 south through Avebury to Devizes; A342 east to Upavon.

Once again here, within the chosen network there lie two landscapes which in this case are so entirely unlike one another as to be almost different worlds: the settled and largely enclosed lowland of the Vale of Pewsey; and the empty, sweeping chalk upland with its unparalleled density of prehistoric sites, evidence of patterns of settlement from a much earlier phase in human history, of which the world-famous Avebury circle and associated monuments are but the most obvious examples. The relation of vale to downs is that of colonized valley to mountain in steeper-contoured country: apart from a few scattered farms and some modern buildings the downs are empty places which, before they were converted to ploughland, had been long divided into sheep-grazing territories that still bear the village names today – Bishop's Cannings Down, All Cannings Down, Horton Down, and so on.

The vale has its stretches of quiet lane: some of these are dead ends, others are unmetalled, but in general this is an area in which you will go for only very short distances before you come to a village. The villages and their outlying hamlets dominate the landscape, particularly in the east, and many of them are still places of great character despite modern intrusions. The vale is a mixed farming area which has partly gone over to large-scale cereal growing, so that in places (for example, to the south near Wilsford) the huge fields – which are at least appropriate to the downs landscape – seem as though they might have slipped from their posts on the upland and found a new resting place between the villages. But in any case it is a long time since the vale has been a well-hedged area. Even when the farms have cattle on them, it is common to see field barriers made of nothing more than few strands of barbed wire nailed to a row of fence posts, whose weathered state betrays their age (a method of division also standard on the hills). Along one short stretch of hedgebank near North Newnton I noticed a single row of spuds growing in place of the hedge – clearly the work of some local as determined to put marginal land into use in his own small way as any barley baron.

The general impression of the lanes in the vale, excluding the small pocket of country around Stowell and Wilcot, is one of scraggy unkemptness. the barbed wire and the often makeshift bits and pieces of fencing filling gaps in run-down hedgerows, the prominent sheds and farm buildings that are frequently patched with corrugated iron, the prevalence of nettles (which easily dominate such cow parsley as there is growing here), all contribute to this effect. Also to be seen half hidden amongst the nettles are the whitened stumps of countless dead elms. Until the advent of Dutch elm disease these formed a major component of the vale landscape, both along the hedgerows where there were many mature trees and even more frequent rows of saplings, and in the pastures, some of which preserve the saddening remains of magnificent trees that no longer offer shade to the cattle which still habitually stand under them. In the late 1970s and early 80s, like so much of Oxfordshire, Wiltshire and Somerset, the Vale of Pewsey has been a landscape in transition. Give it another five years and the wreckage of the elms should have almost entirely disappeared into the locals' woodpiles, but whilst they remain, the dead trees act as a sharp reminder of the beauty not long since to be enjoyed there. Juxtapositions are still to be found of some isolated thatched house backed by the dying frame of a huge elm which looks as if it had been specially made to rear behind the building, its upper branches reaching into the sky like an organic form of fan vaulting, with the green downs slope beyond. In such places one can see as if in diagrammatic form what is soon to be lost. It is a curious irony that elm has traditionally been used in Wiltshire for the making of coffins.

But it must also be said that many of the elms were not *that* beautiful. Many were small, ill-formed trees or untidy clumps and rows of young saplings each choking off the other's growth in unbalanced competition for space and light. Some dead elms are given the illusory appearance of living things by the foliage of the ivy which has long since cloaked them in what is, to my eye, not an attractive outline. And in any case, even in this elm country, not all is lost. The willow and the ash will remain here, in delicate combination, the former's grey-green foliage looking particularly lovely in isolation against the remote greens and fawns of the downs.

The lanes of the vale are more often broad than narrow, many of them having been turned into main lanes. They also run at the same or nearly the same level as the fields, more frequently than in indentations. The result of this in combination with the use of wire fences is that there are many open views, so that even when the lanes have little beauty in themselves there is an almost permanent and very appealing sense of being ringed around with low hills. The downs run in a green and undulating line around the horizon, broken only at the Devizes end, and with the White Horse carved in the turf of Walker's Hill ever present to the north. It is this distinctive sense of encirclement but at a distance which makes the vale lanes worthy of the pootlist's attention. Where the lanes *are* unmetalled here they can be very rough going indeed. One short stretch which gives a vivid idea of how bad the roads must have been in the past lies directly west of Charlton, a village standing at the foot of the chalk hills on the south side of the vale. This track is a churned morass of white earth which is slippery – almost slimy – in wet weather, and which has been visibly gouged out of the ground by the passage of farm vehicles; the kind of road one visits with confidence on a bicycle only after a very long period of drought.

One area of the vale where the lanes are noticeably different from the rest is that around Stowell, Wilcot and Oare, where the presence of parkland and farmland attached to the large houses there has meant that many of the lanes have remained hedged, and in places shaded by woodland or avenues of trees planted along them. At Oare, a lane very close to the main road runs directly and intimately in front of Oare House, a handsome Georgian mansion whose cobbled entrance runs out across the narrow lane surface. Beyond it the lane is a virtual tunnel of trees, and the park fields are thickly enclosed with tree belts. This is so totally different a landscape to that which lies less than 3 km. to the north that it seems as if its owners might have created it expressly in order to shut out the bare eternity of the downs. The lane along Stowell Park is comparably enclosed, and goes around a right-angled bend to follow the line of the Kennet and Avon Canal for a short stretch. The canal is one of three manmade features to bisect the vale in an east–west direction, the others being the main-line railway and a line of pylons. The effect of this is, of course, that anyone intending to explore the area using the figure-of-eight approach is perpetually passing over or under one of these, which is pleasant in the case of the canal, tolerable in the case of the railway, and deeply exasperating in the case of the pylons.

The materials used in all the pre-20th-century buildings in the vale are aesthetically pleasing, both in themselves and, especially, in combination with one another. Thatch is common, and where there is cereal growing the occasional sight of thatched houses barely rising above the crops is reminiscent of East Anglia. As in Devon (though the design differs), the most striking roofs resemble the shapes of fungi, particularly where they run down in a broad, swelling curve almost to ground level. The thatch combines well not only with timber-framed buildings, as at Allington, but also with the attractive orange-red Wiltshire brick, and sometimes quite large brick houses are thatched, for example at Hilcott. But it is the local cottage-builder's ingenuity in combining various materials in his walls which gives the greatest identity to the buildings of this network. Pevsner called Wiltshire "the county of the cottage", and it does seem as though local builders must have lived in sustained competition with one another to find ever new methods of using the available materials. Chalk, flint, sarsen, brick and limestone are all put together in varying combinations and patterns: flint with brick dressings, for example (as in East Anglia and Berkshire), horizontal bands of chalk and flint, sarsen stones and limestone or other materials arranged in a chequer-board pattern (see, for example, the superb farmhouse on a bend of the lane at Draycott Fitzpaine), and so on, with countless variations. Even the makeshift patching of walls of white-gold stone with orange brick – which could hardly have been a source of pride at the time to those who did it – has resulted with the passage of time in surfaces and colour combinations of consummate beauty.

Both the chalk and the sarsen are complemented by the yellow lichens which grow on many tile roofs, for example on the church at Beechingstoke. Striking patterning of materials also occurs in garden and parkland walls such as that at Rockley in the extreme north of the network. In other places, for example at Hilcott and Wilsford, some garden and farmyard walls survive that are constructed out of a compound of chalk, clay and gravel or pounded flints, with or without chopped straw as an additional binding. This must be given a wall-width thatched roof (sometimes later replaced with tile or corrugated iron) to keep out the rain that would otherwise dissolve it. One final small detail which gives a certain quaint personality to some lanesides here – in and out of villages – is the practice of leaving whitewashed stones along mown grass at the roadside to keep the traffic off. This seems to be done more frequently in Wiltshire than in other counties, and rightly or wrongly I am tempted to see in it the influence of the military presence.

The vale landscape ends, effectively, at the stretch of main lane which runs west–east between Horton and Alton Priors. To the north of this, huge expanses of monoculture farming climb gently to the point where the steep scarp slope of the downs begins. Anyone looking at the map of this area will immediately be struck by the number and density of its prehistoric sites: the barrows, the tumuli, the earthworks, the 'giant's graves', the dykes, the strip lynchets and settlements whose names are scattered in Gothic script across an otherwise virtually empty upland. There are very few metalled lanes across this upland; but there is a wealth of tracks and bridleways. This is typical of most chalk downlands in southern England, each of which is crossed by numerous routes that have never been tarred for the benefit of through traffic. By no means all of these are hard-surfaced farm access roads, and some are little more than indentations in the turf, but many are cyclable at least in dry weather. Walking them certainly gives one greater freedom of choice but there is real pleasure in travelling them by bicycle, not least in carrying oneself as far as one can from the routes where the car is king, as deep into the 'primordial' (but in fact for the most part very modern) landscape as is physically possible.

Apart from the steep slopes of the combes and the areas around the earthworks, where there is still a little sheep grazing and some cattle, and certain stretches managed by the Nature Conservancy (for example, Pewsey Down, which includes the White Horse on Walker's Hill), the chalk uplands have been taken over in recent years by the prairie fields of wheat and barley. From the highest points on the hills – the best I have discovered is away from the tracks altogether on Tan Hill, which can be crossed by following the Wansdyke – the land as it rolls down towards the Kennet Valley is like a broader, smoother, and greatly enlarged version of the patchwork quilt of enclosed landscapes, each patch here being 50, 100 or 200 hectares in extent, and divided from its neighbours if at all by wire fences and a little grass, the openness interrupted only by a few strips or clumps of woodland. It is impossible either in words or photographs to convey the graceful sweep of this landscape. Hedgeless and largely treeless vistas *can* have extreme beauty so long as they also have hills and undulations, and the flow of lines across the land on All Cannings Down gives one – I should perhaps say, gives me – the same kind of sensation of freedom and grace as when I look at a piece of outstanding draughtsmanship by, say, Gericault or Gaudier-Brzeska. Were such an idea to be put to them direct (and I must admit I have not tried), the farmers and businessmen who made this landscape what it is today would almost certainly be deeply amused, but the connection remains real enough nonetheless, and can be experienced by default wherever a barn or other large upright object obtrudes into the flow. This flow is, on the other hand, greatly complimented by the tilling of the empty fields where the flints are dragged into a powdering of lines across the fawn earth which often grow more dense, and thus whiter, at one end of each field.

Across this green, yellow and fawn expanse run the tracks – the 'country lanes' of the chalk – white lines scratched into the earth's surface which are so distinct in their appearance, and lead so definitely across the empty spaces, that it is easy to understand how amateur archaeologists have come to invest them with significances that they are very unlikely to possess. It is possible to cross Tan Hill and All Cannings Down by bicycle, to take one example, by following the track which runs directly north of Stanton St. Bernard (at its western end). This route is shared on some days with members of a local hang-gliding club, whom you may notice floating above you in wind-borne ecstasy as you draw closer to the col. The track running northwards from Allington is metalled to beyond the summit: a sign reading 'No Wheeled Vehicles' conveniently keeps the motorists at bay, and one does of course overlook the wheels which happen to be attached to one's bicycle. A little further west from this track lies Harepath farm. The name *here-paeth* was given in Saxon charters to tracks used predominantly for military purposes, and this may therefore suggest a genuine ancient history for the track which runs past this farm, although the origin of the word and its precise use in practice is not clearly understood and it is always possible that the attribution of some military purpose to a road by the Saxons was based on nothing more than legend.

Descending to the villages from this empty upland it can be momentarily surprising to remember that they have churches in them, so strong is the sense of prehistory on the downs, despite all the changes effected by modern farming methods. The edifices of medieval Christianity sit uneasily in the Kennet Valley below the tumuli-clad slopes, and one can have the curious sensation (at its most intense in Avebury at sundown, where the stone circle encompasses most of the village but not the church) that it is the *churches* which are temporary, a mere phase in history, and that the ancient places are waiting in a conspiracy of silence for the time when they will make their comeback. In a car you can get from Alton Priors to Lockeridge in the north along the main and only metalled lane in ten minutes, but cross these downs on a bicycle, and spend your time doing it, and the idea of the villages in the lowlands as quite recent settlements in a vast and inhospitable 'waste' is irrefutable, and is in my experience matched elsewhere in southern England only by the sight of the villages on the fringe of Dartmoor.

At dusk the uplands are strangely foreign, even a little disturbing, whether or not you have read Tolkein and secretly, despite yourself, fear that you may be spirited away by a 'barrow-wight'. Lockeridge, when you enter it, provides only the most qualified of havens. For here in a laneside meadow at Lockeridge Dene there lie hundreds of sarsen stones such as those used in the megalithic barrow tombs and stone circles. It does not help very much to know that these are the glacially dispersed remnants of the hard sandstone that long ago capped the chalk, some of which contain holes worn in them by the roots of the palm trees that grew in England in those less bracing times. They cannot escape association with the megalithic builders, whether one finds them in a village meadow or high on a down, remote from any circle. What is more, they *look* alien, especially in the company of thatched brick cottages, and their traditional nicknames interestingly reveal the polarities of response of earlier inhabitants. Some tried to familiarize them by calling them grey wethers, playing on their odd similarity to sheep lying down, but those who called them sarsen stones had no illusions: 'sarsen' is an abbreviation of 'saracen', in its general sense of non-Christian, heathen, pagan.

On Fyfield Down and the neighbouring country to the north of the main road the sarsen stones are so widespread that the land could only ever have been transferred to arable use by the most massive effort, and much therefore survives as pasture. This is the most distictive and atmospheric stretch of upland in the area, and I extended my original network north in order to encompass it. There are many ways to get up on to Fyfield Down, but the most contrasted is perhaps to go by way of Rockley, where you pass through the architecturally demure and undoubtedly gentrified little village, with its hall and its park, and turn left to climb Manton Down along a noble avenue of tall and slender beeches which strongly suggests that all the country beyond must be a landscaped park. But by the time you have reached the isolated farmhouse which stands in the centre of the 'grey wethers' on Fyfield Down, you could not be further from any product of the 18th-century landscape gardener's imagination. As is my habit I con- trived to arrive at this place not long before sundown, at which time the atmosphere there, and its sense of secrecy, are overwhelming. There are tracks in every direction, some not much clearer in the grass than hilltop sheep tracks – and who uses them, apart from the occasional horse rider or walker? If you take a wrong turn you may well end up wheeling your bike through the stones and the cow-pats, orientating yourelf on some wood as the only easily identifiable feature. At first here you will find the sarsens lying hidden in the long grass at the sides of the main track, but beyond the farmhouse there is a shallow depression which is full of them, ten flocks of grey wethers fixed in unbroken sleep, though in the light of the setting sun they can seem as if with just a little encouragement they might begin to stir. From this site came some of the stones used at both Avebury and Stonehenge.

Christopher Taylor puts forward the view that the main track here is quite as likely to be the remains of one of several neolithic ways to Avebury as the Ridgeway, long regarded as the principal route. The Ridgeway is known to have been in existence before the creation of the Avebury circle, and was used, for example, by traders in flints. It does not run into Avebury at all but sticks to the high ground, continuing southwards to ascend the downs by East Kennett. However, there seems to be no reason why at least some of the pilgrims travelling from the east to visit the temple at Avebury should not have used the Ridgeway, making a last minute right turn towards the object of their journey along some track which has subsequently dis- appeared beneath the plough. The track over Fyfield Down was certainly in heavy use in later times, and indeed up until the 17th century, as part of the main road between London and Bath, which also connected Avebury with Marlborough. If one follows it westwards as far as Avebury it transforms into a field road of the 18th or 19th century, partly walled before it approaches the village, and then cuts through the earth bank surrounding the stone circle.

Above Avebury, the Ridgeway is a broad grass path some five to six metres across, its full width in use by farm vehicles and motorbikes – which have right of access – on the one or two churned-up stretches, but generally cyclable in dry weather. However, in wet weather my most earnest advice to the pootlist is: leave your bike and walk! The track's elevated position gives striking views over the head of the Kennet Valley, and as it descends Avebury Down the view of the heights along which the Wansdyke runs can be quite as broad and grand as in the reverse direction, and is enormously enhanced, indeed made uniquely itself, by the presence of a series of beautifully rounded beech coverts. Because of their shape these woods make fitting punctuation marks in the flowing lines of the landscape, and seem in their own way quite as symbolically and enigmatically placed as the standing stones or the huge rounded earth tump of Silbury Hill. Böcklin, Friedrich, Palmer and Nash would all have found something in them to paint.

Avoid or be prepared for:
Pylons in the Vale of Pewsey as already described; a second line mars almost all views of the Salisbury Plain escarpment to the south; characterless and homogenizing modern road signs and signposts make many lanes into main roads by association; suburbanization or ugly council housing to be expected in most villages other than those mentioned above: at its worst in All Cannings (grey cement clapboard-style council houses and drab 'infilling'), Charlton (alternating thatch and bungalow, finished off with a series of corrugated iron garden sheds and new farm buildings with blinding white roofs), Etchilhampton (desolatingly ugly council housing, with supermarket estate of ready-mades for the better-off next to the main lane to the north); Coate and Little Horton are entirely worth avoiding (all the grossest and nastiest styles of domestic building between 1930 and 1980 seem to have been concentrated along one small street – could be a suburb of Southend but is in fact a suburb of Devizes); Alton Priors (this outstandingly handsome and unusual village now has a back lane to the east filled with a view of grey pebbledash and pink brick walls, garages, American-style open plan gardens, tarmac, and cars; West Overton (the west end is a large housing estate planted next to the downs, swamping the old houses there); Manton (a suburb of Marlborough with an old centre). Except where stated all these villages have something to offer, frequently much, despite the changes in them.

Main lanes: *from the barracks north of Devizes past Alton Priors and through Wilcot Green to Pewsey, has however many good views of the vale and is generally only busy at commuting times; through North Newnton and Alton Barnes to Lockeridge and Fyfield; lane through Rushall is used as main road bypass for Upavon; from A342 past Etchilhampton and All Cannings to junction with main lane in north of vale.*

*(Below)   The view west from Tan Hill. Parallel with
the track runs the earthwork known as the Wansdyke (or
Woden's Dyke), an embankment probably constructed by
the Romano-British population who stayed behind after
the collapse of the Roman Empire, in order to defend
themselves against attack from the north.*

*(Top right)   One of the ways up Tan Hill from the Vale.
(Bottom right)   Near Patney.*

(Top left) Half tamed downs-scape seen along the main lane between Alton Barnes and Lockeridge.
(Bottom left) A track on Tan Hill: early morning.

(Above) Dusk over the downs, from the cross at Alton Barnes.

(Top left) Thatch in its last stages, on a barn by the main lane at Alton Barnes.

(Left) One 'B' road that is well worth cycling: the B4003 out of Avebury, alongside which runs the remains of the 'Stone Avenue' or processional way between the circle at Avebury and the site known as the Sanctuary on Overton Hill.

(Above) Trackside sarsens on Fyfield Down: last light.

Lanes Of King's Sedge Moor, Somerton Moor, Dundon Hill And Sedgemoor Hill

Somerset
OS Maps 182 and 193

Bounded by: B3151 north from Somerton to crossroads on Collard Hill; main lane west along Walton Hill to junction with A361; A361 southwest to Othery; A372 southeast to Langport; B3153 east to Somerton

A lazy squint at the map may well give the impression that this area of country is as bleakly unpromising a subject of exploration as the Cambridgeshire Fenland. The rectilinear layout of farm access roads and drainage channels – which in the Somerset Levels are known as *rhynes*, as opposed to the *lodes* of the Fen – suggests a featureless, rationalized expanse of intensive cultivation stretching forlorn and lifeless to a horizon so distant that it could not be of interest to anyone. Furthermore, there appear from the map to be very few openings within the network I have chosen for the kind of meandering on a bicycle that is possible in other parts of the country.

It is all the more surprising, then, to find that the Levels are (at least at present) places of enormous character, – are indeed unique in the British Isles. Until one has found one's way down on to Somerton Moor, for example, one cannot begin to appreciate just how different it is from any stretch of the Fen you care to name. In the first place there are hills in three directions, and these are far more prominent as features in the landscape than the inexperienced map-reader might guess from their representation as contour lines, so that whichever way one travels the 'moor' is seen in relation to them. In the second place, until recent years almost all of the Levels have remained as areas of natural grass pasture used as summer grazing for dairy herds, and the marshy meadows, unploughed from year to year, possess a variety of plant life which gives each field a personality of its own. So also the uncleared rhynes can be repositories of water-loving plants such as sedges, reeds, water lilies and kingcups, and they yet remain a home for the evanescent otter, as well as for a rich variety of birdlife. As so often, what is 'bad farming' or 'a job yet to be tackled' from the farmer's point of view produces a countryside worth looking at in detail from everyone else's point of view. The Levels also retain many of their waterside trees – aspens, poplars, alders and in particular willows, which either stand in gnomelike groups of pollarded stumps or, where they have somehow escaped human supervision, lie cracked and fallen, continuing to grow in a twisted writhing of branches and leaves that are strangely reflected in the black water of the roadside ditches.

The map supplies many clues to the history of the area, which in this case is a particularly fascinating one. The Levels as we now know them are indeed the product of premeditated hard labour on the part of those who have occupied them, over a period of many centuries. Since the Middle Ages the flood plains of eight rivers running into a confluence which drains into the Bristol Channel north of Bridgewater have been gradually converted from marshland to meadow. The first systematic attempts at land reclamation were made in the 13th century by the ecclesiastical houses at Glastonbury, Muchelney, and Athelney (all outside this network); parts of the then existing marsh were blocked off by walls, the labourers working gradually outwards from the dry ridges or isolated islands which are otherwise known as *burtles*. More ambitious still, the courses of parts of some rivers – for example, the Brue where it runs northwest from Glastonbury – were redirected by the holy men.

But it was not until the late 18th century that the main onslaught on the marsh took place, at which time much of the existing meadows used for common grazing still remained under water for half of the year. The King's Sedge Moor area (partly in the network) was reclaimed and enclosed in the 1790s: the waters of the River Cary were rechanneled into the new King's Sedgemoor Drain, the rhynes were dug for subsidiary drainage, and most of the straight farm-access roads leading into but not all the way through the new fields were also constructed. Small woodland thickets growing in the marsh were cut down, to be replaced by lines of willows planted along water-courses. These were pollarded to supply withies for what became in the 19th century a booming craft industry for the manufacture of baskets, panniers, fish-traps and the like. Some withies are still cultivated in the Levels today in an alternative manner, which is to plant whips as an annual field crop and harvest them, by hand, in the autumn of the same year. I did not see any growing in this network, but I have seen them in the vicinity of North Curry, towards Taunton. They make a unique contribution to the appearance of this farming landscape, and are worth searching out.

The known history of man's activity in the Levels goes back much further, however, than the attempts of medieval monks to drain them. Until the neolithic period, the entire area of the Levels was a shallow bay in which the many tump-like rocky hillocks stood as genuine islands or as narrow, high peninsulas along which settlements of fishermen-farmers not surprisingly came to be clustered. When you are cycling here it is impossible to forget this ancient relationship between island and estuary. As soon as you have dropped down from a hill you arrive at what seems as though it ought to be the 'water level' – and would be, if the land were three to four metres lower. After you have crossed the Level you will experience a distinct sense of 'coming in to shore' as the next hill or island draws nearer, their farms or cottages – as at Henley and Dundon – running along roads which must once have stood very near to the edge of the marsh. On rainy days you can half believe that you are cycling on the surface of the sea itself, and when it is windy, if you are lucky enough to get the wind at your tail, you will be projected along as if your bike had an engine, wrapped in a marvellous silence in which the only perceptible sound will be the minuscule roaring made by your tyres as they keep you in contact with the road. It is of course rather too easy to believe that your rapidity of movement derives entirely from your own highly developed physique, so that the first uphill gradient can come as something of a shock.

The sea began to retreat from the Levels around 4,500 B.C., leaving a swampy estuarine area which was soon taken over by reeds, the accumulation of whose dead matter resulted over many centuries in the growth of peat. The peat of the Levels has been exploited, possibly since Romano-British times, for use as fuel, building blocks and fertilizer. Originally it was cut by hand with the help of specially designed peat-saws and spades. Nowadays the job is done far faster by machines, mostly to supply nurseries and market gardens, but the blocks of peat are still called by the old word, *mumps*, and they continue to be stacked into the rows of odd little piles called *ruckles*, which are another of the defining features of the Levels landscape.

Peat is a great preserver, and quite apart from the famous 'Lake Villages' located in the 1890s to the west of Glastonbury, the remains of over 40 very ancient trackways have also been discovered in the Levels, most of them as a direct result of the enlargement of the peat-cutting industry. These discoveries have mainly taken place in the area to the north of the Polden Hills, and therefore also to the north of this network. Most of the trackways date from between 3,000 and 2,000 B.C. although one, the Sweet Track (which is named after its first discoverer, a sharp-eyed peat cutter by the name of Ray Sweet), has been dated to around 3,800 B.C. This is a walkway of oak planks which was held in place by pegs driven in obliquely, like tent pegs, and like all the trackways it ran across swampy or otherwise impassable ground. At approximately 6,000 years old, the Sweet Track is the oldest 'road' currently known to exist anywhere in Europe, and quite possibly the world.

There is some variety in the design of the neolithic trackways. Most of them are simply pegged-down bundles of alder or birch brushwood cut directly from any convenient spinney growing nearby on the marsh. But some involve a more complex and very strong construction of hurdles which were made from the shoots of hazel, coppiced (and therefore actively managed) on the islands. The hurdles were overlapped, and in very wet patches they were piled on top of one another until the gap was plugged. Amazingly, their design is exactly similar to that still used in present day hurdle-making, and since hurdle tracks have been found dating from 3,000, 2,200, 1,800, 900 and 400 B.C. it can be confidently asserted that the hurdle-making industry has had an uninterrupted existence in the Somerset Levels for at least 5,000 years.

Might there be any coincidence of modern road and neolithic trackway? None is so far known, for the rather obvious reason that archaeological excavation beneath used roads is a somewhat tricky operation, but it seems far from impossible that one or two of today's lanes across the Levels may run along something like the same routes as tracks made 4,000 to 5,000 years earlier – a thought to bear in mind as you are exploring them. At first sight many of the Levels lanes seem as if they are running along causeways, since they are separated from the fields on either side by drainage channels which also serve as aquatic versions of the hedge, containing the livestock and dissuading trespassers. In fact (though there are some medieval causeways which run alongside rivers outside the network), most of the lanes stand at exactly the same height as the fields and would be quite as subject to flooding as they are. Those unused to this kind of landscape will no doubt also think it odd to find gates standing unconnected to any hedge or wall, wherever there is a bridge to link field and lane together. The field bridges are worth a glance in themselves, many being made out of hefty planks supported by solid earth bored through with drains. However, one by one they are being replaced by freestanding metal structures with 'planks' of reinforced concrete. These are by no means so pretty.

With the exception of the almost-main lane running through Nythe to High Ham, the metalled lanes on the Levels here remain delightfully narrow (again in strong contrast to those of the Fen), and they are not even as straight as one might expect from the map, since the metalling along them has not always been laid in a straight line but instead bows away from and curves back towards its intended direction like a long-used poker. On the 'dead-end' lanes (where the metalling runs out), such as that running roughly east–west across Somerton Moor to the north of Whiscombe Hill, the absence of all traffic except the occasional tractor has allowed the superabundant plants of the verges to hang over the tarmac, thus reducing its already limited width even further. For most tourists and weekenders it would seem that the Levels are considered not as places to be visited in themselves, but merely as places to be looked out over from high vantage points. There are at least two such platforms in this network, both National Trust properties, on Walton Hill and Turn Hill, where people park their cars and get out to admire the view of the receding straight (but not straight) lines. This of course is absolutely fine for the pootlist. One of the main reasons that motorists rarely venture into the middle of Somerton Moor, for example, is that there are no through metalled roads; there is, however, at least one through route for the determined cyclist – and even if there were none, he would still be able to apply one of the basic techniques of pootling and explore by following the roads until they petered out, then turn round and come right back again. There is a satisfying sense of being completely off the beaten track in following a lane such as the white road (actually metalled, need I say it?) which runs southwards from the windmill on Walton Hill, or the lane west from Dundon to Dundon Hayes, which curves around its hill and then simply stops dead. One may hear the aggressive snarl of fast-moving traffic on the nearby 'B' road, but none of it is coming this way, and the sense of isolation even in such a small area is enhanced by the absence of anything save a few agricultural buildings on the Levels themselves.

All the more satisfying, too, to find that one can cross Somerton Moor without backtracking, along the 'white' road just mentioned, by taking the Eighteen Feet Rhyne over what when I was there was a highly unstable but nonetheless passable plank bridge, south of which one is directly on to the purplish-brown of the peat, the mud, and the potholes filled with builders' rubble. Or again that one can get from Dundon to Somerton by turning east along a track to Hayes Farm (whose yard is something of a sea, but negotiable with patience) and thence south to Somerton Moor, without recourse to the busy and lorry-infested 'B'. Such routes have to be searched out, admittedly, and one does occasionally draw a blank, but the pleasure of having been into the innermost depths of an unlikely place and come out at the other end through one's own navigation – however straightforward – is worth the risk of a little frustration.

The peat of the Levels can be as much as ten metres deep, and the line of electricity pylons which grazes the northwest corner of this network had to be supported on piles which penetrated to this depth, to prevent them from gradually sinking into the ground. I met a farmer at Henley Corner whose home is built on the peat (unlike most of the houses at Henley, which are more solidly founded on the clay and rock of the nearby 'island'), and he told me that whenever a tractor or lorry goes by his front door, the pictures shift on the wall. He seemed little troubled by this, and the house, which was around 100 years old, had no visible cracks in it. This farmer also advised me to keep my eye on the cattle in the fields if I happened to notice that they were feeling frisky. Apparently – and I repeat this without having witnessed the phenomenon myself – when the cattle run across the peat, they bounce. 'Bounce' was the word the man used, and it conjured up wonderful images in the mind's eye. It seems that the peat gives extra spring to the animals' movements, as if they were running on a large, hard mattress.

The rhynes are cleared out once a year, at least in theory, by the farmers whose land they drain. However, a great variety of conditions can be observed in them, especially in the summer months. Some of the narrow channels are so choked with plantlife that they seem as if they contain no water at all, and there is a non-farmerly enjoyment to be had in finding such products of abstract and reasoned functioning half buried by irrational nature. Others are obscured by a floating carpet of the tiny-leafed duckweed, which looks from a distance like a bright green slime. Even the wider channels, many of which run along the roads, can be worlds within themselves, their still black water overhung by rushes amongst which long-legged spiders spin their webs and silken ropeways by the hundred thousand. At present, many of the rhynes remain the homes not only of the otter but also of the increasingly difficult-to-see dragonfly and glow-worm, stickleback, vole, newt, and toad, and it will be an unusual day for a cyclist in the Levels when his passage does not disturb at least one heron into flight, heaving its great grey wings through the air towards some theoretically safer resting place. It takes only the slightest change of angle to move from the role of hurried passer-by along the lane above to that of fascinated observer of these enclosed universes, which continue oblivious of all human activity around them until such time as men arrive with their ditching apparatuses to demolish them in a matter of a few hours.

The 'islands' and their 'shore' areas (which, when they were muddy, were known as *laggs*) also have individual qualities, even if they are finally less memorable than the Levels themselves. There is a certain pleasure to be had here in guessing where the shore line was in geologically ancient times. As one comes up off the flat land one will find, suddenly, that the ground has a slight slope; there may be hedgerows in place of the rhynes; and oak, ashes, and dead elms, as well as willows. In places, for example looking down to the Levels from the beginnings of the hill by Middle Ivy Thorn Farm, under Walton Hill, and again at Henley, one can see how a field boundary has been drawn at the very end of the gentle and cultivable clay slope. There is hedge, with a line of trees in it; beyond this and parallel with it runs a drainage channel; and beyond this again all is flat, green, and in comparison with the foreground, strikingly devoid of detail, like a landscape imagined by a child.

The rest of the high ground here is typical Somerset hill country, in which medium-to-long and quite hard climbs up winding and sometimes well-tree'd lanes give access to the long views for which the weekend motorists do their driving. Personally I prefer the lower parts of these 'islands', such as the little valley in which Low Ham is situated and the 'shore' area as it runs around towards Henley. Here there are still many small, narrow and unkempt meadows, high-hedged, willowed, overflowing with wild flowers amongst which the cattle trudge. Running up on the steep hill side of the lane there is the occasional orchard in which sheep can be seen, turned to silhouettes in the shade, grazing amongst feather-headed grasses. The lanes have hardly any traffic, and Henley itself is both old and (in 1980) largely unbourgeoisified: not beautiful, but *used*. This too is back-end country, famous for nothing, and delightful for just that reason.

The building stone of the area is blue lias, a limestone varying from entirely bluish-grey to the same hue streaked with pale brown. Not, to my eye, a lovely stone in itself, it is nonetheless vibrantly offset by the older roofs of crinkled pantiles (which are quite similar to those found in north Norfolk): these vary between deep orange and a burnt sienna. Since so many of the fields yet remain as meadows here, the yellows of the June flowers in them, and on dull days the roofs of isolated barns will seem to shine like banks of marigolds. The greyish colour of the blue lias has luckily meant that here as throughout this part of Somerset it has not been difficult to put up modern buildings which blend with the stone, approximately if not exactly. Simulated grey stone and even breeze-block buildings are to be seen in many places, and whilst the majority leave everything to be desired in terms of design, because of their colour they do at least look as if they belong in the area. All the villages, being of the kind that are laid out along their own complex networks of lanes and back lanes, have outbreaks of modern development. But nevertheless each retains sufficient of its old personality to be worth exploring, particularly Low Ham, which has a satisfying straggle of cottages and houses down narrow lanes that are still hedged or walled, and a church which stands stark and without a surrounding graveyard in the middle of a field.

One final significant detail in this network is the signposts: the characteristic old Somerset County Council signpost bears a pyramidal top, on the four faces of which the letters SCC are embossed, and the direction lettering is also stamped out of the metal of each arm and then painted. It may be that such signposts will eventually wear out and be replaced, in which case I very much hope that the County Council will take the trouble either to reproduce their design or to find some new design of equal individuality.

Avoid or be prepared for:
Modern development in villages as already noted; pylons in extreme northwest; and for those who go to the Levels for peace – quite apart from the occasional ear-searing by a low-flying jet – if you go there on the wrong weekend you will also hear a sound in the neighbourhood of Turn Hill which is akin to that made by a swarm of mammoth wasps as dreamed up for some black and white science-fiction film of the 1950s – the long-distance evidence of a

motorcycle scramble, which does not grow more pleasing as you get nearer; rifle range by Low Ham.

Main lanes: *very main lane along Walton Hill, in effect a bypass for Street; much less main lane, not so heavily used as to be worth avoiding, through Nythe, High Ham and Low Ham.*

Local bicycle user, on the lane across Butleigh Moor.

(Below)   A high view across King's Sedge Moor, from
the turn on Turn Hill.

(Top right)   Luxuriance as yet unchecked, along a
'white' (but metalled) lane near Dundon Hayes.
(Bottom right)   Ditchside willows on the moor near Henley.

(Above)   Dundon Hill: a typical Somerset knoll, wooded
at the crest and complete with hill fort deep buried amongst
the trees.
(Top right)   The bridge over the Eighteen Feet Rhyne.
A tentative route for cyclists, pending final collapse.
(Bottom right)   Field gate on the Level, near Somerton Door.

Lanes Of The Little Dart Valley And The Neighbourhood Of Chulmleigh And King's Nympton

Devon
OS Maps 180 and 191 (only a fraction of the area is on the latter)

Bounded by: B3226 southwest from South Molton to junction with A377; A377 south to junction with B3042; B3042 east to Witheridge; A373 northwest to South Molton.

There is an oft-propounded theory about the Devon lanes in general that if you have seen one, you have seen them all. They are pictured as unpleasantly narrow, banked-in, snaking canyons which one traverses much as if one were on the Cresta Run, or riding the fairground ghost train: circuits of confused navigation and countless difficult, dangerous bends and hills, which one enters only with trepidation from the relative safety of the main roads – places, above all, where there are *no views*. But who could possibly subscribe to this opinion except the motorist in Devon? This scurrilously distorted carica-ture of the lanes' actual appearance could only be arrived at by someone travelling in a car – and especially by the kind of motorist who, during a fortnight's holiday at the seaside, make a couple of statutory and perhaps rather grudging forays into the hinterland of Torquay, Ilfracombe or Bideford, only to return with a much-refreshed enthusiasm for the promenade and the Winter Gardens.

But the difficulties of the lanes, and their danger, evaporate when one is on a bicycle – with some qualifications. In place of such difficulties comes the joyous sense of travelling country genuinely free from the urban commuter and the industrial estate, and of looking – it is very often the case, through gates and gaps in banks – at an entrancing variety of the loveliest rural landscapes, which remain unseen from year to year except by the very few precisely because of their so-called inaccessibility.

The inspiration to be had from pootling in the Devon lanes can be summarized in a phrase: expectation and surprise. I first saw these words linked in a book on the English garden by Edward Hyams, where they were used to describe the effect of the layout of the very lovely garden at Sissinghurst Castle in Kent. The effect of what has been done in this garden – the closing off of long views with creeper-hung walls and yew hedges, with moments of 'release' when one walks through an arch into a new but still enclosed space – is intriguingly similar to one's experience in the Devon lanes. The high hedgebanks keep the cyclist in a sustained state of expectation which is momentarily satisfied either by the occasional long view ahead from slopes on the roads themselves or, more often, by glimpses through the field gateways. Landscapes are sometimes more tantalizing and mysterious for being only partly seen. But when the cyclist chooses to halt, snared by what he has noticed, the landscapes in Devon rarely lose their mystery, since each is a localized vista itself enclosed by hills, woods and further hedgebanks. Each is its own place. Such views are lost to motorists who – in these lanes above all others – find it very difficult indeed to stop.

There is a further general beauty for the pootlist in Devon, and this is that along many stretches of road the high banks, topped with their beech hedges, have the effect of focusing one's attention on the sky, especially on days when the weather produces variegated cloud effects. The cyclist rides 'towards' or 'into' the sky along the Devon lanes perhaps more often and more noticeably than in other parts of the country. (This effect is very much in contrast with that to be had in East Anglia, which has been described earlier.)

The hedgebanks typical of West Country landscapes are to be found throughout this network, and on every side of it. They can be anything between one and three metres in height, running along the lanes and also standing as divisions between the fields. The Devon hedgebanks are not so striking as those in Cornwall, since for the most part they are not faced with stone – a few are, in the country east of Tiverton, for example – but as in Cornwall the oldest-timers still call the banks themselves 'hedges'. (The Irish and some mid-Welsh call *their* hedgebanks 'ditches'. I am not sure what if anything they call their ditches proper. In any case it is all part of the same conspiracy to confound people such as ourselves.)

Most of the Devon hedgebanks, as *I* will persist in calling them, retain foliated hedges planted along their tops. The traditional method of planting here is in two rows, one on the field side and one on the road side, and the best of such hedges are those that have been regularly laid. I saw good laying being done along a lane to the north of Week, though this was on a hedge standing at ground level: the cut stems were not being twined around the stakes as they are in the east Midlands, but simply tilted over. I was told by one farmer that any hedge-layer in the West Country who knows what he is doing will make a point of cutting and bending the shrubs away from the direction of the prevailing wind, so that rainwater is less likely to be driven into the cuts. He also told me that the word 'laying' (or *stooping*, or *steeping*, the Devonian variants) is now used by many farmers in the area to mean nothing more than trimming back, a corrupted usage if ever there was one! The great consolation here of course is that even if the bank-top hedges were cut back to their stumps (they rarely are), the banks would remain, most of them twice as high as the average hedge, although they are of little use on their own to the farmer who is trying to keep his sheep in.

The banks themselves are not being much removed at present, except for the occasional field enlargement or blind corner improvement scheme (but see 'Avoid'). If they are not maintained, however, they will in time remove themselves through a combination of water erosion, burrowing by rabbits, and trampling by the sheep which can eventually get on top of them. The end product of this process is a low mound of red earth supporting lines of leggy shrubs or trees, and these are often to be seen where hedgebanks between fields have proved of no further use to the farmers. Maintenance therefore involves digging out what falls or is washed off the banks and chucking it back on top again, or repairing the steep sides by filling in with new earth and then putting a layer of turf over it to hold it all together. The Devon shovel, a tool peculiar to the county, was evolved for this job of turfing: it has a triangular, slightly bowed blade and most users will cut their own handle to suit their individual height and preference.

The hedge plants in this area are predominantly beech and oak, beech being most often used on the upland since it tolerates wind and high altitudes, and also gives a little more shelter during the winter months due to the tendency of its dead leaves to cling on to the branches. Frequently here, as elsewhere throughout the West Country, one comes across magnificent mature beeches, many of them very big indeed, which are to be seen standing incongruously along the tops of the banks, their thick roots running down one side of them to the more extensive supply of soil below. Some of these will have been selected out in the past from the hedgerow saplings and allowed to grow as a timber supply for the farm in question. But others can be seen (though I found none in this network) as lines of trees capping the banks without any trace of a hedgerow left; one may reasonably assume that these are the end-products of an erstwhile beech hedge that has been neglected over a very long period. The pootlist will also sometimes find the ends of the banks at field gateways supported by beech trees growing at ground level; these may double as living gateposts, with big staples driven into them to serve as latches. Another method of support for the banks is a drystone reinforcement made out of small pieces of the local gritstone known appropriately as *quoins*. These are turned at right angles to their position in conventional walling, and held in place through a combination of close packing and gravity. But more often than not bank ends go entirely unsupported, with the result that the roots of the hedge plants become exposed where the earth falls away from them. Their gnarled and knotted outlines lend an attractively grotesque quality to many lanes – so much so that they could be said to be a characteristic feature here.

The inevitable question about the hedgebanks – and it is one which must have occurred with some force to every present-day Devon farmer as he negotiates his cumbersome machinery along routes in no way designed to accommodate it – is why they were put up in the first place. There are several possible answers, but all remain speculative. Firstly, this is another area of England where the farmland which exists today was created piecemeal out of the 'waste'. The nature of such 'waste' in mid-Devon is readily imaginable when one looks at the upland fields where reeds grow abundantly in what is meant to be grass pature (several of these uplands are known as moors, despite the fact that all are now enclosed as fields). As in the Marches, then, the banks would have been used to delimit the physical boundaries of the tamed earth, as well as to distinguish one man's territory from that of another. Their containing nature must always have been useful where livestock was being reared or driven, and it is perhaps possible – a speculation entirely of my own – that some tracks through woodland were banked in to prevent the animals from straying, not least where the woodland was being managed for timber, as it was in the Middle Ages and later.

In some places in the West Country, lanes – as they now are – were originally constructed not as routes but as boundaries to Saxon estates: research has shown that these were dug out as double ditches, with banks being built out of the excavated earth. With the passage of time, and where it proved convenient, they came to be used as roads. Such relatively large earthworks were probably only made in this way on the larger estates whose regal owners would have had control of the necessary labour, in this case slave labour. The fact that many lanes elsewhere now lie lower than the level of the fields beyond the hedgebanks can be explained in two ways. First, water erosion would have carried off a great deal of material over time wherever there was a gradient; and second, it was a common practice during the Middle Ages to dig out the mud and muck which accumulated along the lanes and use it for manuring the fields, and this would also have made its contribution to the lanes' present level, now fixed – at least until the collapse of present-day civilization – by Highway Authority tarmacadam. What is not explained by any of these remarks, of course, is why the makers of this landscape should have erected earth banks, with or without hedges on top of them, in preference to hedges planted directly into the ground or on top of the much lower mounds of earth that were used in other parts of the country. It seems that this is a question which must now remain unanswered.

One of the beneficial side-effects of the hedgebanks on any upland is that they give good shelter wherever they run at right angles to the wind. This is particularly noticeable on a bicycle when the wind is roaring in the laneside beeches and forcing them yet further into their eternally southeastward-bending shape. You can cycle the high lanes behind the unmoving banks with hardly a hair on your head disturbed, except at the gateways where the wind will hammer through, shoving you sideways for a moment with such contrasted power it might be a fist, and sometimes carrying with it a sharp, glinting slant of rain that leaves the banked-in road untouched. There is a pleasantly contradictory sensation in traversing the high 'moors' in such blustery weather, for the most part shut in on both sides by verticals of earth and greenery. When you pause in a leeside gateway it can seem that even the patchwork of banks – with Exmoor always visible beyond it to the north, and Dartmoor always to the south – is perfunctory, and that the intervening moors have in truth never been tamed. Those fields which are little more than barren enclosures of still-wild moorland give added force to the gale-inspired idea that this entire green expanse of upland might somehow revert overnight to its elemental state, with every blade of cropped grass giving way by the morning to heather, bracken and reed, and each of the hedgebanks metamorphosing into lines of rowan and birch.

A wind such as this will sing through the metal field gates in their gaps in the banks, transforming them into crude and bulky aeolian harps. The weird, abstracted sound they produce can seem bafflingly similar to the voice of a woman, humming to herself some distance away – although one can never tell exactly *where*. One gate will be contralto, another soprano, whilst on others the wind may sound low notes as well as high, so that these naiads of the lanes will enjoy the accompaniment of instrumental players as insubstantial as themselves, whose rough-edged, hollow music bears an uncanny similarity to the sound of Andean flutes. The pootlist who stands alone listening to such things as the light is waning will soon be convinced – if he is not so already – that the lanes in Devon have a life of their own.

The remoteness of this country is readily apparent on all but the most major routes. The B3042 through Chawleigh is at the time of writing physically little more than a lane, and the B3226 along the Mole Valley to South Molton, whilst being a more efficiently engineered road, is still quiet and well worth cycling for the beauty of the valley. This has deciduous hangers running along both of the steep valley sides, their rounded treetops merging into a single mass, echoing the rounded shapes of the hills in what is surely one of the loveliest types of natural conformation still to be found in the English landscape. Such main lanes as exist – for example, the ridge road which runs eastwards from Chawleigh across Meshaw Moor and beyond, and that running east from King's Nympton in the same direction – are for the most part quiet. And the banked lanes are used only by those who must – the locals – with apparently very few incursions here from the motorized tourist. The locals, of course, prefer to get on to the major routes as quickly as they can since there is so much work involved in passing other vehicles and navigating the bends on the minor roads. This effectively leaves them – God be praised – to the farmers and the pootlists. But what pootlists? During one day's exploration in this network I travelled for six to seven hours on the least convenient back lanes I could find, and during that time I met the grand total of five farm vehicles and one car. On the main lane just mentioned I passed three cars in an hour. When I stopped along a lane near Affeton Barton I found myself suddenly in the company of two hares, both as big as terriers, which hammered out from underneath a field gate in full confidence that there would be nothing human on the other side. One immediately made off along the lane; the other, stupefied with indecision and amazement, finally slammed back into the field. They were the only other traffic.

The country contained in this network is a solid upland sloping away dramatically at its northern end into the Mole Valley, with sweeping views towards Exmoor. It has been deeply incised by a series of little streams which drain in the direction of the Taw in the west. The cyclist could, if he chose, explore the area by sticking largely to the ridge lanes, which would certainly make life physically easier. But it would also make life far less interesting since the ridge lanes can give a deceptive impression of flatness, and of a landscape lacking in complexity, precisely because they stay away from such complexity wherever they can. However along all the rest of the lanes, which seem to drop off and climb every set of contours they can find, there is complexity in abundance, and travelling them is in my opinion a case of occasional hard work well justified. Not only – naturally – do I advise you to follow such lanes; I also advise you to make deliberately for those stretches where the lanes are marked on the map with those little black arrows that indicate steep gradients (two together means very steep), since it is there that you are likely to find the most secret and memorable spots in the Devon lanescape.

Here in particular the necessary adjustment to the terrain is mental quite as much as it is physical. If you can accept the steep gradients and the extreme slowness of passage through such country as an essential part of the experience of the Devon lanes and, what is more, alter your timetable accordingly (from 'very slow' to 'very, very slow'), then you will find that you can begin to relish it. The upward bits will cease to be an appalling challenge to elasticated muscles, and instead will become another part of the fun; as if in a theatrical transformation scene, their beauty and personality will be suddenly revealed. There is no point whatever in going to Devon on a bicycle only to shun the 'difficult' parts in base and yellow-bellied fear. That would be absurd negative thinking, and anyway it would be about as easy to carry off as going to the Fens and sticking to the hilly parts.

A word more about the hedgebank beeches. To my eye these are one of the defining features of the Devon lanes, particularly on the uplands where they give added height and a sense of magnificence to places which are already high but may not seem so because of the obscuring of the view beyond the banks. The wind does not readily stunt the beeches (as it does the oaks), and so sometimes they will grow to the height of parkland trees even in the most exposed places. There is a Devon beech as there is a north Wales beech, and a Chilterns beech, but the Devon beech is arguably the most beautiful of any. The trunk and branches do not rise straight and slender like those of plantation trees, but have many slight changes of direction, whilst remaining palpably graceful. The bark is a light and almost shiny silver, like a muted birch bark, and the leaves are darker green than in the beeches of other regions; in this colour the russets and maroons of the copper beech seem latent. Along the lanes the beeches have very often been able to grow in groups of three or four together, and in such cases their upper branches will mesh together like those of the downs coverts into one large rounded clump, almost as if they were a single tree.

My first reflective confrontation with the laneside beeches of Devon was in 1969, when I photographed a group standing along the north side of the lane between Cheldon and Affeton Barton. As is so often the case when one first photographs a subject, the moment was a revelation. At that point I recognized something about Devon which earlier I had known only unconsciously. It was a summer evening, and the light from the low sun was shining up into the branches and gilding them so that they gleamed against the darkness of the leaves. By some strange chance I contrived to pass by this same row of trees at the same time of day, at much the same time of year, six years later; and again I photographed them. This time a storn had just gone over, and I took pictures of their shadows falling across a field in the direction of the departing clouds. In 1980 I cycled the lane between Cheldon and Affeton Barton with a third photograph in mind, but I saw no beeches. The next day I returned to the stretch of lane where I believed they had stood, and after a short search I found the stumps. Why they had been felled I do not know; they may have been diseased, of course. No saplings had been planted or encouraged out of the hedgerow to replace them, so that this was now just another piece of neither more nor less memorable banked-in Devon lane.

One old boy I met along these lanes told me that in the past, hedgerow trees were cultivated not only to supply the farms with timber but as a form of homegrown pension for the farm workers. Farmers would allow their employees to select out saplings which they could then watch growing over a working lifetime, felling them for sale in their old age. Hedgerow trees were also grown here as throughout England for countless other purposes:

house building, church building, fencing, gate-making, for shading the cattle, and (in the case of oaks) to supply bark for tanning and fodder for pigs. But no longer: farm workers have another slightly more reliable source of pension money, and if the farmers want timber they go to the sawmills, which in turn go to the Forestry Commission with its vast upland acreages of pine, fir and larch, or they draw on smaller but quite as unbeautiful coniferous plantations of their own. There is not very much practical use today for hedgerow trees (though see page 295); and, as we know, there is no column in the agriculturalist's profit and loss account in which to register uplift of the soul. So hedgerow trees are no longer selected out, unless the individual farmer retains some love of beauty. The hedges are mostly cut down to the same height by machines, and *potential* beauties such as the group of trees which so inspired me are yearly hacked back to the same level – not allowed to begin to come into existence. Speaking as one who knows in the most immediate sense what is being lost, I insist that this should not be the case.

Avoid or be prepared for:
All villages and small towns well worth visiting with the exception of George Nympton, whose earlier personality has been erased by a plethora of bungalows, cement village hall car park, garage, etc.; however – ugly big garage and sea of cars at Drayford; distressingly characterless approach to Witheridge from Drayford, with sandwich-box bungalows boasting U.S.-style non-gardens planted in a dead straight line along the lane there; a couple of atrociously placed bungalows at East Worlington, recently perpetrated, which have as much architectural relation to the good original buildings as cheese spread out of a tube to farmhouse Cheddar; two desirable detached residences at West Worlington, not badly designed in themselves, which nonetheless destroy at a stroke the previously wonderful approach from the southeast by introducing a bland suburban look where it was least appropriate; at King's Nympton bungalows, garage, breezeblock garden walls, a monstrous Victorian brick house and equally horrific car park made out of concrete through which the grass grows to make it look 'rural' do not quite manage to destroy the atmosphere of an otherwise lovely place; modern housing to the north and west of Chulmleigh (hardly surprising in what is a small township), whose centre is nonetheless a place of great character; lane running north from West Worlington to Meshaw Moor (immediately north and south of Lutworthy) provides textbook example of how depressing the Devon lanes could be if farmers decided they had had enough of the banks – passing places installed, road surface widened as far as possible, earth banks replaced alternately on the left and on the right round the corners with an ugly iron fence; banks also removed at some crossroads (e.g. south of Oakwell Farm) and replaced with concrete posts and wire.

(Above)   In the Mole valley, near George Nympton.
(Right)   Steeply down and steeply up: accelerating will
not get you very far up the other side of this hill! North
of West Worlington.
(Opposite)   Steep descent into the Little Dart valley
from, shall we say, one of the larger settlements above
the river.

Preceding pages:
Hedgebanks framing the sky near Romansleigh (left),
West Worlington (top right) and Challacombe
(bottom right).

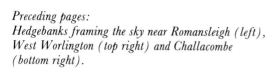

The Cheldon beeches, in memoriam:

(Top left) 1969.
(Bottom left) 1975.
(Above) 1975: the sun casts the shadows of these same trees after a departing storm.

Lanes To The Sea, And Lanes By The Sea: The Environs Of Hartland

Devon
OS Map 190

<u>Bounded by:</u> the coast from Clovelly to the county border; the county border east to the A39; the A39 and the B3237 north to Clovelly.

Farthest from Railways is the title of an antiquated but informative booklet on the Hartland country which is still on sale in reprint form in Stoke church. It is subtitled 'An Unknown Corner of Devon' with all the enthusiasm of a writer who had not witnessed the power of the motor car to make any corner of the land not only well known, but in places thoroughly trampled by the feet of those who had heard – via their reading of booklets such as *Farthest from Railways* – that it was, to date, little visited.

Yet, in a sense, this remains remote country. It is physically distant from any town; and it is remote-seeming also in being shaped into a nose of land which juts out into the Atlantic, so that anywhere near the sea one is forcibly reminded of the fact that Britain is, after all, what one forgets for most of the time: a series of islands. It would be easiest to say, go there in winter to appreciate the area at its best, but the truth is that even in the high summer season one can find lanes in the network, some of which are metalled, some not, that may be followed without encountering so much as a single grockle – discounting one's own reflection in the laneside puddles, of course. The motorized grockles – I will stick with that splendidly disparaging Cornish word even though we are still in Devon – tend to keep to certain beaten paths to advertised coastal venues. They seep into the lanes from the A39 and make for Hartland, which is rife with B&Bs, or Hartland Quay, where there is a well-known hotel, or Hartland Point, where there is a well-known lighthouse. They are distinguished from the local traffic by moving at a third its speed, and some drivers use their lights in the lanes two or three hours before a fine sundown, as if to advertise their alienness. But it is a safe bet that very few indeed of these (one in 50,000, perhaps?) will possess a map sufficiently detailed to enable them to get to the places which the canny pootlist will naturally visit first.

If one assumes that any metalled lane running directly to the coast is likely to be in quite heavy use in summer, that still leaves a lot of other lanes to be explored. I must report, however, that on my last visit to the area I saw two cars parked on the turf above the cliff at Speke's Mill Mouth, one of the area's most famous beauty spots. It must have been a lot more work to drive these objects down the very bumpy unmetalled track which leads to the Mouth than to walk it, and it is some kind of tribute to the drivers' determination never to be out of shouting distance of their machines that they should be prepared to strain themselves in this way in order to despoil what is otherwise a rapturously lovely place.

Despite such incursions, however, this remains 'real' country. There is not a single promenade or holiday camp – for, after all, how could either have been built on such a very rugged coast? – and only one caravan site; whilst Hartland, despite the tea shoppes which are anyway quite unpretentious (and one of which makes its own ice cream), retains an identity as the area's tiny 'capital'. In the most general terms this is the same kind of country as that to be found further east, though rather more austere and barren on the uplands. It terminates abruptly at the sea as though it might have continued forever westward in the same vein had not the land been arbitrarily cut away: here the narrow, deeply indented Devon valleys wind parallel with one another to converge, finally, with the biggest valley of them all.

The high hinterland is moor and banked-in half moor on which trees grow stunted, their crowns planed into ramps by the wind. Tough, close-foliated little oaks stand along the hedgebanks like Japanese miniatures, their branches hung with trailing green beards of *Usnea subfloridana*, a lichen which bears a distinct resemblance to certain underwater plants. The hedgebanks here do mostly obscure the long views that are to be had from gateways or from the open common, of the land sloping gently seaward. Beyond the neat, simple pattern of fields a blue line has been ruled across the lower part of the sky which is of a slightly darker blue or blue-grey than the sky itself, and it always comes as a pleasant shock to see it there when you have been approaching from the east, no matter how clearly you have expected it, or smelled the salt air on the wind. Where there are no banks there are broad hedges, squared off tidily like great green cakes, in which gorse is prominent, and alongside which farms and sturdy stone cottages can be seen amongst their centuries-old groupings of woodland or scrub grown as wind-breaks. As a result one is left with an extraordinary feeling of *destiny* in this landscape, which is further reinforced whenever one descends into the steep, narrow, thickly-wooded valleys where the broadleaved trees grow together in a solid wall of foliage. The apparent solidity of this foliage is hardly lessened in winter when it is seen as an interlacing of branches that appear to occupy every available space above each tree, almost as if one might be able to walk across the treetops themselves without anxiety. I should perhaps qualify this picture slightly by saying that by no means all the houses are quite as sheltered as I have suggested above. Many farms in particular have trees growing for some reason only on their lee sides, whilst others stand entirely naked, foursquare to the gale, with nothing between their living rooms and the Atlantic air but a pane of glass and a thin curtain.

At some time or another most people find themselves looking for a road which leads directly to the sea, and this phenomenon is particularly to be observed whenever one approaches the coast in summertime. It is, of course, one reason that there is so little coast now left undesecrated: the roads have been found, and used, opened up, and built along, over a period of two centuries and more. But the peculiar satisfaction to be had in a network such as this by those who love countryside in its entirely unspoiled state is that of finding one's way along roads and tracks, some of which are little used even by the local tractor drivers, to a handful – a mere handful – of coastal locations where motorists do not or cannot go with their cars. This is indeed a rare thing, in England. There are very few sea roads left along which one can travel without feeling that half the population of the country has been there before you, and most of them yesterday or at best the day before.

The lanes which are frequented by motorists in this network are listed under 'Avoid', with necessary qualifications since two at least are pleasant along certain stretches. But of the others, the 'alternative routes', the best are generally those which are marked on the map as white roads, although as usual this does not automatically mean an absence of metalling. In several cases here, lanes have been tarmacked in the past and are now being left to go back to grass for want of the funds to maintain them, although at present they remain perfectly cyclable despite the odd pothole here and there. Some are marked as 'Unsuitable for Motors', though motors could in practice be driven along them, but the distinction between the drivable and the undrivable roads is blurred. As in the Somerset Levels and elsewhere, some of the metalled lanes can be so deep under the cow droppings near to farms that they appear as a morass until one traverses them, whilst many of those without tarmac have been cobbled with stones in earlier times and remain passable, if bumpy, even in winter. The absence of signposts at some crosses adds to the fun if you do happen to be without a map. Metalling will occasionally turn into semi-metalling, i.e. that having a grass strip along the centre, as though it will at any moment lead into a field, only to connect again with the drivable network; look, for example, at the white road which runs briefly coastwards from the farm at Philham.

One of the most satisfying exploratory routes – not, you understand, that I am stating this as an *instruction* – would involve beginning in the extreme south of this network at Marsland Mouth (having found one's way down there in the first place), and heading northwards along as many of the white roads as possible, making an occasional detour to the coast en route.

Such a journey would be quite hard work, even for those who were expecting it, since almost all the gradients are of the one-in-four variety in these narrow valleys. One stretch of metalled lane which is surprisingly unfrequented by motor traffic and which lies along this north–south path is that running from South Hole towards Elmscott. At one point this lane runs close to the cliff, within earshot of the sea, and with the sloping seaward fields and hedgebanks so arranged that the water is just barely visible beyond them. To the north of Elmscott by a farm called Wargery is a crossroads from which two of four lanes are marked as 'Unsuitable for Motors'. Both are cyclable. The road coastwards leads to Speke's Mill Mouth and makes a better approach to the shore than the bumpy track already mentioned, which runs below it along the streamside. The upper route turns first into a roughly cobbled road, and then narrows to a path as a result of lack of use; at the end of it, before one emerges on to the paths of the common land, there stand a 1930s bungalow that is comical in its incongruity. To the north of the cross one may continue towards Stoke along the other Unsuitable route which remains metalled, in a manner of speaking, for its full length. The great Decorated tower of St. Nectan's church – a landmark in every direction which can be seen from the far upland, silhouetted against the shining sea – fixes the country around it in its period. the complete absence of traffic on this lane enables the cyclist to move towards the village for a brief spell as if he were in some other century, or at least in some much earlier decade of our own. This makes it all the stranger to arrive in Stoke in the summer season, and to come into contact with the transverse road through it, a popular grockle-run to the briny. However, you may immediately leave Stoke by a further non-motor road (metalling with large potholes this time), which drops through woods into the flat-bottomed combe in which Hartland Abbey is situated. This road will take you as far as Blegberry, where a right turn will put you on 'proper' metalling as far as Hartland Point, if you choose to go there, or to Shipload Bay behind Titchberry, which is much less visited and far more beautiful.

A comparable and especially satisfying 'back way' to one of the most popular places in the area is the old road to Clovelly. Instead of following the sensibly engineered 'B' road to the expansive car park like everyone else, the pootlist can turn right along a No Through Road which leads to the hamlet of Wrinkleberry (just outside the network boundary). This dwindles first into a very narrow lane, and then into the nearest thing to a tunnel that you are likely to find on any lane, where the shrubs of mossy hedgebanks have grown delightfully together over the small cobbles. This tunnel opens out into the very beautiful hanging woods which line the cliffs around Clovelly, where the bark of all the trees (grandly mature broadleaved types) is pocked into fantastical shapes by lichens. Here the remains of tarmac on a surface of larger cobbles betray the route's earlier use, and at the bottom you emerge over an anti-car barrier by the ice-cream stall, the donkeys, and the people taking snaps.

The track to Marshland Mouth, south of Mead, *is* a track, an old road to a mill which was never metalled and which remains unusable by anything less rugged than a Land Rover. This (though I know I should not say it) is perhaps the most satisfying lane descent to the sea in the network for the pootlist, because it is the road which lies most unequivocally in the past. It has not been changed, and it is in little danger of being changed in the future. From its head one can also descend steeply into the combe along the old zig-zag track to Morwenstow, south of the border, through woods of undersized oaks that themselves have zig-zag branches in which every line is knobbled and grotesque. At the streamside here there is, in truth, a spot of mud, where one pays the price one *must* occasionally pay, with humbleness of spirit, for penetrating so deep on two wheels.

Once again, it is a price worth paying. In a combe such as this there is absolute shelter, even on a very windy day. The gale may lash the upland and buffet the stunted oaks there until it seems that they will be ripped wholesale from the ground, but in the deep combes only the treetops move, with a cavernous soughing that is mysteriously similar to the sounds one hears in the ancient oak roof of St. Nectan's church in similar weather. No doubt because of the way in which the land was opened up, most of the hamlets and farmstead are built on the high ground, but where cottages do stand in the combe bottoms near to the stream it seems on such a day as though there could hardly be a more sheltered, secure situation in which to live out one's life. There is a sense of expectation to be had in these deep woods, too. On calmer days one will sense the presence of the water at the end of them by the same intuition as when one is approaching the coast from further inland: one *knows* it is there, without having to see it. But on windy days it can seem as if the roar of the waves is carrying along the combe as unarguable evidence of the sea's nearness. Yet is it so, or is this nothing other than the sound of the gale as it races through the treetops?

The frequent appearance of foxgloves along the lanes of this network throughout June and July gives them added poignancy for anyone who knows the legend of the martyrdom of St. Nectan, a Dark Age saint who may have been a Welsh prince in origin, and who gave up his secular life at God's command. St. Nectan was pursued from his hermitage at Stoke to nearby Newton by men bent on assassinating him, and at Newton he was beheaded. This, however, was not the end of the story. The decapitated corpse rose from the ground, grasping his severed head in his hands, and staggered back to Stoke. Here he placed his head on a stone by what is now known as St. Nectan's Well, and only then expired. It is said that wherever drops of the saint's blood fell at the roadsides on this unusual journey, foxgloves sprang up and have grown ever since.

Even the most casual observer might suppose that St. Nectan's return journey to Stoke was exceedingly circuitous, since there are foxgloves along every lane. One possible inference from this, of course, and one that I do not hesitate to make, is that it was only in his death throes that the good saint saw the light and realized that he really ought to have done more pootling – if only on foot and without a head – and determined to make last-minute amends before going to meet his Maker. Such a theory, if it could be proved, would act as essential evidence in support of my theory that so far as pootling is concerned it is never too late to begin. Be this as it may, the event is remembered at St. Nectan's church every Sunday following the 17th of June with a service for which foxgloves are collected from the lanes to decorate the building: this date is known as 'Foxglove Sunday'.

The valley between Stoke and Hartland is in fact unusually well haunted. At the mill on the Abbey River there resides the ghost of a monk who was party to the murder of St. Nectan, and who was later found hanged at a crossroads near Elmscott on a tree which inexplicably vanished not long afterwards. In the woods near the mill there regularly gallops a ghostly white horse, though why it should do so I cannot say, whilst on the bridge below the haunted mill two cackling and (once again) headless old ladies have been picked out by the headlights of passing cars. How they can be judged as old, and even more to the point how they manage to cackle, in a headless condition is something that the narrator of this tale was unable to explain to me. One wonders how they might look in the narrow, flickering beam of a bicycle front lamp . . .

Avoid or be prepared for:
On the lane to Hartland Quay stands 'an unauthorized place within the meaning of the Official Secrets Act', a nasty little clutter of green-painted buildings behind a high wire fence; there is also a small military base on the 'B' road directly to the east of Hartland, whose Nissen huts blend in well with bungalow strip development ranging from the very brash to the very boring; infiltration of some holiday bungalows (as noted) down back lanes and in hamlets, though the dirtiest work seems to have been done in the 1930s, with far fewer incursions in later years.

Main lanes: *from Hartland through Stoke to Hartland Quay is fairly heavily used in the summer, though worth cycling in the off-season; the lane through Titchberry and back towards the B3248 at Velly has had its corners knocked off and passing places inserted to cater for the high level of motorized grockles; main lane, largely unaltered, for coast-seeking motorists from the A39 through Welcombe to Welcombe Mouth (as noted).*

(*Above   Lane at the land's edge, near South Hole.*
(*Top right*)   *Stone-reinforced hedgebank and dead tree
in use as gatepost, near the toll road to Hartland Quay.*
(*Bottom right*)   *A field gate on the B3248, whose posts
bear two inscriptions. The one on the right reads as
follows:*

> '*Alpha thou art first I'm sure
> As Omega is in the West
> And thoult be first for evermore
> Now slumber on and rest.
> This field was once a common moor
> Where gorse and rush grew free
> And now it grows green grass all o'er
> As all who pass may see.*
> > *Js. Berriman, New Inn, Clovelly,
> > Jan. 10th 1902.*'

*The left slab bears an inscription celebrating the
coronation of Edward VII in 1902, followed by a
statement by the same author:* '*I believe in church and
state and all other religions that do good, and to be
patriotic to my country*'.

(Left)   The back lane to Clovelly, at one of the narrower points along the way.

(Above)   The old road from Welcombe to Morwenstow.
(Below)   Above Marsland Mouth.

(Left)   The lower track to Speke's Mill Mouth from the higher, looking landward.

(Above)   The descent to Marsland Mouth.

Part Four:

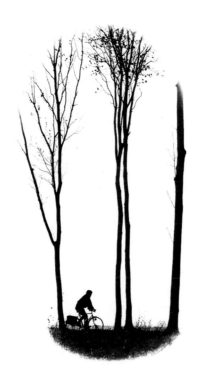

An End To Celebration

"It seems, just now,
To be happening so very fast;
Despite all the land left free
For the first time I feel somehow
That it isn't going to last,

That before I snuff it, the whole
Boiling will be bricked in
Except for the tourist parts – "

     Philip Larkin,
       'Going, Going' in 'High Windows', 1974

I was sixteen or seventeen when first I dimly realized that the things which I happened to find important in the country were not therefore automatically sacrosanct. At that time I went on occasional cycling tours into Shropshire out of the suburbs of Merseyside, usually with one or two like-minded friends. Each time we travelled we made a point of trying to find a completely new route through the tangle of lanes to the south of Chester, but for one reason or another we would often end up crossing a stream which defines one length of the Cheshire–Shropshire border along a particular back lane which we came to think of as our own 'exclusive' route into the still little-known territories to the south. This lane dipped into a wooded dingle, passed the half overgrown remains of a brick watermill whose grindstones could just be made out amongst the long grass and nettles, and climbed the slope beyond as a rough-surfaced bridleway which in June and July was overflowing with wild flowers. There was nothing particularly special about this dingle – nothing, anyway, that we could have put our fingers on – but even so we all tacitly agreed that it was a place worth going back to.

One day I went there on my own, and things were not quite as they had been. Now, I found myself confronted by a new presence on the high land above the mill. You may perhaps be unsurprised to read that this was a bungalow, a bungalow of the 'exclusive, desirable, secludedly situated, ultra-modern' variety. It was clearly visible from below since several trees and much scrub had been taken out around it, as if to display it better to the world. As I remember this building (and I have not been back there since), it was partly constructed in what might be called a Californian 'hacienda' style, with an ornamental tiled entrance arch fronting its drive on the bridle-way, of a kind through which Mexican villains are seen to gallop waving rifles above their heads in the appropriate films. On the side overlooking the dingle the house boasted at least one huge plate glass window which reflected the light with what was to me at the time an unfamiliar, indeed alien, yellowish-brown sheen. Another part of this frontage – evidence, perhaps, of some profound personality split in its designer – was decorated with a trim of varnished boards in unequivocal imitation of a three-star Tyrolean ski-resort hotel. Through the hacienda gateway I glimpsed a neat little scarlet sports car, its colour matching that of the tiles, parked on the fresh gravel in front of the double garage.

It was only then, of course, that I realized what I *had* liked so much about this place: that it *had* been 'remote', that it had *not* been suburbia. But alas, no longer. A piece of the suburbs had somehow overleapt the intervening fields, and landed itself irremediably here. Now, this place was no more than another part of the Merseyside I was seeking to escape; or of Greater Manchester; or of Marin County; or of the Amalfitan Coast; or indeed of all four rolled into one – where previously, in the greenness, and the dilapidation, and the quiet, there had been something of 'old England'.

In his crusading and splenetic book *The Untutored Townsman's Invasion of the Country* (1946), C.E.M. Joad taxed all "producers of 'beautiful England' photographs" with an "obligation . . . never to publish a photograph showing the loveliness of the English country without also and at the same time publishing opposite . . . a second showing the outrages that have been perpetrated upon it." This concluding section has come into being as an acknowledgment of that obligation. It would have been nice to make *English Country Lanes* exclusively a celebration: it would indeed have been nice if the reality had at all times justified such an approach. But any guide, and especially any anti-guide, to the beauties of England today must perforce be angry, if it is to be honest. Nor could the footnotes to each network in Part Three have sufficed on their own: the changes which rural England has undergone, particularly since the end of the Second World War, are of such enormity, and have such profoundly serious implications for all who care about the country, that they demand far more substantial consideration than a few sets of condemnatory footnotes.

The vague and shifting feelings of loss expressed by Philip Larkin in his poem are, finally, neither Larkin's nor mine alone. Increasing numbers of people have been growing concerned at the changes taking place in the fabric of the countryside: not only the 'bricking in' which has affected physically remote country as well as that close to big urban areas, but also the rather more difficult to define changes in the farmed landscape – the most important single artefact of that earlier way of life – the disappearance of hedges and hedgerow trees, the filling-in of laneside ditches, the ploughing of rough pastures for cereal growing, the transformation of many small fields and pocket woodlands stage by stage into a single vast expanse of crops, the decimation of wildlife population.

I have been in love with the English landscape. The making of this book has been motivated above all else by a passion for the country rarely experienced (or so I am determined to believe) by those involved in merely human love affairs. I recognize, of course, that I am not exactly the first to have been affected in this way. But unless the changes which have been taking place in the countryside are halted, and indeed in many places actually reversed, I could well be one of the last. With increasingly clear vision I have watched the sources of my inspiration disappearing, so that now, for me, the sense of loss is predictive as well as retrospective. I am photographing a lane, say, in Shropshire ("But surely," people have said to me before it happened, "what's happening in East Anglia won't happen in *Shropshire!*") – a lane made idyllic by hawthorn hedges in full blossom, and mature, short oaks casting their solid patches of shade across the tarmac: and at the same time, with eyes informed by the misery of actual experience, I see how this place *might* be, with the trees felled and replaced only by empty air, which casts no shade, with the hedges grubbed out and the distant deciduous woodland all gone over to a dark nothingness of cash-crop conifers. When I stand on a hilltop in Warwickshire, gazing out over what is still in the mid-80s the multi-faceted, complex patchwork quilt of the erstwhile English farming landscape, simultaneously and despite myself I see it as the Cambridgeshire Fens, with rectangular slabs of new 'planned' housing inserted amongst the great empty rectangular slabs of green and yellow cattle fodder, and I find myself trying to identify the features which are likely to disappear first. I see "the skull beneath the skin" of the English countryside and in all simplicity I cry out "This must not be allowed to happen!" No: unless he is to remain wilfully and idiotically blind, any celebrant of the remaining beauty of the landscape today must inescapably come to confront the threats to the things he loves. When he does so, his priorities will change.

Tell Me Lies

It is the easiest thing in the world to give the impression in a photograph that everything is fine. But from our own use of the camera most of us who have ever paused to reflect for a moment know that it is a born liar, and that it is perpetually tempting us to play its game. Some of its lies are cheap and nasty, some are wonderful and wonder-eliciting, but in both cases the process of abstracting an image from the three-dimensional, tangible, audible, smellable, *explorable* flux of our own experience must by definition narrow and thus distort the impression it gives of the reality. If I show you a photograph of an apple orchard in full and glorious blossom against an azure sky, the trees standing deep amongst newly opened wild flowers, you may quite reasonably assume that it was taken in an idyllic place which extends in reality, much as it appears in the photograph, for some way in every direction. You may go further and imagine how it might have been to stand in this place, with the spring afternoon sunlight warm against your skin, the scents of the flowers drifting deliciously into your nostrils, and bird-song everywhere.But what now if I tell you that when I took this not entirely hypothetical picture I was at pains to exclude the six tall chimneys of a brick factory belching their yellow smoke into the sky just above the treetops; that a cold wind was throwing down the blossom and gusting the flowers and grasses, whose movement has however been frozen into imperceptibility by an exposure of 250th of a second; that I was standing not knee-deep in flowers but in a lay-by on a roaring, busy, foul-smelling major road, my feet poised amongst the noxious rubbish which had spilled out of an unemptied litter bin?

A collection of photographs such as those on earlier pages is a composite not of how things actually are in the English country lanes, but of how they *can* be, at times, under certain specific circumstances; and by virtue of the fact that I took these pictures; it is also a representation of how I would like the lanes to be at all times. At his most dishonest, the 'beautiful England' photographer not only excludes qualificatory photographs of his subject, he also excludes fundamentals in the photographs themselves, such as the brick factory in the above example. He is quite happy to make idyllic pictures out of corners of the landscape which are in reality far from what his photographs suggest – there is a market for these things, after all, and it's nice work if you can get it. The viewer's imagination, ever regeneratively optimistic, ever wishing to have confirmed that beauty still exists in the 'heart' of the country, does the rest. The myth of old England has been reinforced and reinforced again by photographs of *certain aspects* of the actualities of the countryside. Even today it is still quite easy to go into the nakedest of the agrarian landscapes of Essex or Suffolk and photograph thatch amongst trees with a piece of foreground hedge and perhaps even a pet donkey or goat, and so come back with persuasive images of the old enclosed countryside which did exist there until the advent of factory farming – images immediately eligible for the covers of *Country Life*, *The Field*, or *This England*. It is an unsurprising irony that this photo-mythologising process should have swelled to flood proportions at precisely the time when the subject itself has been undergoing such an unprecedented change for the worse. Will all these hundreds of photographers – myself included – end eventually in some none too distant future, crowding one another out to get the newest and least seen angle on England's Last Oak Tree, situated in England's Last Hedged Field?

What of the photographic lies hidden on earlier pages of this book? One might start, at random, with the top picture on page 66. Here the hill horizon is excluded from the frame, and for good reason, since on the crown of the hill beyond there stands a massive MOD radio mast. The contemporary attributes of this structure – advanced, technology, military communications, the impending holocaust – blend none too well with such ideas as are generally evoked by the sight of a church tower nestling amongst trees. So too the picture of the windmill outside Great Bardfield in Essex on page 68 marginally fails to inform the viewer that when I took it I was standing with my back to one of Great Bardfield's newer suburbs, a line of deeply unexciting modern detached houses. On page 199, the photograph of a winding road in Herefordshire gives no hint that the woodland – which had been beautifully untouched for decades, until not long before I arrived there – was in the process of being felled, so that to the left of the bend there lay a large empty area of tyre-churned mud and broken branches. It would not be difficult to produce more such example, if more were needed.

What follows here is written in two voices, though by no means in two minds. The pictorial catalogue of incursions against the beauty and individuality of lanes and landscape makes no claim to being anything other than a personal and pragmatic selection: these are random examples taken from the many subsequent multiplications of that early moment of disillusionment, anger and disbelief on the border of Shropshire and Cheshire. The second section attempts a more orderly and precise overview, with particular reference to what is unquestionably the most disturbing single phenomenon affecting today's landscapes – the revolution in agricultural methods.

(Opposite)   Machinescape: the intensive farming landscape of East Suffolk.

Incursions And Destruction In The Countryside: A Visual Checklist

"It is quite possible . . . that there will be a great reaction and revulsion against the doings and omissions of the last few generations, and that we or our children . . . will view with consternation the wreckage wrought in our delirium. We shall say, 'Good God! What *have* we done – what have we *not* done – what now . . .?''

Clough Williams-Ellis,
'England And The Octopus', 1928

The Megalopolis: Little-Subtopia-Amongst-The-Fields

Old and new entries to the village of Great Easton, Leicestershire
(The view in the first picture is visible in the distance in the second.)

Up until the 19th century there was town and there was country, and the dividing line between them was clear except at the very edges of the towns and in industrial zones. But with the rapid increase in mobility made possible by the railways and then by the car, urban and rural environments began to get confused, particularly in the decades following the First World War, to the great detriment of the countryside. Unrestrained by planning controls, speculative builders went to the places of least resistance: villages, hamlets, mere crossroads with a pub – anywhere near the big urban centres where land was to be bought was fair game for development.

During the postwar years the tentacles of subtopia have reached far further and far more subtly into what had been completely rural areas than could have been imagined even in the 20s. The countryside's 'sleep of centuries' has been disturbed, and with a vengeance. Now, it is not only the peripheries of the cities which house city people; it is the villages and lanes of country 40, 50,

100 km. away, umbilically connected to the metropolis by the private car. In a sense Leicester, for example, now ends somewhere around Uppingham – and where Leicester ends, Peterborough begins.

In principle, of course, there is nothing wrong with this. Why should the dispossessed urban population not have attempted to recolonize the countryside of its ancestral roots? Why should the villages not have been enlarged? But the overwhelming sadness lies in how this has been done. Once again the most devastating impact has been made – as here, in the early 1960s – by spec builders interested in responding as quickly as they could to a known demand by erecting two or three barely distinguishable estate models (also used in nearby conurbations) on the edges of villages or along the lanes next to existing older houses – anywhere, in fact, where the 1947 Town and Country Planning Act *and its implementation* have not been strong enough to restrain them. No attempt has been made to modify design, materials, siting, colour, or 'gardens' (which are usually unhedged expanses of manicured grass in the Middle American and money-saving vein) so that the new growth connects with what is local and individual in the villages themselves.

This unfeelingly die-straight row of bungalow boxes bears no relation whatever to the old centre, which is of stone with some thatch, its houses standing at many angles to one another, randomly placed by the slow growth of centuries. The insertion of pavements and street lighting, whilst it has theoretical convenience for occupants, is nevertheless one further step towards urbanization. The qualities which are most beautiful and distinctive in the village landscape are precisely those which one does *not* find on the modern housing estate: qualities of enclosure, secrecy, arbitrary placing, the sense of the buildings being connected with the natural world around them. The result of all this, even for the cyclist, can be a profoundly unpleasant sense of claustrophobia. It does seem at times that no matter how far one penetrates into the countryside, one is always in danger of confronting the peripheries of the city – the same dismal peripheries the country over.

Urbanized village approach, Troston, Suffolk
The indiscriminate spread of urban-influenced building in 'deep' countryside has taken two broadly distinguishable shapes. The first might be called Wolverhamptonization, by which I mean the piecemeal development of small sites using mass-produced materials which are mostly of deleterious ugliness, blandness, or tattiness. The use of breeze blocks, unscreened even by bad brick; or of bricks of bilious pink, purple, fawn or yellow; of synthetic *stoneoid* (the makers do not call it that) which fails to come even remotely close to the colour or texture of the natural materials it apes; of aggregate panels and gaudy squares of laminated hardboard, slapped in as 'cost-effective' substitutes for crafted decoration; of gleaming spacecraft-style aluminium window frames (most obscene of all when inserted into old buildings); of 'Texan ranch-style' plank fences, and yet worse still of patterned concrete 'screen blocks' in garden walls, as shown, with the same grey surface and the same crude pattern spreading all across the country from Truro to Alnwick; of the pestilential *Cupressocyparis*

leylandii and *Juniperus chinesis*, those fast-growing TV-dinner substitutes for a proper hedge or wall; of the cement drive, the transparent plastic car port . . . One could go on. Such insertions are almost without exception guaranteed to obtrude both in natural settings (up the lanes) or in the villages, where buildings made of local materials and even the brick villas of the Victorians, those first urban colonists of their own rural backyard, are composed of subdued colours of many subtly related shades.

Here, after the screen block wall and just before the old buildings of the village centre there stands the garage, which trades in used cars – another gross offshoot of the urban road-world whose forecourt of secondhand machines totally dominates the impression of the place. There can be no gainsaying the need for garages in the country, but there remains every reason to speak out against such prominent and uncompromising siting.

The country cottage and its successor: near Polstead, Suffolk

Frequently, even in the quietest rural backwaters, planning implementation has been staggeringly ineffective in controlling the piecemeal spread of new building. This recently completed structure lies along a lane near Polstead in Suffolk – one of the narrowest and (formerly) leat spoiled in Network No. 3. I have a map of the area, which shows that several houses have appeared in similar sites along nearby lanes since the early 60s. Houses did of course appear randomly sited along the lanes in the pre-suburban past. The difference then was that they were built as a result of specific local need, and because they were made out of local materials they *fitted* in the landscape.

Compare this house and the cottage in the photograph below, which stands just outside the centre of Polstead. Where the first is set back from the road as if wishing no connection with it, the second is near to it, and end on; where the first is low, horizontal and broad in its dimensions, the second is vertical and narrow; where the first with its staring picture window suggests a blank and purely rational functioning, the second has a quality of simple dignity and 'uprightness', and because it is made out of natural materials with all their practical inadequacies rather than out of factory-fresh units, the irregularities of

its shape and surface blend far more readily into a country setting. It has also been unobtrusively maintained, although I have to add, alas, that by 1984 its patina of age, and its old windows, had been lovingly removed by builders who would not know such a patina if it fell on them.

This, then, is another detestable form of Wolverhamptonization, currently spreading like wildfire: the self-conscious, demonstrative renovation of old buildings which strips away all but a trace of their original personality, transforming old into 'Olde', so that ancient peasant's home or yeoman's house emerge as species of chintzified, fossilized and *suburbanized* showpieces. Quite as terrible in another way is the warfare being waged against the lesser country buildings, in particular Victorian labourers' cottages, by their new owners, through which all the original stylistic features (e.g. decorative brick window arches) are expensively removed so that the houses end up as *ersatz* modern, Victorian washerwomen grotesquely disguised as 80s punkettes.

Rows of boxes in a river landscape: Layham, Suffolk

Where it is not piecemeal it is large scale; where it is not Wolverhamptonization it is Basingstokeification. The discussions take longer, there are perhaps louder and more articulate objections but, finally, the changes get made and another Wimpeyville of boxes laid out in alienating rows is attached to some erstwhile tiny settlement with which it has no relationship whatsoever. Prior to this development (next to a 'B' road) the view here was of a glassy stream, a mill, a few cottages, and willowed water-meadows. All these are still here, of course, but have lost their original value in juxtaposition with the rows of boxes.

In recent years, most of the steam appears to have gone out of the movement to build new towns. But centre-less, heartless chunks of housing stuck on to villages in places theoretically convenient to the motorist are nothing less than new towns spread more thinly and over a far wider area – a contemporary and bureaucratically approved version of what took place uncontrolled during the 20s. The one ray of hope here – though this is only on the level of design – is that subsequent to the worst prodigies of the 60s there has been a backlash in which some architects and builders have returned (or have been forced by planners to return) to traditional models and materials, designing buildings which do *sometimes* fit in with what preceded them. One can only hope that this new awareness will remain strong, so that the worst horrors of the 20s, 30s and 60s are not reproduced in the passing fashions of later decades.

Road Widening And The Impact Of The Car

Route to nowhere, mid-Suffolk

The first thing which happened to many lanes, of course, was that they were uprated either into 'main lanes' (see Part One, page 54), or into 'B' roads. The latter process did not always mean major alterations, and there are some 'B' roads which remain as lanes to this day. Not so here. This is one of the most depressing views I know in England. The B1078 from Bildeston to Stowmarket was upgraded in the mid 1950s when the nearby air base at Wattisham was enlarged. Work has been done to remake the road along certain stretches in later years, and here the old and the new are seen side by side. The efficient, well-engineered new road cuts across an efficient, intensively-farmed countryside: the Bomb which permanently threatens to drop on Wattisham has been dropped already here. It is another of those wonderful ironies of modernization in the countryside that hedge-removal may 'save' land for agriculture but road-widening schemes – specifically in cases such as this – can then promptly claw back at least a part of the land thus transformed – without, of course, necessarily doing anything to make it feel less desolate.

A hole in the fields, mid-Suffolk

The highway improvers by no means always confine themselves to the main lanes. Single-track lanes can also be subjected to disfigurement, for a variety of reasons, good and bad. Here again in one photograph are the 'before' and 'after': the old lane banked, hedged and tree'd in on both sides of the tarmac, and beyond it the high field on the left bulldozed away to improve visibility and allow passing. On this small scale, an expanse of bare earth (which may of course regenerate some kind of interesting flora, if it is allowed to do so) has taken the place of the old enclosed continuity. This is a lane running from the A12 to Wenhaston: out of view beyond the opened-up stretch is a junction with another lane, on which there is a caravan site which may well have provided the motivation for this piece of engineering. (Caravan sites, it hardly needs saying, are another species of crass defacement of landscape – since one in a hundred thousand caravans is painted in colours which blend in natural settings – that depend for their existence on the car.)

To carve large chunks out of the adjacent fields and leave the junction as a kind of rural miniature of the earthworks found along motorways and urban bypasses is not, in my opinion, the best way to go about things. Why could the field on the left not have been sloped to the edge of the road, and the corner fenced using decorative iron fencing such as that shown on page 195.

In this way the lane would have retained something of its original proportions, and less farmland would have been lost. There is of course some potential for tree planting in the gap – but where are the trees?

Expanse of tarmac (with pub) in Marden, Wiltshire

The central principle in all redevelopment for the benefit of the motorist is that things are opened up: the small-scale is made large-scale, the enclosed is made open, the intimate is made alienating. This pub has never been more than a very modest building, and the garden and inn-yard which once stood next to it may never have been of enormous interest in themselves. But however plain they may be, such elements of the rural and village landscape are, finally, essential to its personality. Imagine this bleak little view with a foreground hedge and a few flowers beyond it, imagine a line of low tiled outbuildings where the nearest car is parked; a different world entirely, and a far pleasanter one. It would seem that the nation's brewers and publicans are, to a man, embarked on a campaign to isolate their drinking houses within the largest feasible areas of unfenced tarmac, perhaps on the assumption that unless cars can be clearly seen to be parked by them, no-one else will ever stop there. English rural Middle America rides again.

Main road furnishing along a back lane, south Herefordshire

In recent years there has been a further assault on the individuality of country places in the shape of signposts such as this, which are of course exactly the same design the country over. In the old days all signposts were made by local firms under contract to the county councils, and designs varied enormously, adding their own small touch of personality to every region of the country. The 'pointing hand' signpost illustrated on page 90, for example, is situated only five km. away from this, at Staunton on Arrow, and proudly bears the name of its makers, Turner Bros. of Newtown. Some county councils do continue to use thoughtfully designed new signposts which look well in rural settings – *and* are no less visible to motorists than the standard model shown here. Sussex County Council, for example, uses a signpost made largely out of wood; this has a number of simple decorative flourishes that make it an embellishment to the county's lanes. Surely the historic road up Stonewall Hill deserves to be pointed out by something more distinctive than the object illustrated?

The British Slob

Over a number of years, out of repeated unwilling encounters with the after-effects of his activity, I have evolved a vivid composite mental image of the person who dumps his rubbish in country places. This person, the British Slob (there is no distinction between English, Welsh and Scottish here), is as I see him by definition a car-bound creature who has lost all creative contact with the natural world. If he visits the country he does so because his wife or girlfriend wants him to, and he tends only to stop in places already pounded to a hardpan by the cars of other motorists. In such spots he deposits picnic waste as prominently as he can, notably beer-can empties which he especially likes to throw under hedges, and on such jaunts he also makes a point of leaving behind the one- or two-pint oil can with which he is perpetually topping up his engine. Sometimes, when he has the energy, the Slob goes out for a nocturnal backseat orgy during which he and whoever else is present will do a lot of heavy drinking, leaving supermarket carrier bags full of empty gut-rot plonk bottles stuffed into field gateways as a record of their visit. Pairs of knickers (though rarely underpants) are also sometimes to be found amongst the long grasses, or hanging beside the catkins – flung aside, it seems, in some dramatic gesture of self-liberation. The Slob either fears the country or despises it, or both at once, regarding it as an irrelevant backdrop to his activities, in any part of which he can relieve himself of what he no longer needs. He carries large-scale waste such as mattresses, prams and old fridges by night to places where he knows he will not be seen, and which are as far as possible from where he himself lives.

Whenever he chooses to drop a newspaper, the Slob receives able and willing assistance from the wind. One single act of casual Slobdom can be totally transformed by wind power in a matter of a few hours. The paper will first be opened, then separated out into its component parts, then spread piece by piece 100, 200, 400 metres

along the lane in a triumphant display of littering which – and this, of course, is the Slob's profoundest unconscious desire – achieves the maximum amount of uglification with the least amount of effort on his part.

A curious but thankfully not too common hybrid of the British Slob is the Slob Farmer who, despite the nature of his work, has inherited a longstanding family tradition of dumping in the few places where wild flora and fauna might otherwise survive on his land. He is also entirely undisturbed by the accumulation of empty polythene fertilizer bags which he leaves wherever they happen to lie once they have been emptied. These are specially coloured a garish turquoise by their manufacturers in order that they will stand out as stridently as possible in whatever natural setting they occupy.

The most disturbing effect of acts of Slobdom for the traveller is that – once more – any sense of remoteness in the country is immediately shattered. Others have been to the dumped-upon place before him, not once but many times; and what is more, these are others who on the evidence have nothing but disdain for the things that he himself loves. I would contend that very few cyclists – and absolutely no pootlists whatever – are Slobs, since they travel slowly enough to see and to be depressed by all the litter. In a car, the roadsides resolve into a vaguely acceptable green blur, but on a bicycle one sees every cigarette packet (the Slob is also a chronic chain-smoker). If the reader objects that the foregoing is a distorted picture, or even (though God forbid) a biased one; if he points out that he knows perfectly pleasant people who also happen, sometimes, to be Slobs; if indeed some of his best friends, or his mother, or his great aunt Regina are occasionally Slobs... then all I can say in reply is that this is the appealing image of themselves which they leave behind, whoever they may be.

This wood is in south Sussex, and is within easy motoring reach of Eastbourne and Hastings. The photograph does little justice to the scale of spoilation involved.

Rural Industry, Services, And The Shadow Of The Military

Slabs on a hilltop, Rutland

What is not often acknowledged either in 'beautiful England' books or indeed elsewhere, is that there is a crying need in rural areas for non-agricultural forms of labour. Only through the introduction of *more* industry than exists already in the countryside can the rural labour force hope to see an improvement in its relatively very low standard of living. For most of this century there have been far too few jobs for the workforce available – hence the drift to the cities and the depression of wages for those who remained. But the city, as we know, now offers very little to drift towards. If one accepts the existence of the problem, then one must also accept the need to find a solution. How might industry be introduced (or in some cases reintroduced) into villages and small towns, without destroying finally and absolutely the qualities for which so many people in the cities turn to them?

This is a huge subject, upon which I am not qualified to write except in the most abstract terms. But certain fundamentals are clear: any village industry, if it is to do no harm to the village as a *place*, must be well sited, physically integrated in the design of its buildings, small scale, not too noisy, ideally related to local produce, and not dependent on a regular stream of big lorries bringing in raw materials and carrying out the finished product. This photograph illustrates an example as good as most of how to get it wrong. Here a series of rectangular concrete boxes have been deposited on the most exposed horizon outside the lovely Rutland village of Wing, so that they totally dominate the previously pleasant valley below the village and shatter all sense of being in the depths of the country. In environmental (rather than in its own) terms this water treatment works for the nearby reservoir is badly sited, built of the wrong materials, crudely shaped, and entirely out of scale with its surroundings. There are far 'prettier' buildings in some of the new industrial estates in places such as Reading or Thetford, which house small-scale manufacturing outfits that might arguably adapt to deep rural locations – electrical engineering firms, furniture makers, printers, manufacturers of agricultural equip-

ment.... Furthermore, there are still many redundant buildings in rural areas – stone and brick barns, in particular – which could be adapted if the will was there. Planning authorities have for some years been geared to treating such proposals sympathetically.

An idyll qualified; near Boxford, Suffolk

A pretty lane to a pretty ford over a pretty stream – the kind of quiet, little-known place where locals go to fish. But lo, in recent years a sewage plant has been sited next to the stream. There can be no disputing the need for sewage plants, but why are they so frequently inserted as display pieces in the countryside? The concrete posts and wire fence here are not only hopelessly ugly in themselves, they also obscure nothing of the installation they protect. On such easy-to-screen sites as this, hedges should be planted as a matter of course, not something which we have to campaign to get. The same applies to the small electricity installations one often finds set down along lanesides without so much as a single leaf between them and whoever passes by – though it cannot, of course, be said about electricity pylons. Until such time as the burial of cables becomes viable – and alas, this seems likely to remain a hopeless dream except in very special places – one can only gnash one's teeth in impotence at their siting. For the traveller, pylons instantly destroy any sense of remoteness from the great conurbations, linking wherever they stand, no matter how lovely or quiet it might otherwise be, with the noise and fumes of the urban and heavy-industrial world. Were there such a body as the Council for the Destruction of Rural England, it would surely have made some of its highest awards for Landscape Spoliation to the Central Electricity Generating Board, which seems to have evolved a policy for routing its lines of fizzing wire through the most beautiful stretches of country wherever possible. (Pylons do supply a kind of shade, in very hot weather, for animals in fields otherwise denuded of trees....)

Nightmare, west Suffolk

About as sensitively designed and situated as a blow between the eyes with a meat cleaver, this fabulously ugly water tower stands on a bend as you come into the embungalowed village of Wood Ditton, Suffolk. The stripped landscape, concrete approach road and concrete (urban-style) lamp standard add their own qualities of desolation to the scene. But water towers do not need to look like this! Not far from Hungerford, Berkshire, for example, there stands a tower in what might be called a 'lighthouse' style, with a tank of simulated boarding, painted white, supported on decorated metal struts and complete (how the Brutalists would have loathed it) with a glazed 'observatory' and weather vane. This actually embellishes the landscape around it, at least to my eyes. The thing illustrated, in contrast, could only supply raw material for one's private imaginings of hell.

Traces of the military, Norfolk

This picturesque structure is one of several buildings still sited on an erstwhile airfield near the village of Cockthorpe: in the many years since they have served any useful purpose, no-one has quite got around to demolishing them. The land has been only partly re-arablized, and broad, cracked concrete runways lie here functionless and void. The one new addition to the scene is a battery turkey

farm – itself a barbarous affront against nature and humanity – whose buildings fit in well with these surroundings. The country is still scarred by numerous such examples of World War Two litter which, it almost goes without saying, should have been properly dealt with by the military themselves long before the land was returned to private hands. The countryside is further and indeed increasingly scarred by today's war games playgrounds, such as those on Salisbury Plain and the Dorset heathlands to the north of the Purbeck Hills, which are entirely to be avoided by those not wishing to experience what repeated rehearsals for war can do to the fabric of previously rural settings.

But the most devastating impact of all on the tranquillity of rural areas is made by the RAF in its fighter aircraft exercises. Much of the 'heart' of the English countryside is, in truth, repeatedly overshadowed by the grey wings of devastation machines. With one exception, in my own experience jets are flown over or very near to every area of country explored for this book. The reasons for their presence above remote country are not difficult to see. The remote country is usually the least densely populated, and apart from *theoretical* safety considerations, thin rural populations have (at least in the past) been able to put up much less of a fight against the installation of 'necessary' military bases. For any traveller tending to anxiety about the impending holocaust, the passage of a low-flying jet above his head, searing the air with its terrible thundering row, is a form of disillusionment unmatched by any other. At such a time – when he had perhaps been quite close to forgetting the subject, if only for a while – he will be more than forcibly reminded that in every sense of the phrase, there really is no escape.

The Inexorable Spread Of The 'Improved' Farming Landscape

Field enlargement in progress near Loddington, Leicestershire

The hedgerow being destroyed here has run parallel to another along the road, and has enclosed a narrow field with thick may bushes and trees, including some ash. For at least two centuries and perhaps for many more, this field had been an individual *place* in the landscape. Soon it will be an indistinguishable part of a very much greater expanse. The same principle applies also to the lanes: when they are enclosed by hedges they have personalities of their own, but when the hedges are gone the lanes are usually reduced to mere functioning units traversing the newly empty spaces. *Was* such destruction inevitable? *Was* there really no other way of utilizing this 'small' field to produce food? Must all farming be carried on as large-scale, energy-intensive, mechanized operations in which human labour is kept at an absolute minimum? Can such methods be sustained indefinitely? And if they were somehow to be sustained for a few decades more, then what hope would there be for the English countryside as we have known it?

The waste land accomplished: near Elmswell, Suffolk

Some farmers may have come to love the hedged landscape as a thing in itself, but most farmers' sense of beauty is bound up with function. "If it's farmed well," they say, "it looks good." and for most arable farmers a 'good-looking' landscape is one over which they hold absolute dominion, and in which there is little or nothing irrelevant to productivity. In this they are not so very different from all we suburbanites who like to see our power over our own little territories expressed in trimmed lawns and neat vegetable patches (there is great scope for 'weed' gardens in suburbia). As discussed in the East Anglian networks, I think that the replacement of the patchwork quilt with huge expanses of tilled earth can, under some circumstances, result in a new visual beauty perceptible to others than the people who farm there. But it can also – and more readily – result in vistas such as this.

No mere appreciation of function by the layman, even if he were able to enthuse about the methods employed (which is highly unlikely), could help to override the feelings of anxiety and desolation which he will feel in such places. This is one of those areas where, as the Nature Conservancy Council put it, there is little left to argue about from the conservationists' point of view, and it provides a depressing model of what the most 'rational' and intensive cereal-growing methods can do to places which previously looked and felt like English countryside.

The waste land with a concrete foreground; Ringland, Norfolk

If, after the hedges have been removed, broad expanses of sensibly functional concrete are inserted into the stripped landscape, the result will generally look something like this: a techno-agrarian nowhereland which might be any place from the Belgian lowlands to the plains of Kansas. All sense of the history of the area has disappeared with its landscape features. In the old days when there were many small fields and many people to work in them, and many children to carry the workers' lunches out to them, every field had a name. In the parish of Colne Engaine, Essex, for example, some 80 km. from this spot, there were fields known as Old Hop Ground, Alder Car, Minnims, Caraway Piece, Nine Journeys, Great and Little Toogoods, Cold Ham Meadow, and Hither and Further Gauls, amongst others. One wonders what names if any will be given to the vast new emptinesses which have been made out of all these once-familiar places, or whether from now on they will simply be numbers registered on some computer printout.

The concrete here is a recently completely entrance to a new set of farm buildings – the usual gigantic rectangular sheds, set nakedly on a horizon. When I was there, the old farm complex nearby stood derelict; it included a well-finished set of brick outbuildings with attractive Dutch gables, and a once superb thatched barn, its thatch now rolled away from the rafters. Prominent amongst the most hideous of new farm buildings are the 'cowtels', as they are somewhat cynically known. These are the equivalent of batteries for cattle in which the poor creatures are penned for most if not all the year, and fed on a rye-grass crop which is cultivated intensively on further sterilized prairie wastes. Such prairies are often created specially for the purpose out of the old flower-bedecked meadows which not long since were occupied by the cows. Thus, even the traditional *pastoral* landscape is no longer safe from the forces of 'improvement'.

Scoured streamside, near Monewden, Suffolk

With the hedgerows have gone many of the hedgerow trees. Since 1950, in some eastern counties *up to 80%* of all trees have been cut down, and even when it is not obvious that felling has taken place, as it is here, it requires only a little rummaging around amongst the long grasses of the lanesides to find rotting stumps which have not been pulled out.

A writer on agriculture of the 18th century, William Marshall, remarked in 1787 that due to the number and great height of the hedgerows in Norfolk "the eye seems ever on the verge of a forest, which is, as it were by enchantment, continually changing into inclosures and hedgerows". So it must have been also in many parts of Suffolk. Only a matter of a km. or so from this scene of recent levelling one can enter a little pocket of the old landscape, which is now thankfully preserved by the local naturalists' trust. Out of the desert of productivity one comes "as it were by enchantment" into a seies of tree- and hedge-lined tunnels running between small and equally enclosed meadows, evidently little changed from the time when it

was mapped by one owner in the middle of the 17th century. The contrast could not be more vivid.

Unless changes are made at national level, hedgerow trees in the open landscape would appear to be doomed. This at least was the conclusion of the 1974 Countryside Commission report, 'New Agricultural Landscapes'. Even if deliberate felling of hedgerow trees were halted, on a national average only one twelfth of the saplings necessary to replace what is being lost (let alone to create landscapes with more trees in them than we see today) are being planted, or allowed to grow up out of hedgerows otherwise uniformly levelled by mechanical cutting. 'New Agricultural Landscapes' concluded that unless something is done, hedgerow trees will gradually disappear from the English lowland countryside.

Relic of a deciduous wood near Ilmington, Warwickshire

This is not, as it may seem, a line of hedgerow trees but what has been left at a wood's edge after clear-felling of the rest, to give – however feebly – the illusion that there is still a wood there during the years that the new crop takes to fill in the gap. I have not been back since I took this picture in 1975, but I can say with some certainty that the chances of the felled trees having been replaced by their own kind is now very slight indeed. Even in such counties as 'Hardy's' Dorset the Finlandization process has had devastating effects on the landscape; 50% of that county's woodland is now coniferous. And where the woods have not been turned into pine dungeons they have been eradicated altogether – with substantial financial encouragement from the Ministry of Agriculture – for conversion to arable use. 30% of woods under 1 hectare were cleared in England between 1947 and 1972. Even before this rape began, England was one of the least well-wooded countries in Europe.

The Battle For The Landscape

> "We fire the fields for harvest,
> The hedges swell the flame,
> The oak trees and the cottages
> From which our fathers came.
> We give no compensation,
> The earth is ours today,
> And if we lose on arable,
> Then bungalows will pay."
>
> *John Betjeman,*
> *'Harvest Hymn' in 'High And Low', 1966*

> "The barrenness of these fields reveals the barrenness of the farmer's spirit."
>
> *Masanobu Fukuoka,*
> *'The One-Straw Revolution', 1978*

The battle for the landscape has begun, and as I write it is growing in intensity. The changes taking place today in England's farmed landscapes constitute the most pressing single issue out of those just dealt with, not because the others are less significant or less deserving of vigorous debate – far from it! – but because such changes threaten us with the most immediate, widespread and irremediable effects. If the diverse mix of hedged fields, small woods and 'marginal' land which makes up what now remains of the traditional English landscape were to be further transformed through commercial pressures, we will never get it back again. We would of course have new landscapes in its place; but could they be in any way its equal? I very much doubt it; and I think that it is worth stressing that this doubt is based on some years of exploration of both the 'old' *and* the 'new' English countryside. The most monstrous, soul-parching prodigies of the most cloddishly doctrinaire architects and town planners of the 60s and early 70s can be made tolerable to live in – if nothing more – by the knowledge that there is pleasant country not far away, to which one may sometimes turn for spiritual refreshment. But when that countryside has itself been converted into an agrarian version of a vacuous concrete piazza, then truly the oppressed urban Englishman seeking beauty or pleasure outside the National Parks, the properties of the National Trust, or at the seaside, will have a few places left to turn in his own country.

All the evidence has suggested that at present nowhere is safe from what is sometimes termed 'improvement'; and that even the landscapes inside the National Parks do not have absolute immunity. All the evidence has further suggested that unless fundamental changes are made in the system of funding agriculture, and unless controls are established *and maintained* over all alterations to the landscape proposed by farmers, then the process by which the eastern counties have been so very quickly turned into the wastes of wheat and barley they are today could continue throughout the rest of England. We might of course try leaving it up to chance and *laissez faire*, but it seems far more likely than not that, if we do, the 'heart' of England will be piece by piece ripped out, until Dorset is simply a slightly steeper-contoured version of Norfolk, Shropshire looks like Essex with the addition of a few preserved, heather-clad hills, and the Somerset lowlands are indistinguishable from most of Lincolnshire*.

Immediately after the Second World War it was inconceivable that farmers would one day constitute the single most serious threat to the continuing beauty of the English landscape. Quite the opposite: at that time, farming was considered to be an activity deserving of the most comprehensive protection and encouragement. Its fundamental importance was well appreciated by a nation still on rationing, and when the Town and Country Planning Act became law in 1947 farming was exempted, almost without qualification. Since then we have watched the landscape change, and because the belief in the inviolable nature of the farming profession (fully encouraged, of course, by the farmers' lobby) has remained until recently almost as entrenched as in the late 40s, most of us have watched it change with a deterministic acceptance. Like the weather, we have felt that it must be this way and that the most painless approach was to accept passively, however little we liked what was happening. After all, we must eat.

I say we have watched the landscape change; but have we, in fact? One of the biggest obstacles to consciousness-raising on this issue is its very invisibility. The disappearance of hedgerows and hedgrow trees, the replacement of deciduous woodland with conifers, the draining of marches, the filling in of ponds, the destruction of all but the line of formerly verdant bridleways, are all activities which may be seen taking place in England from day to day – but for the fact that unless one knows when and where they are to take place (and because landowners are not required to tell us, none do), they are extremely easy to miss altogether. It does not take long to bulldoze a hedgerow, or to fell a tree; and many of the features which have been destroyed were, of course, nowhere near to public rights of way from which their destruction could have been witnessed. Most of the time, one

---

* During the past two years it has begun to be apparent that "the engine of destruction" (in William Waldegrave's immortal phrase) does, after all, have some kind of in-built braking system. But even if EEC measures, still in the melting pot, do succeed in putting an effective curb on today's rampant over-production of cereals, it will remain the case that farmers and landowners will retain the power to alter the countryside as they see fit, until such time as a law is introduced to control such changes which takes into account the views of the rest of the population.

misses them from a distance, with a generalized and vague feeling that all is somehow not as right with the world here as it was before; or one sees some far off, anonymous fire burning as one is rushing up the main road from one urban area to another. This said, however, it is also clear that at a certain stage the changes do show; but by then it is usually too late to do anything about it. I might tentatively define this as being, for the majority of people, the time when the hedges and trees along the roads are taken out – especially where these are 'A' roads – and it can then be seen at a glance that everything else has already gone. At this stage many people find themselves dismayed, without any room for doubt.

Is there an ideal model of the English landscape to which one may turn for reference, in order to highlight the changes where they have occurred? Clearly there is not. The landscape varies so greatly over such short distances, as this book has attempted to show, that no one area can be taken as a typical reference point. But we can say this: the predominant quality of old English farming landscapes – the quality which it may be reasonably claimed has given the greatest joy to the greatest number – is it enclosure, its intimacy. This is quite as true in many if not absolutely all parts of the landscape created during Parliamentary Enclosure as in the more complex landscapes of the west. What has been generally typical of England is a fascinating and mysterious running-together of tens of thousands of individual *places*, each of them small, localized, self-contained, each made up in different parts of hedged fields and meadows, bending streamsides, pocket woodlands, patches of gorse, heather, rough grass or bracken, linked together by a network of zig-zag, tree'd-in lanes.

The key word here is 'individual'. What constitutes a 'place' in the farming landscape? What is it about certain spots which makes us, first, aware of the fact that we are in them and, second, remember them later with affection? It is almost always the features which are now peripheral to the processes of farming: the line of hedgerow trees, the steep, rough slope (inconvenient to the farmer), the patch of wet ground which has to be used as pasture and attracts an abundance of dampness-loving flowers, the unmaintained game covert planted by some huntsman landowner long since departed this earth. It is precisely these features that we have been losing over the past four decades on a day-by-day basis; and when they are gone we are left with the kinds of landscape just illustrated – non-places, parts of a greater expanse that rolls endlessly, homogenously and depressingly away over every horizon. This is the landscape of 20th-century Function, and Function itself is *not* necessarily Beauty. It is this landscape with which we are all now threatened.

A Select Catalogue Of Destruction, And Some Other Observations

Hedgerows

Between 1946 and 1974, farmers took out about 193,000 km. of hedgerows in England and Wales. This is nearly a quarter of those standing in 1946. (E. Pollard and M.D. Moore, *Hedges*, 1974)

In the 1970s, hedgerows in Britain were being removed at the rate of approximately 3,200 km. per annum. (Council For The Protection Of Rural England, 'Landscape: The Need For A Public Voice', 1975)

Between 1946 and 1970, the then county of Huntingdonshire lost 90% of its hedges (8,000 km.), whilst Norfolk lost 45% (nearly 13,000 km.). (C.P.R.E., op. cit., and W.W. Baird and J.R. Tarrant, 'Hedgerow Destruction In Norfolk 1946–70', 1973)

In the Gloucestershire lowlands, single arable fields have been made out of as many as 40 small fields at a time during the postward period. (Radio Four interview on 'Wildlife' with John Hughes, of the Farming And Wildlife Advisory Group for Gloucestershire, 5th May 1981)

For general arable purposes, it was found that fields need be *no larger than 20 hectares* in order to accommodate the necessary agricultural machinery. (A.J. Edwards, 'Consideration Of Field Size And Shape On The Large Arable Farm', a Ministry Of Agriculture technical note of 1965)

Hedgerow Trees And Woodlands

Well over 25 million of the 29 million elms in England, Wales and Scotland are now dead. (Countryside Commission estimate, 1984)

At least as many trees of other kinds have been destroyed in hedgerows alone between 1951 and 1980 as a result of deliberate action by farmers. (Estimate based by Marion Shoard on figures in *New Agricultural Landscapes* by R. Westmacott and T. Worthington, 1974)

In a sample area of approximately 20 sq. km. of land in Huntingdonshire, 2,300 hedgerow trees were found to have been felled between 1947 and 1972.

This leaves about one fifth of the trees that were standing in 1947. (Westmacott and Worthington, op. cit.)

During the latter half of the 1970s, Norfolk was losing about 8,000 hedgerow trees a year. (P. Hardy and R. Matthews, 'Farmland Tree Survey In Norfolk', 1977)

Of the ancient broadleaved woods which had been managed in Britain without very much clear felling since the Middle Ages, nearly a third were destroyed between 1945 and the late 1970s. (O. Rackham, 'Historic Woodlands And Hedges' in The Architects' Journal, 21st January 1978)

'The material demands of society are likely to eliminate such woodland outside nature reserves or other specially protected areas by the year 2025'. (Dr D.A. Ratcliffe, Chief Scientist of the Nature Conservancy Council, speaking at the House of Lords select committee on science and technology, 1980)

Roughlands and Wetlands

Between 1937 and 1971, nearly half the downland turf in Wiltshire was ploughed up for cultivation: an area of some 26,000 hectares. (Estimate based by Marion Shoard on Ministry of Agriculture statistics and aerial surveys held by Wiltshire County Council)

Between 1920 and 1968, 73% of the east Suffolk heathlands were ploughed or turned over to conifers. (C.P.R.E., op. cit.)

25% of Dorset's downland turf was ploughed between 1957 and 1972, and 42% of the Dorset heaths were destroyed between 1960 and 1980. (C.A. Jones, 'the Conservation Of Chalk Downland In Dorset', 1973, and N. Webb and L. Haskins, 'An Ecological Survey Of Heathlands In The Poole Basin, Dorset, England, in 1978', 1980)

Since 1950, the annual area of wetlands to be drained has increased by 600%. 'Wetlands' include water meadows, marshlands, bogs and soggy corners of fields. (F.H.W. Green, 'Aspects Of The Changing Environment', in Journal of Environmental Management I, 1973)

A Ministry of Agriculture survey found in 1969 that there were 2.8 million hectares of wetlands which would still "benefit" from drainage. (E.T. Belding, 'Drainage Surveys Of England And Wales', in 'Agriculture', June 1971)

Wildlife

The Nature Conservancy Council predicts that if "improvement" of farmed landscapes were to continue at the same rate as in the 1970s, 95% of butterfly species would eventually be lost from them. (N.C.C., 'Nature Conservation And Agriculture', 1977)

Under the same conditions, 80% of all bird species would also be lost. (N.C.C., op. cit.)

In some parts of England, frog populations have declined by over 99%. (D.L. Hawksworth ed., *The Changing Flora And Fauna Of Britain*, 1974)

In a single year, between 10% and 16.5% of Sites of Special Scientific Interest had been damaged or completely destroyed. SSSIs cover only 5% of the land surface of Britain. (N.C.C. Survey, 1980)

In the counties of Berkshire, Buckinghamshire, Oxfordshire and Wiltshire, there are 70 SSSIs which are currently under direct threat from farming. (N.C.C., 'Facts And Figures', A.E. Stubbs ed., 1980)

A sample survey in the Isle of Wight showed that 90% of proposed "improvements" to SSSIs actually took place. (Jennifer Tubbs, 'The Concept Of Sites Of Special Scientific Interest: A Review', University of Southampton, 1977)

Of our 43 species of dragonfly, three or possibly four have become extinct since 1953; some species of bumblebee are seriously threatened; 36 breeding species of birds have declined appreciably since 1949, 30 of these being in the lowlands; several of our 15 species of bats are at risk of extinction; and of the 12 species of reptiles, four are equally endangered. Finally, since 1930, ten species of wild plants have become extinct. (N.C.C., 'Nature Conservation In Great Britain', 1984)

The sources have been included in this list since I think it is important to recognise that such data originates largely in specialist research by scientists working in university departments or acting as consultants to organs of government and local authorities. In other words, most of the conclusions and predictions here were made not with alarmist intentions but as statements of fact arrived at through empirical observations in a particular field. It is only when one begins to fit the pieces together (and there are many more such studies upon which one could draw) that the picture grows alarming.

Yet, of course, there is another side to this particular coin. The reader will not have failed to notice that wherever agricultural improvements have been mentioned thus far, the word has been placed within quotation marks. For many farmers and for the Ministry of Agriculture there is – or until only a few years ago there has been – no such qualificatory punctuation. As Howard Newby put it, "the history of the English farmer in the twentieth century is, whatever the vicissitudes, a spectacular success story." It all depends on where you happen to be standing, and by what criteria you choose to measure success.

Vanguard Of Battle

I am indebted for some of the preceding data to homework already done by the writers of Friends of the Earth's booklet 'Paradise Lost?' published in 1980 to launch their campaign to save Britain's wildlife habitats and, in particular, to Marion Shoard's book *The Theft of the Countryside* (also 1980). This book is the most important* single document yet to have been produced on the issues in question. It is quite as relevant now as when it was first published, and I would urge anyone who has read this far to obtain a copy and read it from cover to cover, preferably twice. It puts the subject of change in the farming landscape into a long perspective, making the issues specific and accessible where they have been for most of us, as I believe, so nebulous an experience in the field.

It must also be said of this writer at the outset that she is neither a member of some hypothetical 'old guard' seeking to preserve the landscape for the enjoyment of a privileged minority who already know how to use it nor a 'hopeless sentimentalist', a charge frequently made against those seeking to protect things of beauty in the countryside not only for others' enjoyment, but because they are worth keeping as things in themselves.

---

* A more recent attack on the same subject, confirming that the destruction continued unabated, is *Crisis and Conservation: Conflict in the British Countryside* by Charlie Pye-Smith and Chris Rose (Pelican Original, 1984). Like Marion Shoard, the writers are especially concerned with tackling long-established attitudes, not only widespread views on subjects such as the public responsibility of landowners and the issue of landownership, but also entrenched views of what is valuable in their terms held by some of the older conservation bodies themselves. Particularly useful here is the connection made between the deadlock encountered by environmentalists of all kinds and the lack of public accountability currently enjoyed by the civil service. The writers add to Shoard's arguments for the use of direct planning controls the notion of a land tax, as a method of diverting influence over how land is used, or abused, from owners to the community as a whole.

Some indication of Marion Shoard's main arguments will be necessary in order that the remarks made in the rest of this section shall have a context, – and for another reason as well, viz. that important notions that have yet to be reflected in legislation cannot be repeated too often.

Our Loss, Not Theirs

The first major proposition of *The Theft of the Countryside* is that, whether it likes it or not, the British public has been paying for the desecration of its own countryside: through a system of price support which has guaranteed farmers minimum prices and encouraged them to produce much more food than we need; and through a system of capital grants which are made out of taxpayers' money by the Ministry of Agriculture in order to stimulate increased efficiency in agriculture through the modernisation of farms. So in 1980–81, over £191 million was paid out in the shape of capital grants to farmers. Of this, perhaps two thirds served to finance activities which may be described as damaging to the environment. (By way of contrast, the entire operating budget of the Nature Conservancy Council during the same year was £9.384 million). Such grants are given not only *without any test* being made by the Ministry of Agriculture of each project's actual potential, but also without any consideration of the wealth of the applicant; and very few applications are ever turned down. This system means that in pure accountancy terms, any patch of ground which is not being used to a maximum level of productivity – i.e. for factory farming, in the shape we now know it – is money down the drain as far as the farmer is concerned. Any hedgerow which does not serve to contain cattle in a field, any hedgerow tree whose roots impair the efficiency of ploughing, any small field at present inaccessible to cultivation machines, any old orchard no longer harvested for profit... all those peripheral details of the landscape which give it individuality and glory, are money down the drain to the farmer. It would be a foolish farmer indeed – in pure accountancy terms – who did not take advantage of the offer which has been made permanently available to him with no strings attached by the Ministry of Agriculture on behalf of the unconsulted British public, whereby he is enabled to transform his leaden farm into a golden one, and to *produce more food*.

But we do not need more food! Indeed, as most of us should be only too well aware by now, the EEC can only benefit from an overall *reduction* of the amount of food produced within its boundaries. Yet as the system has been operated, vast sums of taxpayers' money have been poured into an unchecked expansion of farming capabilities, whilst yet further vast sums are poured into disposal of the surpluses produced. In other words, we are being made to pay twice over for what we do not want in the first place. Surplus food production is, indeed, the biggest administrative problem of the EEC, and the methods currently used to deal with it range from the morally questionable to the tragi-comic. One method of disposal of surplus skimmed milk, for example, is to feed it to cattle, which then produce more milk, which is converted to skimmed milk and fed to yet another cattle, and so on *ad infinitum*. Do individual cows ever find themselves drinking their own milk, one wonders, and if so, do they recognise the taste?

Two arguments have been repeatedly put forward in favour of the continuance of this Laputan system. These are: (1) that since we have only limited control over the price of imported food, increased production at home guarantees supplies of some commodities at low prices, and (2) that in some global emergency such as a third world war we would need to use the surplus, since not enough could be produced at home to feed everyone. Marion Shoard disposes of both these arguments, showing in the first place that there is by no means so much to fear as is often claimed in the fluctuating prices of the world market, and that in any case the protection we enjoy from such viccisitudes (which is, of course, much greater than its defendants generally like to acknowledge) is won only at a cost that is out of all proportion to its visible benefits. In the second place, Shoard draws on the findings of two scientists who have concluded, through researches conducted independently in recent years, that even if all food imports were to be cut off we could still grow enough food in Britain to guarantee a healthy diet – always assuming of course that there were enough people left alive to do the growing, or the eating. It comes as no surprise to learn that this would involve modifying the Briton's habitually meat-heavy diet to one in which vegetables predominate.

The question arising naturally out of such considerations, which is now (at last) being aired on a far wider public platform than that of the journals of environmentalists, is this: if it can be shown that Britain's farmers are at present producing more food than we need, and that its existence is a chronic problem and indeed – as a result of the existence of protectionist trade barriers, and the dumping of some surpluses in Third World countries – an international scandal, then why on earth do we continue to encourage our farmers, by way of the capital grants system and by way of a number of other massive if less immediately visible diversions of capital into farming, to increase levels of productivity around the country? For in the process we simultaneously exacerbate the existing problem, and further assist in the destruction of the countryside!

A new style of farmer

One result of state support for agriculture, and one that has been encouraged by successive governments, is that many small farms have been amalgamated into single large units, so that in some parts of the country the small farmer is now a rare creature indeed. The 1982 Minister's Annual Review of Agriculture reports that the total number of holdings in the UK in 1981 was about 242,300: in 1953 the figure was 454,000. Where, one wonders, have all those hundreds of thousands of farmers gone? As Richard Body puts it in *Agriculture: The Triumph and The Shame*, "what has happened over most of England is that the small livestock holdings that were predominantly given over to pasture have been amalgamated into substantial farms, and the pasture ploughed up to grow corn." He goes on to observe that it has become increasingly difficult for any young person wishing to set up a farm on limited capital to do so, because of the existing system.

Amongst the largest owner-occupiers there is also an entirely new group, – the financial institutions. These were initially attracted into farming by the massive increases in land prices in the early part of the 1970s, and they were not slow to appreciate that these values could be further augmented by increasing the efficiency of each holding. Some evolved subsidiary companies (Fountain Farming Ltd. is one of the best known) which could act as finely-tuned 'improvement' machines and simultaneously operate as tenants of the farms they were transforming. The institutions also had the enormous advantage over the small owner-occupier of being able to borrow anything up to 90% of the land's original value in order to finance intensification schemes of the most Draconian kinds.

The absence of effective restraints

Marion Shoard writes: "It might be supposed that in return for the support farmers receive from the community at large they could be expected to pursue their activities in ways which would harmonise with the needs of the rest of the community." It might indeed be expected: but we have the evidence all about us that – at least so far as *some* farmers are concerned – we can expect until we are blue in the face, and it will make no difference. Such farmers, or companies, will continue to farm in ways which are convenient and highly profitable to them, and severely detrimental to the richness and beauty of the landscape, until such time as they are restrained. There is at present no effective method of restraining them. The existing planning machinery is all but impotent in matters of landscape conservation: the use of tree preservation orders, the constraints on the siting of farm buildings, the six months' notice rule where moorland is to be ploughed, are all the merest drops in the ocean, nor are they in themselves necessarily effective. Over the wider changes there are no controls at all, and Shoard provides a detailed study of a case in which one of the most lovely patches of West Sussex downland, which had been singled out by the County Structure Plan as one in which changes in land use were not to be encouraged, and was situated right in the middle of an 'Area of Outstanding Natural Beauty' (a label meaning precisely nothing in effective planning terms), was converted to ploughland despite anything which objectors could do. The objectors did, indeed, do everything that they could do: they went through all the possible procedures but they had no real power, nor any real hope of preventing the destruction from taking place.

The picture is hardly any brighter when one considers the activities and powers of the other bodies directly concerned with the constitution of the countryside. The *Forestry Commission* is responsible for the issuing of felling licences for all woodland clearance and could therefore, in theory, do a great deal to slow or modify the destruction of our remaining broadleaved woodlands. In practise, felling licences for such clearance have been only very rarely witheld. The *Nature Conservancy Council* supervises reserves around the country, but its powers are absurdly limited. It does its best within the limits of its tiny budget; it attempts to inform the public of the issues and the need for action; but at present it can *guarantee* to save only a very little. A mere quarter of the 134,000 hectares of National Nature Reserves are actually owned by the NCC, and only on these 35 sites are the rights of wildlife inalienable: the others are leased or managed through agreements with the landowners, and these have no guarantee whatever in perpetuity.

The *Countryside Commission* has developed a programme of educating farmers into the principles of conservation, and has laid out a code of practise subsequently endorsed by the National Farmers' Union and the Country Landowners' Association. The education programme may, it is true, have some effect in time: at present no-one seems able to say for certain either way. But even if it does work, such an essentially toothless approach will take so long to alter farmers' attitudes (and it is of course the attitudes of the least compromising which matter most) that we are not likely to have very much left of the old landscape for a new generation of conservation-conscious farmers to conserve. We would, it is true, have the *National Parks*, – so long as proposals are not put into practise such as those submitted in 1979 by the Countryside Review Committee, whereby protection would have been effectively removed from 80% of their total area. We are still able to withdraw into the National Parks, and enjoy the *wild* country they encompass. But I for one want to enjoy much more of England than the freedom of 'the tourist parts', and I want to be sure that what I already love, in the prosaic as well as in the obviously pretty places, remains there to be enjoyed. Not atrophied, you understand; not preserved in aspic; but in a state of sustained change – which has been a constant of every farmed landscape since time began – that nevertheless guarantees some maintenance and some replacement of the features which have given it beauty and variety in the past.

A Way Forward

So then: what can be done? Marion Shoard's suggestion, which she lays out at length and in informed detail, is that farming be brought fully under control of planning bodies specially created for the purpose. These Regional Countryside Planning Authorities, as she calls them, would be so constituted that they would represent not only the opinions of the people in each rural area which they administer, but also the opinions of the people in nearby urban areas who most use such stretches of country for recreation. Their evolution would not involve any fundamental change in the existing planning system, – merely an extension of it to bring under control for the first time any agricultural activity which affects the ecological balance and/or overall appearance of the landscape. Such changes would thereafter be defined as 'development'. The Town and Country Planning Act does, after all, contain the word 'country' in its title; and whilst it has in the past provided a system whereby the spread of building and industry in rural areas may be controlled, it allows no means of safeguarding that very non-urban environment – against which all such spread is rightly seen as a potential incursion – from undesirable change within itself.

Against the cries of "Unfair!" which would be bound to reverberate from the agricultural lobby if this proposal came anywhere near to being put into practise, Marion Shoard has this to say: "property speculators, mining companies, those who would pull down historical buildings, retailers, industrialists and householders have all been required to operate within the requirements of the rest of the community. I ask no more of farmers." None of this – as farmers' representatives have been so frequently heard to say – is purely a country matter, about which we urbanites know nothing, and about which they *must* know best, as if by inheritance through the genes.

I think it is worth stressing that the scheme which Shoard proposes does not mean that henceforth the landscape would be prettified by the repressive actions of unrealistic bureaucrats into an unchanging pastiche of its earlier state. Farmers would be able to state the case for change just as industrialists, retailers and home-owners are able to do; and there would naturally be times when their case would be found to be wholly justifiable, others where some compromise could be achieved. In such situations, Shoard's argument runs, we would at least know that the opinion of representatives of *the community as a whole* had been sought, and that the community as a whole could therefore be said to have decided to support the changes made. It is cheering to find that even Howard Newby, by no means the most ardent supporter of environmentalism, comes separately to a very similar conclusion:

"In the future a diverse ecology will only be able to coexist with an efficient agriculture within the context of a *planned* land-use strategy, and such an attempt to resolve the various and conflicting demands on the countryside cannot be successful without farmers surrendering at least some of their freedom of action to do as they wish with their own land."

Elsewhere he writes:

"It now makes sense economically and – bearing in mind the umbrage of consumers – politically to withdraw some marginal land from production, or at least not allow its productivity to be expanded, when the extra production will only be used to further enlarge existing surpluses."

Some Quibbles, And Some Counter Arguments

It will have been apparent earlier in this book that my own reactions to the modernised landscapes of East Anglia and elsewhere are not always entirely negative. Unlike Marion Shoard, I still find parts of the Wiltshire uplands beautiful, even under crops rather than downland turf, and there are indeed *some* stretches of open prairie country – the upland to the south of Avebury is one, the area of the Essex 'hills' just west of Saffron Walden is another – where I would find myself inclined to kick up a fuss if I discovered that through some further unexpected development in agricultural methods plans were afoot to re-enclose them. Openness can be beautiful, especially where the land curves. The sweep of huge mechanically cultivated fields can be breathtaking when the light is hitting them in the right way, and the symmetries and precision of ploughlines can appeal very strongly to that side of our nature which craves order and admires technique. The very earth itself is beautiful, especially in flint country.

It has to be asked, then, whether for our nature poets and landscape painters, latent as well as actual, the endless empty earth would always be totally uninspiring. *Would* they cease to experience any kind of spiritual uplift in the new countryside? *Would* the sense of otherness be totally lost to them? Would they not know the joy of being surrounded by growing things? Would they not in any way be able to sense the ancientness of the land they stand on? I think that the answer to all these questions, based on personal experience, must be 'no – not always'. All is not entirely lost in the landscape of the cattle-fodder factory. There is still hoar frost in winter, heat haze in summer, winds off the sea, the passage of scudding clouds, and all the associations which old buildings (especially isolated churches) can call up in the imagination.

Even now – through photography in particular – we are evolving a new aesthetic which may help our children to see the beauty where it exists in hundred hectare fields, in much the same way that our experience of artists such as Constable and Palmer has helped us in the past to see more in the old landscapes. Such factors must be borne in mind in the debate about the countryside. If we can recognise the occasional virtues of the new farming landscapes as well as their obvious failings, it may better equip us to tackle the main problem which now confronts us: how to restore to them something of what has been lost.

Another niggling question which remained in my thoughts as I read *The Theft of the Countryside* (and which Marion Shoard also confronts and answers) was: who exactly is this 'we' for whom the countryside should be protected? In other words, how many members of the British public do in fact use the farmed landscapes for recreation? For how many of these is it an essential of living? For how many of the rest is it little more than an abstract green backdrop to the occasional car-bound picnic?

The danger in claiming that one wishes to protect the country for everyone is that it may sound as though one merely wishes to protect it for oneself and a like-minded minority whom one knows will treat it with respect; – in the words of Philip Lowe, as quoted by Howard Newby, "preservation for the nation, but not necessarily for the public". The Countryside Commission has for some years found itself caught up in precisely this contradiction (although it should be noted that, given the number of recent recruitments to its leadership of former officers of the National Farmers' Union and Country Landowners' Association, the Commission may not be unduly agonised at its position).

Whilst one of its functions has been to help to make the countryside more readily accessible to the public, another has been – usually via local authority initiatives – to provide honeypot sites near to large urban areas: the country parks and picnic sites developed along disused railways, in woodlands or old gravel pits, along stretches of riverside and such like places, replete with homogeneous picnic tables and discreetly placed toilets, to which the weekend 'explorer' of the country can drive and park his car. Even the establishment by the Commission of the long distance footpaths (about which intrinsically I am not in any way complaining) can be seen as a kind of honeypotting, which serves to draw quite a number of hiking-booted wasps and flies away from the 193,000 km. of by no means so well publicised or used field paths and bridleways which exist throughout the rest of England and Wales. Even the Youth Hostels Association, an organisation which has in the past been second to none in the business of encouraging people out into the country under their own steam, has aided and abetted in this particular process by opening new (and of course in themselves perfectly useful) hostels along the routes of the long distance paths whilst at the same time it has allowed its less profitable hostels in the less frequented areas to close without replacement. All such areas have innumerable lanes, and innumerable paths, but how many Y.H.A. members ever find their way on to them?

The Countryside Commission's 1977 'National Household Survey' found that about 21% of 5,000 people questioned during three summer months like – or said they liked – "long walks, hikes or rambles" better than any other form of outdoor activity. 33% liked "drives, outings and picnics" best. The rest were divided amongst a number of activities: visiting the coast, stately homes or safari parks, watching or participating in sport, fishing, horse riding and pony trekking. No-one seems to have mentioned cycling – nor, as the dawn had not then begun to break, pootling. The survey also found, interestingly, that *nearly half* of interviewees preferred to be in "the working countryside" (which heading included canals, lakes and reservoirs).

As we know, statistics can be misleading. It may be that this cross-section of 5,000 people is not characteristic of the public at large: certainly 21% seems a rather large percentage to like long walks, hikes, or even rambles when one bears in mind the Sports Council's estimate of $2\frac{1}{2}$ million keen or moderately keen walkers in the country as a whole, and the relatively small membership (50,000 in 1985) of the walker's most vocal representative organisation, the Ramblers' Association. But it does seem that the minority of explorers of 'real' countryside who are prepared to use their muscles and – when necessary – to get mud on their feet, is not quite so small as one might have feared. Yet how many of these are true explorers? This same survey, as already mentioned in Part One, identified a convervatism and uncertainty in those who go to the countryside, and *New Agricultural Landscapes* showed that in many cases in its various test areas, which are located broadly across the country, field paths were barely or never used. There are certainly very many lanes that are, to date, quite as little used by cyclists.

This is fine, of course, for those who love solitude, and I include myself amongst them. The solitude dilemma in this overcrowded country was well summarised by C.E.M. Joad, using as an example a Sussex common which was at the time threatened with development and which, the developer argued, there was every reason to use for building since few ever went there. But, says Joad, "it was precisely the fewness of the people that constituted the attraction of the place to the few. If everybody enjoyed the pleasures of Midhurst Common, nobody would enjoy them because there would be no beauty left to enjoy. You cannot appreciate solitude if a multitude is busy appreciating solitude at the same time." Indeed you cannot, although even in the company of a lot of people there might perhaps be "beauty left to enjoy". There would not have been much beauty left on Midhurst Common, however, if the Midhurst Brick and Lime Company had put up its proposed works there.

But let us suppose that no-one had ever used the Common. In that case, would not the industrialist's arguments have been acceptable? If no-one ever went there to be distressed by the uglification and environmental damage to the place, then why not build a brick works on the site? In confronting this question one must come to recognise a principle which underpins all 'environmentalist' activity, and this is that such places or features (or animals – the otter, for example, which hardly anyone ever actually sees in the wild) are worth preserving in themselves, and for themselves. In helping them to remain in existence – in knowing that through our efforts they survive, even though we may never see them – we also help ourselves since at the same time we preserve something of the morality, and perhaps also the optimism, of our own species. This may appear to be a deviation from the line of my argument, but on the contrary it is very much bound up with it. For if we can say – speaking of the landscape – that places are worth preserving *in themselves*, then whether or not people go there to be alone in them becomes a secondary issue.

Marion Shoard's method of tackling the problem of identifying the potential group for whom the old, intimate countryside should be preserved is both pragmatic and direct. She devotes one chapter of her book to a presentation of the views of a number of children in a Kentish village which had not long since lost a buttercup meadow and a row of old trees through farming intensification. Both the meadow and the trees had been used by the children as impromptu playgrounds, and both had been missed by them once they were gone. The enjoyment of these children was simple and straightforward, as one would expect, requiring no special training, no knowledge of painting or nature, landscape design or local history. It would follow, then, that if those who use the country to the full – who plumb its depths – are at present a minority, this can only be because the majority has been unlucky, and does not yet know what it is missing.

How then to set about transforming the majority who appear not to know (or care about) what they are missing into a majority who will make full use of the countryside resources which remain there for the taking, and who will at the same time treat them with respect? In what is perhaps the most radical chapter of her book, Shoard argues that instead of attempting to focus the public into 'safe' and specially prepared country playgrounds, the relevant bodies should be continually reminding people of their rights of access in the countryside, and actively encouraging them to get out there and enjoy it. I think the land could take it. Those who go to the country with love for it in their hearts to not destroy it. They do not set light to it, or leave its gates open, or allow their dogs to worry its sheep. Nor, if the public took *en masse* to the lanes on bicycles, or to the paths on foot, would they wear holes in all their surfaces (as is sometimes ludicrously argued) like the holes worn along the paths of over-popular summits such as Snowdon or Ivinghoe Beacon. There are a lot of lanes, and a lot of paths. They can absorb people both physically and also, I think, in that other way about which the solitude-seeker is so concerned. A person met by chance on a remote field path is a fellow-traveller, a creature of common interests, not an enemy. He does not spoil the appearance of the landscape, or even dispel its mystery; indeed, he is quite as likely to stop and discuss these very things with whoever is coming in the opposite direction.

So, then, if this 'we' is not yet everyone, this does not mean that the campaign to save the landscape must therefore and for all time remain a campaign specifically for the benefit of a countrywise minority. Hand in hand with any such campaign *must* go an anologous campaign to persuade the remaining majority of what they may be missing. Only when many more people realise the great joys to be had from exploring the countryside in depth will they begin to care about the threats to all the very sources of such joys. And what this indefinable majority should know, and care about knowing, is so very simple. As I see it, we need only two things in order to begin to enjoy the country to the full. The first is the knowledge (or confidence) that we may use it, – that rights of access do exist; and the second is an Ordnance Survey map, and an understanding of what its symbols mean, – especially those little red dots which lead out across open country where there are not even any roads or tracks!

This is where education has a fundamental role to play. Now, of course, we have the Scouts and the Guides, and the Duke of Edinburgh's Award Scheme, through which *some* children and young people can gain the necessary know-how. We have 'O' Level Geography, which includes training in map reading, – in order to get through an exam at the end of it. And we have some teachers, in some schools, who take their pupils on field trips through which they can relate map-reading and a theoretical knowledge of rights of way to the actuality. But we also have the evidence of studies such as the 'National Household Survey': if education in access to the countryside were truly universal and effective, then it is highly unlikely that so many of those who visit the country who are in fact able to go further would do so merely to put themselves on two hundred metre leashes, the other ends of which are firmly tied to the bonnets of their cars. One Junior School teacher I know who has taken her pupils for walks along the otherwise unused field paths near her school told me that when she looked for books, leaflets and teaching aids on the subject of access to the countryside which were pitched at the appropriate level, there appeared to be very little available, apart from yet further versions of the 'Dont's' list of the Country Code. Yet it is precisely at this level that such education should begin, throughout the country and especially in urban areas, as a creative combination of 'Dont's' and 'Can Do's.'*

The Ordnance Survey map is, potentially, *the* universal panacea so far as access is concerned, provided it is used with the right attitudes. It tells us what is on the ground, and it tells us where we may go on that ground. Armed with it, the countryside explorer will find to his pleasant surprise that he has no further use (if he ever had any) for the country parks, and the neat wooden signs pointing the way along the long-distance paths. Even those little arrows painted on trees by enthusiastic local ramblers' groups to show the way through woodland will be of only intermittent value to him. He will, finally, be able to find his own way; and he will want to do so, turning his back for good on all professional paternalists. All it needs is a little right-headed professional paternalism – encouraging vigorous and responsible independence – at the right moment, early on in life. I was lucky in this respect: I had a good geography teacher (even if I did not know it at the time), and what he taught me stuck.

This process of thought leads back inevitably to the theme of the pootling revolution. Strangely, bicycles are omitted from Marion Shoard's arguments on how the countryside might be opened up to more people. Instead, she puts emphasis on the development of recreational bus routes so that individuals who do not have cars can at least get out into the country cheaply and reliably at weekends. This is valid, of course: there will always be those without cars who prefer to walk, or amble, for whom buses would be invaluable if they did run regularly into the country. But those who choose to cycle have no need of buses. They may have need of trains, of course, especially where they live in a metropolis. In less enormous towns the difficulties of getting out into the country are far less great, but no less real. It is never much fun cycling along a busy (and often potholed) urban trunk road, especially for those still unsure of themselves on a bike, and there is an urgent

* As of March 1985, we have had the Countryside Commission's Access Charter, and its booklet 'Out In The Country' which tells people their rights as well as their responsibilities. It arrived not a moment too soon and, quite unsurprisingly, it has proved extremely popular.

need for the further development of 'green routes' out of every town and city in the country – such as those which have been made in Bristol, for example, by the cycling campaign group Cyclebag. These at present run along a disused railway and what was until not long ago a very muddy and little-used riverside footpath which is now a smooth, wide and quiet bikeway that makes an ideal alternative to the only road – a very busy trunk road – which runs in the same direction.

The pootling revolution could and would help to foster that other revolution in awareness in the British public by which we will all become far more discriminating about landscape than we have been in the past. By the same token that the pootlist is not a litterbug because he sees what litter means, so also he opposes the felling of hedgerow oaks and the ploughing of meadows thick with flowers because he has seen for himself what *that* means, retrospectively if not on the actual day of destruction. As pootlists and walkers multiply, so increasingly public opinion must be mobilised against the changes in the countryside. Struggles to implement the one revolution and as a matter of course you are struggling to implement the other.

Norfolk lane-users.

The third general area of objection which is likely to occur to any reader of *The Theft of the Countryside* concerns the issue of compulsion. Now, as many of us are aware, by no means every farmer is a rapist of landscape, even in the 1980s. Amongst people in my own acquaintance I can think immediately of one who is for most of his time a businessman but lives on and runs a smallholding of a few tiny fields, which will remain tiny under his ownership, and has a flock of sheep to his name; another who is a fully professional farmer who moved from northern Oxfordshire to western Devon partly because he could not bear to watch what some of his fellows were doing to the (in both senses of the word) former landscape; another who is not a farmer as such but maintains his old country house parkland in its original state as a sanctuary for wildlife and lets out the pastures to a farmer; and yet another who is now getting on, has run a traditional mixed farm in the same way all his life, loves the hedges and trees as things in themselves, and would not dream of damaging them if he can help it. It is also important to remember that – as Richard Body puts it in his invaluable book *Farming in the Clouds* (1984) – there are quite a number of farmers who have been "goaded" into high input/high output production in order to stay in business at all. Concern about the state and direction of British agriculture is widespread amongst the practitioners themselves: the only parties who would seem to be entirely happy with keeping the machinery running as it does are that minority of large, rich arable farmers and intensive livestock breeders, and their efficacious representatives in the NFU and the numerous London-based producers' associations.

But for this very reason, until fundamental changes are made, the general threat to the countryside will remain. Farms are sold daily, and those who have maintained or improved landscapes may pass their property on to others who will immediately set about undoing all their good work. *We have no guarantees, and guarantees are precisely what we need.* Generalised promises from the lobbyists, now fully alerted to public conern, are not enough. If we had been sufficiently naive or ill-informed, then publications such as the NFU's pamphlet 'Caring for the Countryside' (1977) might have been taken as the harbinger of some new and effective determination by farmers to conserve the landscape. This pamphlet contained the following statement, for example:

"The Countryside Commission and the Nature Conservancy Council have recently identified critical conservation issues and suggested possible remedial action. We have accepted in response the need for action. The question is not whether but how this action should be taken."

The pamphlet went on to advise farmers to retain and conserve landscape features "wherever practicable and appropriate". There are, of course, as many ways of interpreting that qualificatory phrase as there are farmers, or barley barons. Such a statement of intent is about as much of a guarantee that *all* farmers will preserve the old landscape as a promise made during a sober moment by a hardened alcoholic that this time he really will come off the bottle. "As farmers and landowners," the pamphlet concluded, "we are the custodians of the countryside". But if farmers are genuinely custodians then *where has so much of the countryside gone* since 1945 under that custodianship?

If there is still any trace of doubt in the reader's mind on this matter, let him turn to the *New Agricultural Landscapes* report and make a comparison between two diagrams of the sample area surveyed in Huntingdonshire. The diagram showing the replanting which the consultants suggested would most benefit this miserable landscape is quite a complex one, with a lot of lines across it: the diagram showing the replanting which the farmers of the area *might* have been prepared to allow is virtually a blank piece of paper. Indeed, update material published by the Commission in 1984 shows that of the skeletal remains of the old hedged landscape which survived in the study area up to 1974, a further 20.5% have been hacked out during the intervening decade. Clearly, unless a system is brought into being whereby the major decisions about the appearance of the countryside are put into the hands of a body other than those of such farmers, Huntingdonshire is extremely likely to remain what it is today, a dreary, depressing and (in terms of wildlife) sterile tract of England. Unless such a system is brought into being, there is nothing to *guarantee* that much of the rest of England will not also very quickly end up looking like Huntingdonshire.

Planning For The Lanes

Suppose for a moment that the battle for the landscape was won, the imbalance of power redressed, and the Regional Countryside Planning Authorities proposed by Marion Shoard established as a reality. As has been said already, these bodies would be centrally concerned with the maintenance, protection and reconstitution of landscape features and wildlife within their allotted areas. What might happen to the lanes, in such a newly civilised state of affairs?

There is already evidence that the flora and fauna of the lanes, being in part on publicly owned land, are better off than on much marginal farmland. Public reaction was certainly effective against the relentless methods of mowing and the sometimes monstrous use of weedkillers along roadsides by highway authorities during the 1960s. As Richard Mabey recounts in *The Roadside Wildlife Book*, many highway authorities reacted to criticism by introducing programmes of mowing which are design to encourage roadside flora, using a 'zoning' system by which the plantlife closest to the road surface (in a stip between $\frac{2}{3}$m. and 2m. wide) and plantlife on all sight-lines (bends, etc.) is mown the most frequently, and land further from the road is left alone for most of the year. Some highway authorities have also collaborated with county naturalists' trusts in identifying particularly valuable stretches of verge, and some verges are now designated as nature reserves and marked with posts at either end (as for example in Kent and Cornwall), to warn off the mowers. Rightly so: over 600 of our 2,000 species of flowering plants have been recorded on the estimated 202,000 hectares of verges and ditches in Britain, and they are of course also heavily populated, or used, by animals, birds and insects. The verges are in a sense another surviving sector of the country's roughlands, and since they are seen by so many they are of prime importance.

However, by no means everything is well with the roadsides. Mabey details the destruction of roadside ditches – which can be environments of distinct ecological importance – once again with the assistance and encouragement of grant-aid. In prairie farming landscapes where hedges have been removed it is a common sight to find the earth tilled virtually to the edge of the tarmac, or with little more than a foot of beaten, dead-looking grass between the two. Also, whilst many highway authorities are enthusiastic about flowers, far fewer are particularly keen on trees: *New Agricultural Landscapes* details four main objections made by the authorities to trees and tree-planting, all of which are connected with road safety. Plausible as these may be as generalisations, they are inapplicable in so many currently treeless places along the roadsides that one cannot take them very seriously. Good work is currently being done here by some highway authorities – notably Wiltshire and Lincolnshire – but even so, only a tiny fraction of the possibilities are being realised on a national basis. The one centrally planned policy for tree planting is – bitterest of ironies – along the motorways, where trees have been planted in their millions in order to relieve the visual tedium which otherwise hypnotises drivers into a comatose state. Such tree planting can hardly be claimed to improve 'the landscape': all it does is to make the motorways themselves marginally less vile. In order to improve the landscape as a whole, we need many millions more trees along the trunk roads and the lanes which – unlike motorways –remain a *part* of each locality they traverse. Clearly, then, tree planting alongside roads should become one of the duties of the RCPAs. They would be able to administrate planting schemes not as a secondary activity (as it has always been for highway authorities, whose main concerns must, of course, lie elsewhere) but as an immediate priority, discussing and if necessary debating the sitings in each scheme with the highway authorities concerned.

The RCPAs could also take it upon themselves to restore run-down roadside hedgerows by laying and planting in gaps, and to maintain ditches in such a way that their wildlife was safeguarded or restored. If the reader objects that this would inevitably necessitate the use of manual methods, and that such labour-intensiveness would cost a great deal of money, I can only refer him once more to *The Theft of the Countryside*. A combination of the redirection of a *very small proportion* of the money which has been used for landscape destruction, and the use of some volunteer labour (we already have quite a number of keen amateur hedge-layers and wallers the country over) could begin to achieve the desired ends, without inordinate demands on the taxpayer's already lightweight purse.

Particular attention could be paid by every RCPA to the maintenance of unmetalled tracks within its area, especially those with known wildlife or historical value. Where it could be shown that the plantlife of formerly hedged and tree'd tracks with public rights or access had recently been des-troyed by farmers, these could be reconstituted by new planting (although it goes almost without saying that there is no substitute for a thousand-year-old hedge but another thousand-year-old hedge). Whether this should be done by the farmers or by the RCPAs themselves is one of the touchiest aspects of the subject. I think that the best way in many cases, whether it be along the tracks, the metalled lanes or the trunk roads, would be for a system of (if necessary compulsory) purchase to be established which could be used in all cases where collaborative methods failed, through which the RCPA would in effect 'nationalise' the land concerned.

A Landscape Movement

> "Our England is a garden, and gardens are not made
> By singing: – 'Oh, how beautiful!' and sitting in the shade,
> While better men than we go out and start their working lives
> At grubbing weeds from gravel paths with broken dinner-knives..."
>
> *Rudyard Kipling,*
> '*The Glory of the Garden*', *(1911)*.

As the debate on farming methods continues, more and more people are developing a newly critical awareness of the rural environment, and it would be good to see this put into practical and creative use. The RCPAs might take on the role of the new architects of the countryside, but all those who think and care about the subject should be able to feel that they too can collaborate in the process of conserving and remaking it, constantly feeding the authorities with suggestions (based, naturally, on informed knowledge of what is appropriate in each case). The existence of the RCPAs – the fact that there was at last somewhere to write where one's opinion would not only be heard but could also be acted upon – could not fail to generate public involvement and interest. Energy, and emotion, could be harnessed productively.

But what of the farmers? Their response to public control over their activities will no doubt depend to a large degree on what else is done to modify the system which underpins their livings. Richard Body may well be right when he suggests that we can only steer British farming away from its present course by withdrawal from the Common Agricultural Policy and by a unilateral declaration of free trade, which will be one step towards encouraging the production of foodstuffs, on a global scale, in the places that are actually best suited to them. Certainly so long as arable crops can be profitably grown here on Grade III land that is far better suited to pastoral use, farmers will continue to want to grow them there. The source of this profitability is, of course, the system of price support and grants towards mechanised, chemicalised farming methods: take away these fiscal props and the pastures would be more likely to remain as pasture.

Even so, in 1986, there is still a proportion of farmers who are genuinely inclined toward conservation, and as is documented in *Working the Land* by Charlie Pye-Smith and Richard North, a handful of farmers have even succeeded in going back to running their businesses using variants on the old mixed farming system. No doubt many more would do the same once the political stimulus toward intensification was removed. In the meantime – and the next decade will be crucially important in this respect – we *must be sure* that we can begin to save the countryside from further unnecessary change, and this may well mean that where farmers are not genuinely conservation-conscious, individual battles must be fought.

In the longer term it will also help, I think, if the difficult-to-teach but essential subject of landscape aesthetics were to take a place on the curricula of agricultural colleges alongside ecological management, which is already taught in some of them. A concerted attempt could then be made by emergent farmers to consider the features which make farmed landscapes beautiful and how these can be maintained or indeed 'produced', in much the same way as food is produced.

I can hear the reactions to this even as I write. The notion of the farmer as blunt, good natured, down-to-earth individual narrowly intent on feeding the nation is so deeply entrenched in most people that such a suggestion is bound to be greeted with derision from some quarters. But what is education if it is not a broadening of awareness? Surely the most immediately relevant place to discuss landscape aesthetics is one in which those who maintain the landscape get their education?

For the RCPAs, the new 'marginal land authorities', the possibilities are rich indeed. Their representatives too would have to be well educated, and they would need to maintain the closest working links with all conservation bodies, both national and local to their areas. Every stretch of country has its own special features, and whilst it is clear that the most important of these from the conservation point of view must be itemised and surveyed without further delay (a task which the Nature Conservancy Council has identified as a priority, although it would be good eventually to see such places cared for as far as possible on a parish basis), it is also important that all those less rare but perhaps equally loved features which in accumulation give an area of country its personality should be noted before they disappear. In west Oxfordshire as it runs up into the Cotswolds, to take a less obvious example, the frequency of willows in hedgerows as well as streamside areas means that in July and August the landscape there is striking: at that time the golds and yellows of the ripening crops combine with the dark masses of the hedges and the silvery shades of the willows to beautiful effect. In such an area the planting especially of aspens and poplars as well as further willows, all of which have shining leaves, would greatly enhance this existing beauty; whereas for example the planting of oaks or chestnuts in any number – wonderful trees that they are – would not contribute to what is already distinctive in the area. We need to look at every stretch of the country in this way.

In the old enclosed landscapes, then, the key words would be preservation, replacement, or extension of such valuable features as remain, but it is in the new prairies that the most exciting possibilities lie, not just in terms of reconstituting wildlife habitats in places from which they have been entirely removed but, again, in terms of establishing new features with something of a painter's eye. I can think of a hundred – no, a thousand! – places in East Anglia where a single line of trees along a naked stream, or a single small clump of beech or oak, would transform the present cropped waste into something quite other: a landscape which has personality, memorability, upon which the creative and reflective hand of man is evident, – a new kind of idyll, in which the existing potential for beauty in the open landscape is defined and enhanced.

On a more practical level there is also a very good case for re-hedging roadsides in all areas that are prone to heavy snowfalls. The removal of hedges has resulted in many villages being cut off by snowdrifts in winter where previously the roads had been at least partly protected: in some places the hedges could be re-trained from still-living root systems which the farmers never got around to grubbing out. It is an encouraging thought that 'quickset' will grow, or re-grow, into a substantial hedge in as little as eight years: the vacuous nonscapes of Lincolnshire, for example, may be transformed in the mind's eye by imagining what could be done with the county's surviving hedges alone, most of which are currently trimmed down to a couple of feet above the ground.

In the same way, hedges could be replanted in the gaps between existing fragments, and in the long term it should be possible to use the evidence of the earlier field systems, which is readily available on Ordnance Survey maps, to reconstruct the most important elements of pre-prairie landscapes. In some places, and some only, roadside tree planting of the appropriate species could be enough to give prairie countryside some kind of sense. The photographs below show a stretch of country near Greenstead Green in Essex, which looks as it does now as a result of the removal of the hedgerows and the retention of some mature hedgerow trees along the roadsides. Blocks of old deciduous woodland in the distance are important in giving this area its individuality, and in such a context the avenues of oaks along the lanes are sufficient to lend definition to the foreground area. The isolation of the boles of the mature oaks against the expansive sweep of big fields or against the sky is definitely pleasing here. Even so there is an important distinction to be made: you may be able to grow a passable hedge in under a decade, but it takes ten times as long to produce a mature oak.

In certain places – and one must acknowledge that there has been *some* change in very recent years – natural regeneration and/or planting by highway authorities, landowners or parishes is already helping to establish trees in this way. But this is the merest fraction of what can and must eventually be done. From the wildlife point of view, of course, single avenues even of noble oaks are no substitute for more complex habitats. For this purpose, it would be valuable to establish tree or shrub belts of say 3 to 6 metres in depth along both sides of roads where land can successfully be liberated from the tyranny of the plough. Such features would also serve to improve the appearance of the prairie voids out of all recognition. In some cases, where footpaths are nonexistent in neighbouring country, these could be encouraged along the centres of such woody strips, in parallel with the road. Such a type of landscape with tree belts can already be seen, for example, in the Norfolk Breckland, and rather more attractively in the Hampshire hill country to the north of Andover: anyone exploring these areas will be quick to see the potential for such a type of layout in country where the fields are large and symmetrical. Finally, I should mention that there is at least one practical use for the timber from well matured roadside trees, which could return a worthwhile profit to landowners in the long term, and this is in the production of hardwood veneers for furniture-making. Hedgerow trees are ideal for slicing into veneers since they grow in the uncramped conditions which are most likely to produce the thick, straight trunks and boughs that are essential for the process. If local authorities (which do not often die) owned verges then it is arguable that investment by planting for the far distant future could once more become a viable proposition.

One further word about the issue of enclosure. Having called for at least two revolutions already in this book, I may be risking charges of excess beyond excess if I end it by calling for a third, but sure it is that this is one area in which even a rigorous planning authority would be hard put to make changes, so that if anything is to happen it must be through a revolution in individuals' attitudes. I am thinking of what we put around our country (and for that matter our town) gardens. Is it not time to have done with cheap and nasty substitutes for hedges and walls, and to enclose the windswept, littered grass piazzas of US-style housing estates? The revolution I hope to see here is a mass return to comforting, solid hedges of box, privet, hawthorn and yew, and to walls made out of whatever walls *should* be made out of in each area concerned – brick, flint, limestone, granite – not just around the older houses but also around the new. One way of at least partly absorbing brash suburban monstrosities into the landscape is to screen them with visual barriers which do in themselves fit. But how to effect this? If I were dictator, I would have owners of 'Texan ranch-style' plank fencing banished to the oil-producing zone to which they so evidently aspire, and I would have all planters of *cupressocyparis leylandii* consumed on pyres made out of their own superficial plantings. But this is no doubt by the way. One can live in hope.

In Conclusion

Wherever you travel in the countryside today you are likely to hear the buzz of chainsaws. You may not see them, but you hear them. Many are being used to take down the elms, others to thin or fell conifers – but not all. Since my own awakening to the destruction around me, each time I have heard a chainsaw I have felt subdued panic. What is being lost now? Should I not hurry on to the next beautiful place and see it, drink it in, memorise it, photograph it, before 'they' get there and start to destroy it? But no. I for one have had my fill of rushing from place to place like a wild animal driven out of one piece of cover in search of another. When the cover is exhausted, some cornered animals can put up a tough fight. The most important question is whether there are yet enough of us who feel similarly. I think that there are.

The battle lines are clearly drawn up. The cameras of media and press have long been turned on localised battlefields such as Exmoor, the Norfolk Broads and the Somerset Levels. The National Farmers' Union, that gigantic wolf in shepherd's clothing, continues to ply the media with material designed to put the public's mind at rest – insofar as it can – whilst at the same time it prepares itself for changes that are now inevitable. Since the publication of *The Theft of The Countryside* and partly as a result of it, the subject of change in the landscape as a whole has moved much closer to centre stage than ever before, and there is no doubt that it is now a live political issue engaging the attention of all parties. Most notable amongst several relevant parliamentary debates was one in February 1981 in which Chief Opposition Spokesman Lord Melchett tabled an amendment to what was then the Wildlife and Countryside Bill, drawing directly upon arguments in *The Theft of The Countryside*, whilst early in 1982 a Hedgerows Bill designed to give statutory protection to hedges of historical or amenity importance also went before the House of Commons. In the autumn of 1983 both Labour and Liberal parties approved resolutions for the protection of countryside and wildlife at their annual conferences, whilst during the following summer the subject of the damage done to the environment by modern farming practises was at last examined by a House of Lords Select Committee, much to the discomfiture of the MAFF and the NFU. In January 1985, the House of Commons Environment Committee published a report which described the Ministry of Agriculture's attitude towards conservation as complacent. In an 11th hour attempt to erect a mask of concern in front of its otherwise unsmiling features, this same Ministry has established an 'environmental co-ordination unit', which the report accurately described as a 'gesture' towards conservation. Unfortunately but quite predictably the report endorsed the voluntary approach in conservation matters, but it did usefully call for the preparation of a White Paper on the broad issues surrounding land-use in the countryside. At much the same time a bill was tabled by Labour MP Dr David Clark in an attempt to close some of the more astounding loopholes in the present Wildlife and Countryside Act: this was passed, in much modified form, in June 1985. Finally, in September 1985, the Labour Party published its Charter for the Environment, which promises that a future Labour government will establish planning controls over farming, forestry and water operations, introduce a *new* Wildlife and Countryside Act, and institute a complete ban on straw burning.

The resounding failure of the Common Market summit conference of December 1983 served to focus attention on the fact that the EEC was in imminent danger of running out of money, and commentators – the prime minister amongst them – were not slow to remind us of the absurdity of continuing subsidies to agriculture under the Common Agricultural Policy at existing levels in such circumstances. Pressure on the EEC to reduce its grain production has also come from America, whose Secretary for Agriculture said in mid 1985 that the US was prepared to engage in a trade war with the EEC if the latter did not take direct measures to end its dumping of grain surpluses on the world market. The first of such measures was proposed in the EEC Green Paper on agricultural policies of July 1985: this involves price cutting, with some proposals for financial support for small farmers unable to subsist on reduced incomes. A structures regulation published in March 1985 also included a potentially important scheme allowing (though not yet funding!) new grants systems to encourage farming practises which conserve wildlife and landscape in so-called 'environmentally sensitive areas', which are to be defined individually by each member state.

In Spring 1984, Friends of the Earth announced the publication of its own consultation paper containing proposals for a Natural Heritage Bill which would replace the still highly unsatisfactory Wildlife and Countryside Act with much stronger measures. These would, once again, include the extension of planning controls to cover intensive agricultural and forestry operations, the institution of grants to be paid via the Ministry of Agriculture to farmers who wish to encourage wildlife on their land, and the establishment of legislative protection for Sites of Special Scientific Interest similar in nature to those afforded to Listed Buildings. Friends of the Earth is already highly active in encouraging direct public involvement and local action, and now has more than seventy Countryside Action Groups dedicated to disputing the future of individual sites wherever they are seen to be threatened. For the immediate future, the most constructive action by members of the public must remain such local, neighbourhood action – a patch of marsh saved from draining here, a hedgerow saved there – and it will be partly by the proliferation of such activity the country over that centralised change will be effected in the long run.

FOE's campaign is absolutely in harmony with the view of the Nature Conservancy Council expressed in 'Nature Conservation in Great Britain', published in June 1984 as a response to the World Conservation Strategy. Quite as much of a model of restraint and balanced argument as one would expect to see emerge from an independent government agency, this document does nonetheless confront the disastrous changes of the past few decades with an unflinching gaze, laying blame not only on the incompatibility of modern agricultural techniques with conservation, but on conservationists themselves in failing to win sufficient support for their cause from central government. The expansionist mania of the CAP is, once more, identified as a major factor in the destruction of habitats, and the paper calls for a halt to further damage to such fragments of the wild as remain in lowland landscapes whilst at the same time acknowledging that the power of vested interests will ensure that the road to such changes is a long one. Amongst the many objectives of its strategy for future nature conservation in Britain, one in particular stands out: this is that conservation should be established in the minds of politicians and public alike as a *socially necessary activity*, and that this necessity should be defined not only in terms of recreational needs and possible job creation, but in terms of spiritual needs as well.

The Countryside Commission meantime, even in the face of the overwhelming evidence contained in the NCC report, continues to toe the middle line in reaffirming its espousal of the 'conservation-by-persuasion' approach. Even so, the Commission has finally found its way round to declaring – in its 1984 policy statement on agricultural landscapes – that *if* this approach is seen to fail then it, the Commission, will be prepared to endorse legislative methods to ensure conservation of the landscape. It would of course be possible to protract almost indefinitely any admission that the 'persuasion' approach has failed – the material contained in the Commission's own 1984 update on *New Agricultural Landscapes* is in itself sufficient evidence of failure – but such a change of heart on the legislative approach is nevertheless significant, and may be read as symptomatic of the changes now taking place in the political climate so far as conservation issues are concerned.

The Forestry Commission has also at long last modified its own position, by the publication in 1984 of a report entitled 'Broadleaves in Britain'. This paper carefully sidesteps the key issue here, the extent of the destruction of ancient semi-natural woodlands – for which the Forestry Commission, as administrator of felling licences, must be seen to be directly responsible – but in its list of recommendations it does reveal a new determination to tighten up controls over the felling of broadleaved woods in future. The new policy, if implemented, will mean that remaining ancient woodlands can be managed – with the help of grant aid and tax reliefs – so as to perpetuate their individual qualities, and that landowners wishing to fell broadleaved woods will 'normally' be required to replant with the same kinds of trees, thus maintaining the broadleaved resource at roughly its present extent. There are those amongst us who would say that by rights all those formerly broadleaved sites which have been stocked with conifers during the past four decades should also be gradually returned to something like their earlier state; even so, the policy changes suggested here are substantial enough in themselves to give cause for a glimmer of hope so far as woodlands are concerned.

It has long since been time to stand up and be counted. A national opinion poll conducted at the time of the debating of the Wildlife and Countryside Bill showed that it was the opinion of no less than 78% of the people interviewed that the second most important job for any future government was to provide effective protection for the countryside. In a BBC radio programme 'You The Jury' broadcast in June 1984, prior to the debate taking place 56% of the audience supported the motion that farming operations should be brought under planning control: after the debate this figure has risen to 81%, despite the fact that all the farmers' representatives opposing the motion emanated reasonableness of the sweetest kind. Those who are not farmers and landowners outnumber those who are by approximately 200 to 1, so that there would seem to be rather more than a fighting chance that a mass outcry by those who care but who have, until now, felt powerless to do anything, will be enough to bring the matter to a head in the corridors of power.

In 1980, Marion Shoard wrote that "another 30 years of huge economic incentives, coupled with the exclusion of farming operations from our planning machinery, will mean the end of the English landscape." Since then, the fact that policy-makers in the European parliament have begun to come to grips with the problems caused by over-production makes it seem far less likely (though not, of course, impossible) that the insanity of production incentives can continue in any form for very much longer. Indeed, just before this book went to press, a draft report prepared for the Nature Conservancy Council predicted that during the next decade and a half, over $2\frac{1}{2}$ million hectares of farmland could be *taken out* of production. The catch for those concerned about the countryside is that if this happens, and clearly one should remain sceptical, then it is most likely to happen where the soils are poorest, in counties such as Shropshire, Staffordshire and Warwickshire. Some farmers may stop growing cereals on land that was never naturally suited to them in the first place, but this in itself will do nothing to alter the imbalance in the prairie zones, where the soils are richest, nor will it *guarantee* the immunity of surviving marginal land in other areas from future incursions. EEC quotas will hit individual farmers, but in themselves they will do nothing to restore the countryside.

The countryside is far, far more than a food factory and that, finally, is why we need legislation to protect it and plan for it on a national scale. A few years ago, the Church of England issued an official statement to the effect that the British public is now amongst the most secular in the world. If, then, it can be assumed that few of us now cling to any hope of a life after death in which some at least will gain admission to a celestial Paradise, is it not all the more to the point – all the more pragmatic, if you like – to maintain some elements of a Paradise which can be enjoyed on earth, now, whilst the blood is still flowing in our veins? We can *make* the 'better place beyond the town' which the urban person sometimes dreams of, and where it exists already, we can maintain it. The resources of this man-made Paradise lie all around us: it is simply a question of putting them to sensitive use, and substituting for the buzz of the chainsaw and the roar and whine of the bulldozer the quieter sounds of digging and tending. Why, after all, should the needs of the stomach and the needs of the heart and mind prove incompatible? Why should it be impossible to reconcile agriculture and Arcadia?

In an earlier, more confident, less secular age Kipling could conclude his poem:

> "So when your work is finished, you can wash your hands and pray
> For the Glory of the Garden, that it may not pass away!
> And the Glory of the Garden it shall never pass away!"

Never? Oh yes it can, Mr. Kipling, if we let it.

POSTSCRIPT

During the twelve months since this part of the book was completed, the countryside debate has altered its focus of attention. Where, only a matter of 18 months ago, conservationists were still confronting the imperative need to find effective means of holding the state-supported expansionism of farmers firmly in check, the process of expansion itself has now gone into reverse, as inevitably it had to do once the EEC began to tackle the problem of food surpluses, and the debate is centring on how best to deal with land that is expected to go out of production. The fact remains, however, that the countryside is no safer from deleterious change than it was before this news broke. The Thatcher government's proposals of February 1987 for making partial use of such land by turning it over to forestry (two thirds of which would be conifers) or, yet worse, to the expansionist mania of another group, the property developers, only confirms yet once more the need for a comprehensive, sensitive plan for the preservation of such quality as survives in the landscape today, and for the re-creation of its most cherishable features on land taken out of production in every prairie zone. Such a plan would be national in scope but drawn up through detailed groundwork and observation of what is most valuable, on a parish-by-parish basis. *Only* within the framework of such a plan, backed by the appropriate legislation, can surplus farmland be coherently harnessed, and the immemorial qualities of the English landscape be preserved.

Select Bibliography

A reading list on the subject of the English countryside and its lanes could quite easily run to book length. All I have detailed here, therefore, are the publications which I have myself found most useful as aids to exploration, and a selection of the books which have proved to be most influential in consolidating my ideas on the countryside.

Aids To Independent Exploration

The Department of the Environment's list and map of historic monuments is published by Her Majesty's Stationery Office, and can be purchased at the larger monuments.

Gardens Open To The Public In England And Wales is published by the National Gardens Scheme in March/April of each year, and is available from newsagents.

Historic Houses, Castles and Gardens is published annually, usually towards the end of March, by Historic Publications, and is also available from newsagents.

For reading after rather than before one gets to know an unknown region, the excellent *Making Of The English Landscape* series is published by Hodder and Stoughton.

The National Trust's list of properties open to the public is sent free to members, or can be purchased at any of the larger properties.

Nikolaus Pevsner's staggeringly comprehensive reference series *The Buildings Of England* is published by Penguin Books, one book to a county. It should be used with restraint, since the amount of detail is likely to distract from essentials.

Richard's Bicycle Book (1975) by Richard Ballantine is published as a Pan paperback.

The *Shell Guides*, as mentioned in the text, are published by Faber and Faber on a county by county basis.

Aids To Inspiration, Reflection, And Debate

Aldous, Tony	*Goodbye Britain?* Sidgwick and Jackson, 1975
Barr, John	*Derelict Britain*, Penguin Books, 1969
Blythe, Ronald	*Akenfield*, Penguin Books, 1972
Body, Richard	*Agriculture, The Triumph And The Shame*, 1982, and *Farming In The Clouds*, 1984, both published by Temple Smith
Brooks, Alan (ed.)	*Hedging – A Practical Conservation Handbook*, 1975, published by and available from the British Trust For Conservation Volunteers
Dyos, H.J. and Aldcroft, D.H.	*British Transport*, Leicester University Press, 1969
Ewart Evans, George	*Ask The Fellows Who Cut The Hay*, 1956 and *The Pattern Under The Plow*, 1966, amongst several others published by Faber and Faber
Fukuoka, Masanobu	*The One-Straw Revolution: An Introduction To Natural Farming*, Rodale Press, 1978

Hoskins, W.G.   *The Making Of The English Language*, Penguin edition 1970

Hyams, Edward and Smith, Edwin
                       The English Garden, Thames and Hudson, 1964

Joad, C.E.M.   *The Untutored Townsman's Invasion Of The Country*, 1946

King, Angela and Conroy, Czech
                       Paradise Lost? 1980, published by and available from Friends
                       Of The Earth

King, Angela and Clifford, Sue
                       Holding Your Ground, Temple Smith, 1985

Mabey, Richard   *The Roadside Wildlife Book*, Sphere paperback edition 1978,
                       and *The Common Ground*, Hutchinson, 1980

Morton, H.V.   *In Search Of England*, Methuen, 1927

Nairn, Ian   *Counter Attack Against Subtopia*, Architectural Press, 1957

Nature Conservancy Council
                       'Nature Conservation In Great Britain', 1984

Newby, Howard   *Green And Pleasant Land?* Hutchinson, 1979, reprinted 1985 by
                       Wildwood House

Parker, Rowland   *The Common Stream*, Paladin, 1976

Pollard, E., Hooper, M.D., and Moore, N.W.
                       Hedges, Collins, 1974

Pratt, E.A.   *History Of Inland Transport And Communication In England*, Kegan
                       Paul, 1912, reprinted by David and Charles, 1970

Pye-Smith, Charlie and North, Richard
                       Working The Land, Temple Smith, 1984

Rackham, Oliver   *Trees And Woodland In The British Landscape*, Dent, 1976

Schumacher, E.F.   *Small Is Beautiful*, Abacus, 1974

Shoard, Marion   *The Theft Of The Countryside*, Temple Smith, 1980

Taylor, Christopher   *Roads And Tracks Of Britain*, Dent, 1979

Westmacott, R. and Worthington, T.
                       New Agricultural Landscapes, 1974, and *Agricultural Landscapes:
                       A Second Look*, 1984, published by and available from The
                       Countryside Commission

Williams-Ellis, Clough
                       England And The Octopus, 1928, reprinted by Blackie and Son,
                       1975